# UTTARA

Arshia Sattar is already acknowledged as our most sensitive and perceptive translator of the Ramayana: her text glows with her love for the epic about this Most Perfect of Human Beings. Uttara however starts with an act of Rama's which is difficult to condone, and here, along with an equally nuanced and luminous translation, she takes us through subtle analyses of the moral and emotional ambiguities of Rama's acts which make this text so disturbing. Riveting, even for those who, like me, were brought up on that epic.

– Girish Karnad

Both a terrific read and a revolutionary contribution to our understanding of the Valmiki Ramayana – and of the many Ramayanas that followed. The translation is smooth, spirited, and accurate, and the seven essays brilliantly illuminate the text. Together they show why this largely unknown final book of the Ramayana is the answer to many of the enigmas in the rest of the text and the explanation of much of the worship of Rama that is to come.

– Wendy Doniger

# UTTARA
# THE BOOK OF ANSWERS

TRANSLATED AND WITH COMMENTARY BY

ARSHIA SATTAR

HarperCollins *Publishers* India

First published in India by
HarperCollins *Publishers* in 2019
An imprint of HarperCollins Publishers
HarperCollins *Publishers* India, Cyber City, Building 10-A, Gurugram, Haryana-122002, India
www.harpercollins.co.in

2 4 6 8 10 9 7 5 3 1


P-ISBN: 9789353572594
E-ISBN: 9789353572600



Typeset in 11.5/15 Arno Pro at at
Manipal Technologies Limited, Manipal

Printed and bound at
Manipal Technologies Limited, Manipal

*

HarperCollins *Publishers*, Macken House, 39/40 Mayor Street Upper, Dublin 1, D01 C9W8, Ireland

*And again, for Sanjay*
*who always had the right questions*

# *Contents*

# ACKNOWLEDGEMENTS

In 1996, almost exactly twenty years ago to the release date of this book, Penguin India published my abridged translation of the Valmiki Ramayana. David Davidar had commissioned the book and Ravi Singh was my editor. I was told to keep to a strict seven hundred English pages, and how and what I edited out of the Sanskrit text was entirely my choice. I chose to abridge my translation for the 'main' story, so, apart from shortening repetitive passages, I chose to slash away at the Yuddha Kanda where this one killed that one. More critically, I chose to miniaturize the hefty Uttara Kanda, picking from it what I considered (at the time) the most important narrative moments – Sita's banishment, Rama's reunion with his sons and Sita's final and irrevocable departure. The rest of the Uttara Kanda, I thought, simply retold stories and created backstories for the characters in the preceding books of Valmiki's text.

As the story of Rama became more and more politicized in contemporary India, I was forced to look back on my own work, to see it for what it was, for what it might be seen as, for what I had intended it to be. In that sense, I was forced to confront my own politics about the Ramayana and how I understood and re-presented the Valmiki text in English. After 2002, I had the opportunity to teach and talk about the Ramayana in many places. Often, students and audiences asked me questions about why things in the story had happened the way they had, why we received the Ramayana in the way we did. These were questions for which I had only tentative suggestions rather than the definitive answers they expected from an 'expert'. At some point, I began to see these questions as germane and inherent, even, to the Valmiki text itself. I realized, then, that perhaps many of the problems twentieth- and twenty-first-century readers had with the text might have their answers in the Uttara Kanda, the book that I had failed to truly acknowledge in my translation of Valmiki. This volume is, in many ways, in recompense for not having previously understood the significance of the Uttara Kanda and what it does to Valmiki's story of Rama.

It was the Ramayana scholar Paula Richman who first suggested that I should do a stand-alone translation of Valmiki's Uttara Kanda. I did not think that anyone would care to read it. But she persisted in her gentle and persuasive way. Other gentle persuaders made the same suggestion soon after, among them Rustom Bharucha. Without the faith and conviction that Paula and Rustom expressed in a new reading of Valmiki's Uttara Kanda, I would not have had the courage to suggest this as a book to R. Sivapriya, my then-editor at Penguin. Sivapriya's commitment to the idea of the book made it real and I thank her for her unstinting belief in my work and the secure confidence she radiated about why such a book had to be done. Always, the lodestone of what I write about the Ramayana is Wendy Doniger – my constant teacher, personal Sanskrit dictionary and grammarian, on-call editor, fastest emailer in the West, ready reckoner for anyone and anything in myth and epic – but more than all of these, a loving and beloved friend. This book would not exist without Paula, Rustom and Sivapriya, but it exists as an altogether better book because of Wendy.

I have used the fourth edition of the *Srivalmikiramayana Satika* published by the Nirnay Sagar Press, Bombay (1938), for this translation. For the US edition, thanks are due to my indefatigable agent, Priya Doraswamy, and to Chandni Ananth for her patience with the index and for casting one more critical eye on the text.

Time and space to write was provided by Sangam House and, in the last phase of untying the knots in troublesome and often garbled thoughts, by D.W. Gibson's generous invitation to Writer's Omi in the spring of 2016.

More and more, I learn that I can be who I am because of my mother Nazura, the backbone of my adult life. For all that she has remained critical of what I wear, she has always supported what I do and how I do it. From letting me cross turbulent waters to go away to graduate school, to years later insisting that I remain true to my desire to teach and read and write in the face of other pressures, Nazura always made me believe that what I was doing was not simply the right thing, it was the only thing I could and should do. No thanks will ever be enough for that.

For love and strength and food and drink and flowers when there weren't no sunshine, thank you Anna Hammond, Bob Madey, Bronwen Bledsoe, Priya Sarukkai Chabria and Rachel Saltz.

Tyler Norman, when I count my blessings, I think of you.

Anmol Tikoo, Arati Rao, Aseem Shrivastava, Lynne Fernandez, Maya (who used to be called Digger), Mrugank Sanghvi, Mythri Surendra, Nayana Currimbhoy, Pascal Sieger, Pavi, Raghu Karnad, Raghu Srinivasan, Raghu Tenkayala, Rahul Soni, Rohan Agarwal, Shai Heredia, Sonali Sattar, Sunil Shetty, Tabasheer Zutshi, Trupti Prasad, Vivek Madan – you helped me to keep singing when the music died. This book is for each of you as much as it is for our beloved Sanjay.

# INTRODUCTION

What we call the Valmiki Ramayana consists of seven books or kandas – Bala, Ayodhya, Aranya, Kishkindha, Sundara, Yuddha and Uttara. They vary in length and, often, in language and style. Even the most inexperienced Sanskrit reader will notice that the greatest variation in these elements is evident in the difference between the Bala and Uttara Kandas and the so-called middle books of the text. The poignant human emotions in Ayodhya, the exquisite beauty in Sundara, the leaps of imagination in Kishkindha, are all replaced (barring a few magnificent passages such as the rape of Rambha) by largely uninspired language in the Bala and Uttara Kandas. In these, the first and the last books, the fundamentally prosaic and essentially narrative metre of the shloka is punctuated by formulaic constructions rather than elevated by the soaring images that rip through it in the middle books. While the middle books feel like 'kavya', the poesy to which the Ramayana stakes claim, the first and the last books resemble sectarian Puranas in both language and attitude.

Much has been written and said about Valmiki's composition. Some of that writing has concerned itself with text-critical issues. Text-based scholarship is largely agreed that though we regard the Valmiki Ramayana as a unitary text, it cannot have been composed by a single person at a single time. It is very likely that the story of Rama, the exiled prince whose wife was abducted during their time in the forest, was in circulation for a long time before it came together in the Sanskrit poem that we attribute to

Valmiki, who is perhaps a construct rather than a flesh-and-blood writer. While this does not matter in most instances (the text we have is the text we know and love and cite as such), there are times when the idea of a single author and a continuous period of composition for the Sanskrit Ramayana becomes problematic, most especially when these ideas impinge upon our understanding of the text as a whole.

Of all the many realms that the Ramayana inhabits – the literary and the religious, the devotional and the poetic – and for all that it signifies to the people of the subcontinent and beyond, it also, more or less, conforms to the generic idea of the Indo-European epic in its structure and its concerns. One of the theories that underpins the idea of the epic as a literary genre is that epics are a record of what happened, albeit retold in a hyperbolic and exaggerated style. The idea that Valmiki put together a story that was already in circulation serves the purposes of those who would like to believe that the story of the Ramayana is true, that all Valmiki did was record these real events in the most beautiful language available to him. While it may well be that there was once a prince who was unjustly exiled after a palace intrigue that placed his younger brother on the throne, and it may also be that when he lived in the forest, his wife was abducted by the powerful ruler of a distant land and it may further be that the exiled prince had to find allies and fight a great war to win her back and regain his kingdom, that story is not the Ramayana. The Ramayana is a story where monkeys fly and demons have ten heads and creatures change their shapes and forms at will. It is a story that contains flying chariots and magical weapons powered by secret utterances. It is a tale where dharma and karma act together to make things happen, where making the right choice does not always lead to the right (or the happiest) consequences.

Eventually, over centuries of tellings and retellings, of religious shifts and reforms, the story of Rama becomes a story of a god acting on earth, in the world of men. But until that theological moment which occurs in historical time, the story, as exemplified in Valmiki's telling, is many things, including an epic. Once Rama is established as a god, as Vishnu descending to earth as an avatara to restore dharma, the Ramayana becomes a Vaishnava text. It is unlikely that it was always thus – the composition of the Sanskrit Ramayana pre-dating the appearance of Vaishnavism as a sectarian creed by several centuries. However, throughout the Valmiki text, there are instances of Rama being referred to as a god and of people around him behaving as if he were a god. Despite this, Rama does not actually exhibit the special powers of a god. His extraordinary gifts and talents, like Ravana's or Hanuman's, appear to be the generic qualities of a hero and predicated on the narrative necessities of the Ramayana as an epic rather than on Rama's uniqueness in his own story.

One of the most poignant existential moments in the Valmiki text is at the end of the Yuddha Kanda, when all the gods have gathered to celebrate Sita's triumph at the trial by fire that she puts herself through to prove her chastity to her husband and his allies.

> [The gods] raised their strong arms that were adorned with jewels and addressed Rama, who stood in front of them with his palms joined.
>
> 'You are the creator of the worlds and the foremost of the wise! How could you let Sita walk into the fire? Don't you know that you are the greatest among the gods?
>
> 'Long ago, you were Ritadhama, the best of the vasus. Then you were the self-born Prajapati, the creator of the three worlds. You were the eighth rudra and the fifth panchama. The ashvins are your ears, the sun and the moon are your eyes. You are visible in the time between the end and the beginning of the worlds. And yet, you have humiliated Sita as if you were an ordinary man!'
>
> Rama, the lord of the worlds, the best among those who practise dharma, said, 'I always thought I was human, that I was Rama, the son of Dasharatha. Tell me who I am. Where did I come from? Why am I here?'[1]

The question of whether Rama is aware of his divinity in Valmiki's text has been asked and answered many times over the centuries. As one might expect, for such a crucial and multilayered question, the answers have been multiple and complex. Each of us who reads the Ramayana chooses the answer that suits us, for there are a number of possibilities with regard to

---

[1] Arshia Sattar (tr.), *Valmiki's Ramayana* (New Delhi: HarperCollins India, 2019), chap. 67.

the extent and knowledge of Rama's divinity within the text. But since we know that the text we call Valmiki's was compiled over a long period of time and through several moments in the history of what we now call Hinduism, we presume that passages and verses were added and subtracted, each transaction shading the larger narrative not simply with a theology but also with a politics. Nowhere in Valmiki is this theology, of Rama as Vishnu, more emphatically stamped on the story as it is in the Bala and Uttara Kandas. In the Bala Kanda, the gods together beseech Vishnu to take human form to deal with Ravana, who cannot be killed by gods, gandharvas, yakshas and danavas because of the boon he secured from Brahma.

> Praised by all the gods, Vishnu humbly asked them a question, although he already knew the answer. 'How can this king of the rakshasas be killed? Tell me and I will use that very method to kill this creature who torments the rishis!'
>
> The gods cried out together, 'Be born as the son of a mortal woman and kill him in battle! O scorcher of your foes, Ravana practised severe austerities for years and gratified Brahma, the creator of the worlds, the most revered. Brahma was so pleased that he gave Ravana a boon by which he was invulnerable to all beings except humans. In the old days, Ravana scorned humans and so he did not include them in his boon of invulnerability. O enemy-burner, Ravana can only be killed by a human.' Vishnu considered the words of the gods and decided to choose King Dasharatha as his father.[2]

In the Uttara Kanda, Rama rejoins his divine essence after Time comes to tell him that his days on earth are over.

> Rama went forth, wearing dazzling white clothes, carrying a bunch of kusha grass in his hand and uttering mantras to invoke Brahma. He left his home and walked down the road shining like the sun. He did not speak to anyone or look at anything, Shri walked on his left holding a lotus, the Earth walked on his right and his own majesty walked in

[2] Sattar, *Valmiki's Ramayana*, chap. 4.

> front of him. His great bow and all his arrows took human form and followed him. The Vedas appeared in the form of brahmins and Savitri, the protector of all, and the sacred syllables were also there.
>
> ...
>
> After going one and a half yojanas, Rama came to the clear, pure waters of the Sarayu that lay to the west. At that moment, Brahma, the grandfather of the worlds, arrived, surrounded by all the gods and great sages in their wondrous vehicles. Flowers rained from the sky and a gentle breeze blew. Thousands of gandharvas and apsaras came there as Rama approached the Sarayu on foot.
>
> 'Welcome, Vishnu!' Brahma's voice rang out from the sky. 'It is our good fortune that you have returned to us, Rama! Enter your own body along with your godlike brothers!'
>
> Rama did as Brahma said and entered Vishnu's effulgent and splendid body with his brothers. The gods and heavenly creatures and celestial beings all worshipped him, praising him and saying that the heavens had been purified by his arrival.[3]

The Uttara Kanda lulls us into equanimity, into a state of quiescence, by telling us stories after the exhausting events and extreme emotions that have preceded it in Rama's life. It is the book that establishes Rama's unchallenged rule in Kosala and the surrounding lands, it reiterates the Bala Kanda's idea of Ayodhya, now a ramarajya, where all is calm, all is bright. Perhaps Rama, too, needs to sit back and consider all that he has done and all that has happened to him. We listen to these stories with him, even stories that we have heard before. But through these modified stories, there are other larger corrections that are also being undertaken and these will be examined through the essays in this book.

On the one hand, we could say that nothing much happens in the Uttara Kanda, that it exists only to reinforce the idea of Rama-as-Vishnu. The overall atmosphere of the kanda is calm and serene. Secure in his kingdom, Rama listens to the stories that Agastya tells him, mainly stories about Ravana's ancestors and the rakshasa clan to which he belongs. On the other hand, we

[3] Sattar, *Valmiki's Ramayana*, chap. 71.

could say that everything that is of any lasting significance happens in the Uttara Kanda: Rama banishes his beloved Sita because he is persuaded by town gossip that a good man would not take back a wife who had lived in the house of another man; Rama kills Shambuka, a low-caste man practising austerities that are above his station, in order to secure the health and well-being of the brahmins in his kingdom; Rama is reunited with his sons, whom he now believes to be his legitimate heirs, at the sacrifice that he conducts, the same sacrifice at which he loses his wife forever; Rama watches over the voluntary death of his devoted brother Lakshmana who submits to the curse of the sage Durvasas.

The Uttara Kanda is the seventh and last book of what we call the Valmiki Ramayana. The word 'uttara' has many meanings, among them, 'after', 'epilogue', 'ultimate' and 'answer'. This Uttara Kanda performs the functions of all those meanings: it comes after Rama's adventures as an exiled prince and then as a reinstated king are over; it acts as an epilogue to the main story where loose ends are tied up and narrative closure is provided with Rama's ascent to heaven; it is the ultimate moment in his long tale and in his theology; and it provides a series of complex answers to questions that the previous story suggests. For this volume, the most important aspect of the Uttara Kanda is that it provides answers – not simply to questions that had actually been raised, but also to questions that might have been imagined then and might be imagined even now.

The most obvious ways in which the Uttara Kanda provides answers is by telling and retelling stories. In the Kishkindha Kanda, it is from Jambavan that we learn about Hanuman's super-simian powers by hearing the story of his birth and all the boons he received when he was struck down by Indra's thunderbolt. Hanuman also hears this story, perhaps for the first time, and he is immediately both empowered and inspired to leap over the ocean in search of Sita. At that moment, a discerning reader might ask, how come Hanuman didn't know he had these powers? But the larger story rushes onward, flying with Hanuman to the next narrative moment, and has no time to answer that question. The Uttara Kanda has, however, noted that lacuna, that dangling thread, and neatly weaves it into the multiple closures that an epilogue can provide. Agastya tells Rama the story of Hanuman's birth because he has never heard it. And Agastya's version adds the crucial episode in which young

Hanuman, made mischievous by his many boons, starts to harass the sages as they perform their rituals. The sages curse him to forget his powers until he is reminded at the moment when he most needs them. The discerning reader is now satisfied, the narrative has corrected itself and the story can go further without embarrassment.

These corrective mechanisms demonstrate that the 'text' knows itself.[4] But they also indicate that some parts of the text (and even perhaps of the story itself) came later. Scholars are more and more clear (with more and more evidence to support their argument) that the Bala and Uttara Kandas are later additions to what we call the Valmiki text. Given the language and tone of these first and last books, they clearly come from a later linguistic and, more importantly, a later theological period when Vishnu has become a deity who has avataras, a deity who acts in the world for the benefit of human beings. This he does by 'saving' dharma in various ways, usually by killing those who perpetuate adharma, for example, Ravana. The Bala and Uttara Kandas are also the books in which it is explicitly stated that Rama is a god, that Vishnu was persuaded by the other gods to take human form and kill Ravana. Rama's story as a god later becomes a central part of Vaishnava bhakti as versions of the Ramayana appear in different languages across the subcontinent and beyond.

The Bala and Uttara Kandas are also the only books of the Valmiki Ramayana where Valmiki himself appears, framing, as it were, the story that he is about to tell, a story that will eventually be presented to Rama by his estranged sons. Valmiki is in the opening verse of the Ramayana, but he is not in its last few pages. He appears to exit the story after Sita enters the earth but in an unexpected Moebius strip moment, it's entirely possible that he stays in the wings of the action and continues to narrate/describe the rest of Rama's life as it happens.[5] Valmiki's presence in only the first and last books

[4] I don't mean to essentialise the text or to suggest that it has some mysterious autonomous agency. Obviously, there are self-conscious composers and redactors at work in the Bala and Uttara Kandas, with political and theological agendas that need to be communicated.

[5] For more on this, see Arshia Sattar, 'Inside/Outside: Where is Valmiki in the Story He Tells', in *Lost Loves: Exploring Rama's Anguish* (New Delhi: HarperCollins India, 2019).

might also reinforce the idea that these were written later, bookends for a story that has suddenly changed its tone and purpose.

Apart from the Rama-as-god theme placing the Valmiki Ramayana in a wholly different universe of texts, the politics of the Uttara Kanda also seem to diverge from what we experience in the middle books. In the Uttara Kanda, Rama, who had taken Sita back after her captivity on Ravana's island, is persuaded to send her away because of what people are saying. Narada convinces Rama to kill a low-caste man who is practising austerities. Lakshmana wilfully places himself in the way of a curse that will end his life and Rama does nothing to prevent the curse from being fulfilled. There is a noticeable difference in the way the story now reacts to so-called transgressions (of dharma) by women and lower castes. Rama must act as a king at all times, whether it be towards his wife, his brother or his citizens.

Like all epilogues, or books that provide answers, the existence of the Uttara Kanda demands that we then read the text backwards, or rather, retrospectively. From the stories that the Uttara Kanda tells, we learn why people did what they did, what they had done before and what their motives for their actions might have been. Because we are placed in a universe where boons, curses and past lives are all operational, we find also that our characters move further away from making free choices to their lives being determined by their past actions. The way we see Rama and his story after reading the Uttara Kanda is substantially different from how we would see it if we had stopped reading the story at the end of the Yuddha Kanda.

Ravana, in particular, is dogged by a series of curses that affect his actions and make his death at the hands of Rama a certainty: Vedavati declares that a woman will be the cause of his death; Rambha ensures that he cannot touch a woman against her will; Nandi predicts that monkeys will be responsible for the death of his clan; Aranyana promises that an Ikshvaku king will be born for his destruction. When a text employs such a multitude of causes for a single event, we see the narrative strategy of overdetermination at work. Leaving nothing to chance, the text and its creators make sure that Ravana will be felled by one of the many reasons that his backstory provides. We might want to ask why the Uttara Kanda is so anxious that Ravana's actions and his death be so utterly overdetermined. And that we be reminded many times over that he is a rakshasa, and that he has the nasty temperament as well as all the predilections of that antagonistic category of being. Could it be because the middle books of the Ramayana hint at Ravana's nobility, his majesty? Or, do some parts of the main story stretch credulity, such as a powerful rakshasa king and his kingdom being defeated by a ragtag army of forest dwellers armed with trees and stones? Or, does the Ramayana hint at Ravana's genuine love for Sita? Or, are there other books (Puranas and the like) being composed at the time of the Uttara Kanda that have turned Ravana into a Shiva bhakta, respected and protected through hard-won boons by the god who is Vishnu's sectarian rival?

In the overdetermined case of Ravana, we see that the Uttara Kanda attempts to answer all of these questions, some of which have only been alluded to by the story as it unfolds. None of these questions have actually been asked, inside or outside the text. We have moved from anticipating the discerning reader to cutting off the arguments of the suspicious reader, the sceptical reader.

And so we see that there are many agendas at work in the Uttara Kanda, which together make the entire story all the more subtle, ethically complex and therefore, fascinating. This powerful text provides an emphatic (if not satisfactory to all) conclusion to the story of King Rama as well as to the story of Rama-as-Vishnu. As a king, Rama reverses his previous act of taking his wife back after she has been in the custody of another man because the queen and the king must be above reproach. Also as a king, Rama ensures that a strict hierarchy of caste behaviour prevails in his kingdom by killing Shambuka. Further, he makes sure that all unruly elements around his kingdom are subdued (for example, Lavana) by his brothers. He conducts the sacrifice to establish the supremacy of the Ikshvakus in the region and, eventually, settles his nephews and sons in kingdoms of their own. Having ordered his temporal tasks, he completes his divine duties by ascending to heaven to rejoin his real essence as Vishnu. As a god acting in the world of men, he has restored dharma by killing Ravana, as an avatara should.

But the neat end that the Uttara Kanda offers has consequences, both social and political, for the way the entire text of Valmiki's Ramayana is read and inhabits our culture. It also points to the enormous changes that occurred within Hinduism and its surrounding polity in the centuries between the time when the first and the last verses of the Valmiki Ramayana were composed. It is important that we receive and read this foundational text of religion and literature as a reflection of the historical moments through which it has passed.

# UTTARA

## SARGAS ONE TO ONE HUNDRED

## Sarga 1: The Sages Come to Rama's Court

When Rama had regained his kingdom after slaying the rakshasas, all the sages came to honour him: those that lived in the east, Kaushika and Yavakrita and Raubhya and Chyavana and Kanva, the son of Medhatithi; those that lived in the south, Shvastatreya and the venerable Namuchi, came along with Agastya; those that lived in the west, Prishadgu and Kavasha and the great sage Raudreya, came too, along with their disciples. The seven great sages, Vasishtha, Kashyapa, Atri, Vishvamitra, Gautama, Jamadagni and Bharadvaja, each of them distinguished and blazing like a sacrificial fire, arrived at Rama's palace and waited to be let in.

The doorkeeper went immediately to where Rama was, and when he saw him, shining like the full moon, he quickly told him that Agastya had arrived with the sages. As soon as he heard that the sages, who were as bright as the morning sun, had arrived, Rama told the doorkeeper to let them come in at their convenience. Rama stood up and joined his palms and greeted them respectfully when they entered. He ordered seats to be brought for them.

When those bulls among sages were comfortably seated on grass mats decorated with gold, Rama asked after their welfare and about their disciples and their mentors. The great sages, who knew the Vedas, said to Rama, 'Joy of the Raghus, strong-armed Rama, we are well in every way. And we see that you, too, are well, after killing your enemy. You have conquered the three worlds with your bow – Ravana, king of the rakshasas, was obviously no obstacle for you. Well done, Rama! You killed Ravana and his sons and grandsons and we are fortunate to see you today, victorious and in the company of your dependants. Well done! You killed the night-ranging rakshasas Prahasta, Vikata, Virupaksha, Mahodara and the dangerous Akampana. You felled Kumbhakarna in battle, Rama, larger than whom there is no known creature. Well done! You were victorious in the duel with the king of the rakshasas, who is invulnerable even to the gods. Defeating Ravana was a mere trifle. Well done! You killed his son, too. Luckily, strong-armed one, you were set free when that enemy of the gods came charging towards you like death itself. You were victorious. We were surprised to hear that you had killed Indrajit – he is invulnerable to all living beings and a master of illusion in war. Well done! You have given us an auspicious gift – freedom from fear. May you grow in victory, tormentor of your enemies!'

Rama was very surprised when he heard what the enlightened sages had to say. He joined his palms in respect and said, 'Gentlemen, you dismiss such great and heroic rakshasas as Kumbhakarna and Ravana. Why do you praise Indrajit? You dismiss such courageous rakshasas as Mahodara, Prahasta and Virupaksha. Why do you praise Indrajit? What is his power, of what manner are his strength and courage? How and why is he considered greater than his father? I do not command you, but if you can, please tell me. If it is a secret that can be told, I wish to hear it. Tell me, how did Indrajit gain his boons and how did he defeat Indra?'

Kumbhayoni Agastya, the effulgent one, heard great-souled Rama's words and said, 'Listen, king, and I will tell you how he came by his power and his strength, how he could kill his enemies and not be killed by them. I will tell you, Rama, about Ravana's race and his birth and the boons that were conferred upon him and how he got them.'

## Sarga 2: The Birth of Vishravas

'Long ago, in the Krita Yuga, there lived a brahmin sage named Pulastya, a son of Prajapati, who was like Brahma manifest. His virtues and fame were all rooted in dharma and they are not easy to describe. It is enough to say that he was a son of Prajapati. For reasons of dharma, that bull among sages went to the Trinabindu hermitage on the slopes of Mount Meru and began to live there. The very soul of dharma, he performed his austerities and his studies and undertook the control of his senses. But some young women went there and disturbed his practice. They were the daughters of the gods and the serpents and the royal sages and apsaras, too, and they would go there to enjoy themselves. Because the place was so lovely in all seasons and the woods were so pleasant, the young women went there often to play. The effulgent sage was enraged and said, "Whoever comes within my line of sight shall become pregnant!" When they heard those words from the great-souled one, the young women became afraid of the brahmin's curse and stopped going there.

'But the royal sage Trinabindu's daughter did not hear them and she went to the hermitage and wandered around without fear. At that time, Prajapati's son was reciting the Vedas, shining with the light of his austerities. When she heard the sound of the Vedas and saw that man, rich in austerities, her body turned pale and began to show signs of pregnancy. She grew agitated when she saw the change in herself and she realized what had happened. She said, "What is this?" and went to her father and stood in front of him. Trinabindu looked at his daughter and said, "Why is your body in this peculiar condition?" The poor girl joined her palms and said to her illustrious father, "I don't know, father, why my body is like this. A while ago, I had gone to the heavenly hermitage of the enlightened sage Pulastya to look for my friends. I did not see my friends there but then I noticed this change in my appearance and so I came here."

'Trinabindu, shining with the light of his austerities, entered into a meditative trance and saw that this was a result of the sage's actions. The enlightened one understood the curse of the great sage and taking his daughter with him, he went to Pulastya and said, "Venerable one, here is my daughter, adorned with her own virtues. Accept her as an offering, great sage, she has come here of her own free will. Your limbs are tired from the practise of austerities, there is no doubt that she will serve you continuously." The brahmin was eager to take the young woman and so when he heard the words of the righteous king, he agreed.

'The king returned to his palace after he had given his daughter away. And the girl stayed there, gratifying her husband with her virtues. Filled with affection, the effulgent sage said, "I am pleased with your wealth of virtues, my dear. And so, today, I will give you a son who will be my equal in his attributes. He will continue both our lineages and he shall be known as Paulastya. And because you heard me reciting the Vedas, he shall without a doubt be known as Vishravas." The young woman was thrilled to hear this and before long, she gave birth to that son.

'Vishravas, bull among sages, became known in the three worlds for his integrity and righteousness and, like his father, he was yoked to the practise of austerities.'

## Sarga 3: The Birth of Vaishravana

'Vishravas was truthful, courteous, alert, dedicated to studying the Vedas, pure, detached from sensual pleasures and devoted to cultivating righteousness. The great sage Bharadvaja learned how he lived and gave his own daughter, Devavarini, to him as a wife. Vishravas, bull among sages, took Bharadvaja's daughter in marriage and was happy. The soul of dharma, he fathered a marvellous son on her, full of energy and vigour and with all the virtues of a brahmin. His grandfather was overjoyed when the boy was born and named him in consultation with the gods and the sages. "Since he is the son of Vishravas and is just like his father, he shall be named Vaishravana," they said.

'Effulgent Vaishravana went to a forest where austerities were performed and there, he blazed brighter, like a fire fed with oblations. While he was living in the forest, it occurred to that great soul to always practise dharma, for dharma is the highest goal. He practised austerities in that vast forest for a thousand years, living according to the prescribed rules – first living on water, then on air, then on nothing at all – and the thousand years passed as if they were a single year. Effulgent Brahma was highly gratified and he went to that hermitage along with Indra and the hosts of gods. He said, "Sage of true vows, I am pleased with your actions, my child. Ask for a boon, my dear, for in my opinion, you deserve one."

'Vaishravana said to Grandfather Brahma who stood before him, "Blessed one, I wish to be a guardian of the quarters, the one who protects wealth."

'Pleased and satisfied in their minds, Brahma and the hosts of gods agreed. Brahma said to Vaishravana, "I was just about to create the fourth guardian of the quarters. Yama, Indra and Varuna are the others in the position that you desire. Knower of dharma, go and take your place and become the lord of wealth. You shall be the fourth guardian of the quarters along with Yama, Indra and Varuna! There is a celestial vehicle named Pushpaka which shines like the sun. Take it and become equal to the gods. May all be well with you. Now, we shall go as we have come, child, for we have accomplished our purpose by giving you these great boons."

'When Brahma and all the gods had departed for the heavens, the lord of wealth spoke respectfully to his father. "Blessed one, I have obtained boons from lotus-born Brahma but he did not appoint a place for me to live. Find me a place to live, lord, a place where no living beings will be harmed." Vishravas, bull among sages, said, "Knower of dharma, listen. There is a beautiful city called Lanka, built by Vishvakarma for the rakshasas, as Amaravati was for Indra. The city has gateways of gold and precious stones but it was abandoned by the rakshasas long ago because they feared Vishnu. There are no rakshasas there now because they all retreated to the underworld. Go and live there as you please. Your stay there will be without blame and you will not bother anyone!"

'The great soul listened to his father's righteous words and went to live on a mountain peak in Lanka. Before long, and because of his rule, Lanka became prosperous and was filled with thousands of happy and contented rakshasas. The great-souled king of the rakshasas, the son of Vishravas, lived happily in Lanka which was surrounded by the ocean. Using Pushpaka, every now and then, the gentle lord of wealth would happily visit his mother and father. He was praised by the gods and gandharvas as well as by the siddhas and charanas and he shone with rays like the sun himself.'

## Sarga 4: The Birth of Sukesha

Rama shook his head and, for a moment, he gazed at Agastya, whose body shone like the three fires on a sacrificial altar. He said, smiling, 'Blessed one, I was surprised to learn that Lanka already belonged to the flesh-eating rakshasas. We had heard that the rakshasas were born from the bloodline of Pulastya. Now you are suggesting a different origin for them. Were they more powerful even than Ravana, Kumbhakarna, Prahasta and Vikata? And Ravana's sons? Who was their ancestor, brahmin? What was his name and how strong was he? For what crime were they driven out so long ago by Vishnu? Relate all this to me in detail, flawless one. Dispel my curiosity as the sun dispels darkness.'

Agastya was surprised when he heard Rama's elegant words and he said to him, 'Prajapati Brahma, born from a lotus, created water and then created living beings to protect the waters. Living beings were tormented by hunger and thirst and they presented themselves humbly before Brahma and said, "What shall we do?" Brahma smiled and said, "Protect these waters!" Some of the hungry ones said, "We shall protect!" and others among them said, "We shall worship!" Brahma, the creator, said to them, "Those who said that they would protect shall become rakshasas and those who said they would worship shall become yakshas!"[6]

'There were two brothers, Heti and Praheti, both bulls among the rakshasas. They oppressed their enemies, like Madhu and Kaitabha had done. Praheti, the righteous one, wanted to live in the forest but Heti tried very hard to find himself a wife. He was extremely clever and very strong. He married Yama's sister who was truly frightening and so was named Bhaya. He fathered a son on her who came to be known as Vidyutkesha, thus making her the best among those with sons. Heti's son, effulgent Vidyutkesha, was as bright as a blazing fire and he grew like a lotus in the waters. When that night-ranging rakshasa became a young man, his father made efforts to find him a wife. Heti, bull among rakshasas, chose Sandhya's daughter, who was like Sandhya, for the purpose of engendering sons. Sandhya decided that since she needed to give her daughter to somebody, she gave her to Vidyutkesha. Once he had obtained Sandhya's daughter, Vidyutkesha enjoyed many pleasures with her, as Indra does with Paulomi.

'In time, just as rain clouds swell with water drawn from the ocean, Salakantaka became pregnant by Vidyutkesha, and the rakshasi went to Mount Mandara to have her baby, like Ganga did when she had Skanda. After she had given birth, she desired Vidyutkesha. She enjoyed herself with her husband and forgot about her son. The abandoned baby, who was like the autumn sun, began to cry softly. He put his fist in his mouth and roared

---

6 In Sanskrit, 'rakshami' means 'I protect', hence 'rakshasa' and here, 'yakshami' means 'I worship', hence 'yaksha'.

like a thundercloud. Shiva, destroyer of the three cities, who was seated on his bull with Parvati and flying high above, noticed the wailing rakshasa baby. Parvati felt pity and made the child the same age as his mother. She also made him immortal. Because he loved Parvati, Shiva gave him a celestial city. Then, your majesty, Parvati also gave the rakshasi a boon – that she would conceive at once and that her children would immediately reach the same age as her. Now that he had received the marvellous city as a boon from Shiva, Sukesha, who was mighty and extremely clever, became arrogant and wandered around the skies like Indra.'

## Sarga 5: Malyavan, Sumali and Mali Are Born

'A gandharva named Gramani, who was like Indra, saw that the rakshasa Sukesha had been given these righteous boons. He gave his daughter, Devavati, who was like a second goddess of good fortune, to Sukesha according to dharma, as Daksha had given away Shri. Devavati was as pleased with her loving husband, who had been made glorious by boons, as a poor man who has found wealth. United with her, that night-stalking rakshasa shone like a mighty wandering elephant born from Anjana. Sukesha, king of the rakshasas, fathered three rakshasa sons on her, Rama – Malyavan, Sumali and Mali, who was the strongest of them all. They were as steady as the three worlds, as firm as the three fires on a sacrificial altar, as formidable as the sacred chants, as terrible as disease. Sukesha's sons blazed like the three fires and they grew quickly, like a disease that has been ignored. When they learned that their father had obtained his boons through great austerities, the brothers went to Mount Meru, determined to perform penances. The rakshasas accepted harsh rules, best of kings, and began their penance which terrified all living beings. They heated up the three worlds, the gods, the asuras and humans, by these practices and by truthfulness, self-control and good actions.

'Eternal Brahma, the four-faced one, arrived in a flying chariot and said to the rakshasas, "I have come to offer you boons!" Realizing that Brahma, surrounded by Indra and the hosts of gods, was going to give them boons, the rakshasas shook like trees. They joined their palms in respect and said, "If you are pleased with our austerities and wish to give us boons, then make us unbeatable, killers of our enemies and long-lived. Let us be superior to others and attached to one another."

'"It shall be so," said Lord Brahma to Sukesha's sons. After that, Brahma, who loved brahmins, returned to his realm.

'Then, Rama, when they received those boons which had made them fearless, the night-stalking rakshasas began to obstruct the gods and the asuras. The gods and the sages and the charanas were troubled but they could find no one anywhere who would protect them and they suffered like men in hell. The three rakshasas were filled with happiness and they went together to ageless Vishvakarma, the best of builders. They said to him, "Sir, you build houses for the gods according to their hearts' desires. Build a house for us, too, wise one! Build a house like Shiva's in the Himalayas, close to Mount Mandara or to Mount Meru!"

'Mighty-armed Vishvakarma told the rakshasas about a house that was like Indra's Amaravati. "On the southern shore of the ocean lies the mountain named Trikuta. Among its peaks which are like clouds, there is a rock that even birds can't reach because it is chiselled on all four sides. I built a city there, on Indra's command. It is called Lanka. It is thirty yojanas wide and has doorways made of gold. Best of rakshasas, you are unassailable, you can live in that city, as Indra lives in Amaravati together with the gods. You are subduers of your foes. When you occupy the fortress of Lanka along with other rakshasas, it will be impregnable to enemies." Hearing Vishvakarma's words, Rama, those rakshasas went happily to Lanka, which was circled by deep moats and had hundreds of houses made of gold. They settled there with thousands of their followers.

'There was a gandharvi named Narmada, who enriched all kinds of dharma. She had three goddess-like daughters – Hri, Shri and Kirti. Even though she was not a rakshasi, she happily gave the girls, whose faces were like the full moon, to the rakshasas in order of age. She married her three fortunate gandharva daughters to those excellent rakshasas under an auspicious star. Once Sukesha's sons were married, Rama, they took pleasure in their wives as immortals do with apsaras.

'Learn, now, about the children that Malyavan fathered on his lovely wife, Sundari. They were Vajramushthi and Virupaksha and the rakshasa

Durmukha, and Suptaghna and Yajnakopa and Matta and Unmatta. Sundari also gave birth to a lovely daughter named Anala.

'Sumali's wife had a face like the full moon. Her name was Ketumati and he loved her more than life itself. Sumali fathered children on Ketumati. Learn, your majesty, who they were, in order of birth. There were Prahasta and Kampana and then Vikata and Kalakarmuka, Dhumraksha and then Danda and then mighty Suparshva, Samhradi, Praghasa and then the rakshasa Bhasakarna and the daughters Raka, Pushpotkata, sweet-smiling Kaikasi and Kumbhinasi. These are known as the children of Sumali.

'Mali's wife was the gorgeous gandharvi named Vasuda. Her eyes were like lotus petals and she equalled the best of the yakshis. Listen, Rama, as I tell you about the children that Sumali's younger brother fathered on her: Anala and Anila and then there was Hara and then Sampati. These sons of Mali were Vibhishana's ministers.

'And the three of them – Malyavan, Sumali and Mali – bulls among rakshasas, proud of their courage and strength and surrounded by their sons and other night-stalking rakshasas, began to obstruct the gods led by Indra and the sages and the nagas and the danavas. They wandered together through the universe like the wind and they were the very image of death in battle. Made arrogant by the boons they had received, they disrupted sacrifices and sacred rituals all the time.'

## Sarga 6: The Gods Ask Vishnu to Protect Them from the Rakshasas

'Along with their wives, they tormented gods and sages rich in austerities, who sought refuge with the god of gods, Shiva. They joined their palms in respect and in voices that trembled with fear, together, they said to him, the three-eyed one, enemy of the triple city, enemy of Kama, "Blessed one, you are the tormentor of your foes. Both kings and commoners are being obstructed by the sons of Sukesha because of the boons they received from Grandfather Brahma. Our hermitages, which were our shelters, no longer provide refuge because of them. They have driven the celestials out of heaven and are now playing there as if they were Indra and the immortals. 'I am

Vishnu', 'I am Rudra', 'I am Brahma', 'I am Indra, king of the gods', 'I am Yama', 'I am Varuna', 'I am the Sun and I am the Moon', say these rakshasas and their forebears. They have been made arrogant by their boons. They take pleasure in battle and they obstruct us. We are frightened. You must free us from fear. Take on your inauspicious form and eliminate these thorns in the sides of the gods!"

'Purple-hued Shiva with the knotted hair had some affection for Sumali. So he said to all the gods who had beseeched him, "I will not kill those demons for they cannot be killed by me. But I will give you advice about who will be able to kill them. Bulls among the gods, you must seek refuge with Vishnu for this plan to work. He is the lord, and he will kill them." The gods praised Shiva with cheers of "Victory!" Still oppressed by the fear of the rakshasas, they went to Vishnu, holder of the conch and the discus, and honoured him. Greatly agitated, they spoke to him about being oppressed by Sukesha's sons. "The three sons of Sukesha are like the three fires on a sacrificial altar. They have taken our homes because they have those boons. They have established themselves in an impenetrable city called Lanka on the peak of Mount Trikuta and they get together and obstruct us! Do us a favour. Kill them, killer of Madhu! Cut off their heads with your discus and offer them to Yama as if they were lotuses, their heads as well as the heads of all those who are with them! Rid us of our fear, as the sun melts the ice."

'Addressed thus by the gods, Vishnu Janardana, god of gods, who creates fear among his enemies, said to them, "I know Sukesha, who is arrogant because of the boons he received from Shiva. I also know his sons, the eldest of whom is Malyavan. I will subdue these rakshasas who have crossed all limits of decency in battle. Worry no more, gods!" The gods praised him and, filled with joy, returned to their respective homes.

'When Malyavan learned what the gods had planned, he said to his heroic brothers, "The gods and the sages have gone together to three-eyed Shiva, calling for our deaths. They said, 'The sons of Sukesha, dreadful in form, are bloated with arrogance because of the boons they have received and they obstruct us every step of the way. These rakshasas have defeated us, Shiva! We are so fearful of them that we cannot stay in our own homes. Kill them for our sake, three-eyed one! Burn them up with your roars!' When the thirty gods said this, Shiva, the howler, killer of Andhaka, shook his head and his hand and said, 'Gods, I cannot kill Sukesha in battle. But I will give you advice about who can kill him – yellow-robed Vishnu, holder of the discus and the mace. He can kill them. Seek refuge with him.' When they received this advice from Shiva, the enemy of Kama, they bowed to him and went to Vishnu's abode and told him everything. Vishnu said to the gods led by Indra, 'I will subdue these enemies of the gods in battle! Worry no more!' Bulls among rakshasas, Vishnu has promised the frightened gods that he will destroy us. What do you think would be appropriate? He has killed Hiranyakashipu and other enemies of the gods. It is not easy to defeat Vishnu who wants to kill us."

'Sumali and Mali listened to Malyavan's words and then they spoke to their elder brother as the ashvins would to Indra. "We have studied the sacred texts, we have given charity, we have performed the required rituals, we have guarded our power, we have obtained long lives free of sickness and we have stood firm in our own dharma. We have plunged into the imperturbable ocean of the gods with our weapons. We have always defeated the gods in battle, we have no fear of death. Vishnu, Rudra, Indra and even Yama, all of them are afraid to stand before us. Vishnu has no reason to fault us. The gods have turned Vishnu's mind against us. Surrounded by all our armies, we are ready to take on the gods who are the cause of this disorder."

'The rakshasas Mali and Sumali and the eldest, Malyavan, announced their plans. Angrily, they went forth into battle, like mighty Jambha and Vritra. With their battle chariots and their elephants and horses that were as large as elephants, mules, cattle, camels, porpoises and serpents, crocodiles and tortoises, and fish and birds that were like Garuda, and lions and tigers and boars and deer and various other animals, the rakshasas, enemies of the gods, proud of their strength, left Lanka and marched towards the realm of the gods to do battle.

'The other creatures that lived there were filled with fear and despair for they realized the calamity that would befall Lanka. Commanded by Time, terrifying omens predicting the destruction of the rakshasa leaders arose in the sky and on earth. Clouds rained bones and hot blood, the ocean breached its shores and even the best of mountains shook. Thousands of creatures rushed around as if they were dancing, making sounds like the rumbling of thunder or a horse laughing. Great vultures spewing fire from their mouths, wheeled above the rakshasas like death. But the rakshasas were proud of their strength and ignored these omens. They did not turn back, moving forward as if drawn by Yama's noose.

'Malyavan, Sumali and Mali went ahead, blazing like sacrificial fires. As the gods take refuge in Brahma, so the rakshasas depended on Malyavan who was like Mount Malyavan. Under Mali's control, the army of rakshasa leaders rumbled like a thundercloud as it moved towards the realm of the gods, eager for victory. Lord Vishnu made up his mind to do battle when he heard about the rakshasas' plans from a messenger of the gods. Praised by the gods, siddhas, sages, the best of the gandharvas and the apsaras, Vishnu, enemy of the enemy of the gods, came forth, holding the discus, a sword, the bow and the conch. The rakshasa army trembled, shaking like the peaks of the Blue Mountain. Their flags were scattered by the wind from Garuda's wings, their weapons were in disarray. Thousands of rakshasas, rangers of the night, surrounded Vishnu who shone like the fire at the end of time, and began to attack him with their excellent weapons which were sharp and tipped with blood and fat.'

## Sarga 7: Vishnu Fights Malyavan, Sumali and Mali

'Like clouds raining down upon a mountain, that rumbling horde of rakshasas rained its arrows on Vishnu. Surrounded by dark-skinned rakshasas, blue-black Vishnu appeared like a mountain of collyrium being rained upon by clouds. Lightning-like arrows were released from rakshasa bows, like locusts to a paddy field, like insects to a tree, like bees to honey, like sea creatures to the water. They were sped by the mind and they entered Vishnu like the worlds at the end of time. There were charioteers with chariots and elephant riders with elephants, soldiers on horseback, and foot soldiers as well. They were all in the sky. Mountain-like rakshasas attacked Vishnu with their arrows and spears and swords, stopping his breath as breathing exercises would stop that of a brahmin. As heavily assaulted by the night-stalking rakshasas as the ocean is replete with fish, Vishnu stretched his bow, Sharnga, and loosed his arrows upon them. Vishnu cut the rakshasas down by the hundreds and thousands, chopping them to the size of sesame seeds with arrows that were as fast as lightning and as swift as thought.

'Putting the rakshasas to flight the way the wind does the rain, Vishnu Purushottama blew his conch, Panchajanya, born of the waters, and it sounded to all living beings like the roar of the ocean at the end of time. It terrified the rakshasas as the roar of a lion, king of the beasts, would terrify elephants in a forest. It made it impossible for horses to stand, elephants were humbled and weakened warriors fell from their chariots. Fine-feathered arrows, released from Sharnga, sharp as lightning bolts, passed through the bodies of the rakshasas and pierced the earth. The rakshasas fell to the ground like mountains struck by lightning. Like streams of red ochre that flow in the mountains, blood flowed from the wounds of the rakshasas caused by Vishnu's discus. The voices of the rakshasas were drowned out by the sound of Panchajanya, best of the conches, the twanging of the bow and Vishnu's own roars. Hundreds of thousands of arrows flew swiftly from Vishnu's bow, like rays from the sun, like massive waves from the ocean, like great snakes from the mountains, like showers of rain from a cloud. Like a lion chased by a sharabha, like an elephant chased by a lion, like a leopard by a tiger, like a dog by a leopard, like a cat by a dog, like a snake by a cat, like a rat by a snake, so ran the rakshasas from Vishnu in battle. Others fell to the ground. Vishnu, slayer of Madhu, killed thousands of rakshasas. He filled his conch with air as Indra, the king of the gods, fills the clouds with rain. Tormented by Vishnu's arrows and befuddled by the blaring of the conch, the rakshasa army was crushed and turned towards Lanka.

'When the rakshasa forces had been destroyed by Vishnu, a rain of arrows from Sumali covered Vishnu on the battlefield. The rakshasa raised his bejewelled arm like an elephant lifting its trunk and roared with pleasure. He was like a rain cloud limned by lightning. Vishnu cut off the head of Sumali's roaring charioteer with its shining earrings and the horses dashed around in confusion. Like a stumbling, senseless person, Sumali, lord of the rakshasas, was dragged hither and thither by the panic-stricken horses. Then, Mali entered the battle. He grabbed his bow and arrows and attacked Vishnu. His arrows, adorned with gold, entered Vishnu's body like birds flying to Mount Krauncha. And though Vishnu was hit by thousands of Mali's arrows, he was not disturbed while fighting, just as a man who has controlled his senses is not distracted by anxiety. Then, Vishnu, creator of all beings, holder of the mace, twanged his bowstring and released a flurry of arrows which were streaked with lightning. They entered Mali's body and drank his blood like the serpents drank nectar long ago.

'Vishnu routed Mali with his strength and caused his crown, his arrows, his battle banner, his chariot and his horses to fall to the ground. Now without his chariot, Mali, the best of the night-stalking rakshasas, picked up his mace and charged towards Vishnu like a lion from a mountain peak. He struck Garuda on the forehead, like Shiva had struck Yama, as Indra strikes the mountains with his thunderbolts. Garuda was grievously wounded by that blow from the mace and he was tormented by pain. He took Lord Vishnu away from the battlefield. The rakshasas raised a huge roar when the god left the battlefield because of Mali. Vishnu, Indra's younger brother, was facing away from the battlefield but when he heard the rakshasas' roar, he hurled his discus towards Mali, intending to kill him. Like the wheel of time itself, the discus shone like the sun and lit up the worlds as it cut off Mali's head. Sliced off by that terrible discus, the head of the rakshasa king fell to the ground spewing blood, as Rahu's head had fallen long ago.

'The gods were overjoyed. They roared like lions, shouting, "Excellent!" Sumali and Malyavan burned with grief when they saw Mali dead and along with their armies, they went quickly back to Lanka. Great-souled Garuda had recovered. He was angry and he returned, sweeping away rakshasas with the wind from his wings. The rakshasas fell from the sky into the ocean – some with their lotus-like faces slashed by his discus, others with their chests crushed by his mace, others with their necks severed by his plough, some with their heads split by his club. Some were torn up by his sword, some were pierced by his arrows. Vishnu shot arrows like lightning from his bow and wounded the rakshasas whose dishevelled hair streamed in the wind. The rakshasa army was confused. Their umbrellas were smashed, their weapons had fallen, their clothes had been ripped by arrows, their entrails hung out and their eyes rolled in fear. They were chased by Vishnu like elephants are chased by a lion, and the rakshasas screamed and ran away with their own elephants. Covered by Vishnu's arrows and dropping their own, the rakshasa hordes fled like a black cloud chased by the wind. Rakshasa leaders fell like mountains, their heads cut off by the discus, their limbs crushed by the mace and sliced by the sword. They fell to the ground with their pearl earrings and jewelled necklaces and it seemed as if the Blue Mountain itself had fallen.'

## Sarga 8: Vishnu Defeats the Rakshasas

'As that army was being destroyed from the rear by Vishnu, Malyavan returned, as the ocean does after touching its shore. His eyes bloodshot, his head shaking in anger, the rakshasa said to Vishnu, "Narayana, you do not know the eternal kshatriya dharma. You are killing us, who have no mind for war and are terrified, as if you were a base creature. Lord of the gods, you cannot obtain heaven if you kill those who have turned away from battle. Heaven is only obtained through good deeds. Bearer of the conch, the discus and the mace, if you are keen to fight, then I stand here. I will challenge your strength, show it to me!" Vishnu, the mighty younger brother of Indra, king of the gods, said to that leader of the rakshasas, "I have freed the gods from their fear of you. In doing so, I am fulfilling a promise I made to them with regard to the rakshasas. I will always give up my life to do what is dear to the gods. And so, I would kill you even if I were in the underworld."

'As the god, whose eyes were like the petals of the red lotus, was speaking, the lord of the rakshasas, greatly enraged, pierced him with a spear. The spear hurled by Malyavan tinkled with bells and shone like lightning in a thundercloud. It struck Vishnu in the chest. Vishnu pulled out the spear and threw it back at Malyavan. Released from Vishnu's hand, the spear approached Malyavan like a meteor hurtling towards a mountain of collyrium, as if it had been hurled by Skanda, the god of war. Like a lightning bolt hitting a mountain, it struck the lord of the rakshasas' broad chest, which was adorned with necklaces. Malyavan lost consciousness when his armour was pierced but when he recovered, he stood up again, immovable as a mountain. He struck Vishnu fiercely on the chest with an iron spear covered with spikes. The rakshasa was eager to fight. He hit Vishnu again with his fist and stood a bow length away. A great cry arose from the sky, "Well done, well done!" After he struck Vishnu, the rakshasa also hit Garuda. Garuda, the son of Vinata, was enraged and he blew away the rakshasa with the gale force of his wings as a strong wind does dry leaves. Sumali hastened towards Lanka with his army when he saw his elder brother being tossed about by the wings of that bird who was the best of the twice-born. Repelled by the wind from the bird's wings, Malyavan also made for Lanka with his army, covered in shame.

'And so it was, Rama, that the rakshasas were defeated several times in battle by lotus-eyed Vishnu and they lost many of their leaders. They left Lanka and went to live in the underworld with their wives, unable to face Vishnu in battle and tormented by fear. Those who were descended from Salakantaka and famous for their valour, joined the rakshasa Sumali. The rakshasas that you killed were all descendants of Pulastya. Mali, Sumali and Malyavan were all more fortunate and stronger than Ravana. No one other than Vishnu – the lord of the gods, Narayana, holder of the conch, the discus and the mace – could have killed those rakshasas. You are that four-armed god, the eternal Narayana, the invincible and imperishable lord, born to kill the rakshasas.'

## Sarga 9: Ravana and His Siblings Are Born

'After a while, the rakshasa Sumali came up from the underworld and wandered through the world of mortals. He was blue as a cloud and wore earrings of beaten gold. Once, while he was with his young daughter – who was like the goddess of wealth without the lotus – Sumali saw the god of wealth, Vishravas, going by in his chariot, Pushpaka. Vishravas was like an immortal, bright as a fire. The rakshasa said to his daughter, who was named Kaikasi, "Daughter, the time has come to give you away. Your youth is passing. Because we are righteous in our minds, we have made plans that will be to your advantage. Little daughter, you are virtuous and like the goddess of wealth herself. But suitors have kept away from fear of not winning you. Being the father of a daughter is the greatest of all worries for those who seek respect, for you never know who will accept your daughter in marriage. An unmarried daughter causes uncertainty in three families – her father's, her mother's and the family into which she will be married. Go, then, my daughter, to Vishravas, the best of sages, born in the line of Prajapati, descendant of Pulastya. Choose him for yourself. Undoubtedly, my daughter, you will have sons like him. He is the lord of wealth and equal to the sun in brightness."

'At that time, Rama, the brahmin son of Pulastya was performing the agnihotra sacrifice, blazing like the fourth fire. Concerned for her father's honour and unaware of the dark hour, the girl went and stood before him, looking down at her feet. When he saw that girl with the lovely hips, whose face was like the full moon, that magnanimous one, blazing like a fire, said, "Whose daughter are you, my dear, and why have you come here? What is your purpose? Tell me truly, my pretty one." The girl joined her palms and said, "You should be able to guess why I am here with your powers. Know that I have come here on the orders of my father. My name is Kaikasi. You can know the rest."

'The sage entered a state of contemplation and spoke. "I can see what is in your heart, my dear. You have come to me at this dark hour, so listen, for you must know what kind of sons you will bear. They shall be dreadful – dreadful in appearance and friends with dreadful people. My lady with the lovely hips, you shall give birth to rakshasas of cruel deeds!" She bowed to him when she heard those words and said, "Sons such as these cannot be born from a brahmin!" The sage replied, "The last son that is born to you will be righteous, in conformity with my lineage."

'In time, the girl gave birth to a dreadful creature who had the repulsive form of a rakshasa. He had ten heads and huge teeth, he was dark as collyrium, he had coppery lips and twenty arms, huge mouths and flaming hair. Jackals spewed flames from their mouths as he was born and carnivorous beasts circled him in the inauspicious direction. Indra rained blood and the clouds rumbled menacingly. The sun dimmed and huge meteors fell. His father, who was like Grandfather Brahma, named him. "Since this one has ten heads, he shall be called Dashagriva!" Mighty Kumbhakarna was born next, the likes of whose enormous strength had never been known before. Then, the girl named Shurpanakha, with the hideous face, was born. Kaikasi's last son was the righteous Vibhishana.

'They grew up in that great forest, cruel and energetic. Ten-headed Ravana became capable of tormenting the worlds. Kumbhakarna, wicked and blundering, wandered through the three worlds, harassing and devouring sages who were devoted to righteousness. But noble Vibhishana stood always in the path of dharma. He studied the Vedas, ate sparingly and controlled his senses.

'After some time, the god of wealth, Kubera, arrived in his chariot, Pushpaka, to visit his effulgent father. Kaikasi saw him blazing with splendour and the rakshasi said to Ravana, "Son, look at your brother, resplendent

Vaishravana! You are his equal since he is your brother. But look at your state! Ravana, you with the ten necks, you of immeasurable prowess, make an effort, my son, so that you become like him!" Brave Ravana grew exceedingly angry. He made a promise when he heard his mother's words. "I swear to you, truly, mother, that before long, I shall be my brother's equal. I will surpass him. So give up the torment in your heart!" In a fit of anger, Ravana fixed his mind on penance and declared, "I will get what I want through austerities!" He went to the auspicious hermitage of Gokarna with his brother to fulfil his goals.'

## Sarga 10: Ravana and His Brothers Earn Their Boons

Then, Rama said to the brahmin Agastya, 'How and what kind of austerities did those brothers of mighty vows practise in the forest?'

Agastya said, 'Each of the brothers entered into a practise that was appropriate for him. Kumbhakarna, steady and controlled and keeping to dharma, stood in the midst of four fires with the burning sun overhead for the whole of the hot season. In the rains, he was drenched by the clouds and knelt on one knee. He passed the winter submerged in water. He lived ten thousand years standing firm on the path of truth and striving for righteousness. Vibhishana, pure and dedicated to dharma, stood on one foot for five thousand years. Flowers rained, troupes of apsaras danced and the gods sang in celebration when his period of restrictions was over. He stood for another five thousand years with his arms above his head, concentrating on the sun because his mind was set on studying the Vedas. Vibhishana passed ten thousand years of restrictions in this way, as if he were in Nandana, Indra's celestial garden.

'Ten-headed Ravana went without food for ten thousand years. At the end of every thousand years, he sacrificed one of his heads to the fire. Nine thousand years passed and he gave nine heads to the fire. He got ready to offer his tenth head at the end of ten thousand years. Righteous Brahma, the grandfather, came to him. Brahma was pleased and stood there, surrounded by all the other gods. "Ten-headed Ravana, I am pleased with you, son!" he said. "You know dharma, pick a boon that you wish to have. I will give you what you want, your efforts shall not be in vain!" Ravana bowed to him, his heart overflowing with happiness. In a voice trembling with joy, he said, "Blessed one, death is the constant fear for all living creatures."

'"You cannot be perfectly immortal. Ask me for something else."

'"Lord of all creatures, let me be unslayable by winged creatures, by yakshas and nagas, by danavas and daityas and by the gods. You are worshipped by the immortals! I do not worry about men and other beings for I consider them equal to straw."

'Grandfather Brahma said, "It shall be as you say, bull among rakshasas! But listen, you have pleased me. I have another boon for you! You are without sin, rakshasa! The heads which you threw into the fire shall be restored to you, just as they were before." As he was speaking, the heads that had been sacrificed to the fire by the rakshasa rose again.

'Grandfather Brahma then said to Vibhishana, "Vibhishana, my son, knower of dharma, you stand in the path of righteousness. I am pleased with you, you are a creature of good vows. Choose a boon!" Righteous Vibhishana, surrounded by virtues as the moon is by moonbeams, joined his palms and said, "Blessed one, it is enough for me that the lord of all creatures himself is pleased with me. If you still want to give me a boon, then listen. Let it be that all my thoughts are appropriate for the stage of life that I am in so that I always act with righteousness and uphold dharma. Generous one, this is the boon that I consider to be the best. There is nothing in the world that cannot be achieved by those who are committed to righteousness." Prajapati Brahma was pleased. He said to Vibhishana, "It shall be so, son, because you are righteous. Although you are born from a rakshasa womb, tormentor of enemies, your consciousness was not born in adharma. I grant you immortality!"

'When he was trying to grant boons to Kumbhakarna, all the gods joined their palms and together they said to Prajapati Brahma, "You should not give any boons to Kumbhakarna. You know how that wicked one has been harassing the worlds. Seven apsaras from Indra's garden, Nandana, ten of Indra's attendants, as well as sages and men have been eaten by this fellow. You are of unlimited brilliance! Instead of a boon, give him the gift of stupor. The world will remain safe and his honour will be maintained." Lotus-born Brahma concentrated on the goddess Sarasvati and she appeared at his side. Sarasvati joined her palms and said, "I am here. What would you like me to do?" Prajapati Brahma said to Sarasvati, "Become the speech of this leader of rakshasas, as the gods wish!"

"'It shall be so," she said and entered Kumbhakarna's mouth. Then Prajapati Brahma said, "Kumbhakarna, mighty one, choose the boon you want!" Kumbhakarna heard that and said, "God of gods, I wish to sleep for many years."

"'It shall be so," said Prajapati and left with the other gods. Sarasvati also went back to heaven. But wicked Kumbhakarna thought sadly, "How did a sentence like this come out of my mouth just now?"

'The brothers, who blazed with splendour, went to the Shleshamataka forest and lived there happily after they had received their boons.'

## Sarga 11: Ravana Takes the City of Lanka

'Sumali heard about all the boons that his scions had obtained. He overcame his fear and rose up from the underworld with his companions. Maricha, Prahasta, Virupaksha and Mahodara, who were his ministers, also rose, full of excitement. Surrounded by those bulls among rakshasas, Sumali approached ten-headed Ravana. He embraced him and said, "Son, by good fortune you have obtained the boons that your heart desired from the greatest of all in the three worlds. The enormous fear of Vishnu, which made us abandon Lanka and settle in the underworld, has now vanished, mighty-armed one. We had to leave our home when we were defeated and we entered the underworld together with our distraught followers. The city of Lanka, where your wise brother the god of wealth now lives, was always a place where the rakshasas had lived. Our goal will be quickly accomplished if it can be won by diplomacy. Or by force. Or by gifts. Without a doubt, my son, you will be the ruler of Lanka. You shall be the lord of us all!"

'Ravana said to his maternal grandfather who was standing there, "The lord of wealth is our elder. You cannot speak like this!"

'Prahasta, the rakshasa, offered Ravana this pertinent advice: "Mighty-armed Ravana, you should not speak like this. There is no brotherhood among the brave. Listen to my words. Aditi and Diti were sisters. Together, they were the beautiful wives of Prajapati Kashyapa. Aditi gave birth to the gods, the rulers of the three worlds; Diti gave birth to the daityas – both are the descendants of Kashyapa. Knower of dharma, in the past, this earth with its forests and oceans and mountains belonged to the daityas, for they were powerful. Vishnu defeated them in battle and brought the three worlds into the unassailable control of the gods. You will not be the only one who has acted perversely. The gods themselves have behaved like this before. These are my words." Spoken to thus by the wicked Prahasta, Ravana thought for a moment and then said, "All right!"

'Heroic Ravana was pleased and along with the rakshasas, he went to a nearby forest. The rakshasa with the ten heads established himself in Trikuta and then, he dispatched eloquent Prahasta as a messenger. "Go quickly, Prahasta, and relay my message to the god of wealth with all due courtesy. 'King, the city of Lanka which you have occupied belongs to the great-souled rakshasas. You are without flaws, this is not worthy of you! You are of immeasurable valour, you will make me happy and you will uphold dharma if you return this to us now.'"

'Instructed thus, eloquent Prahasta set out and conveyed Ravana's words to the god of wealth. Vaishravana, skilled in words, listened to Prahasta's message and replied, "Go to Ravana and tell him that this city, this kingship and all that is mine is his to enjoy without any hindrance. Soon, I will do everything that will make you happy, lord of the rakshasas. I shall go and inform my father while you wait." The lord of wealth went to his father, greeted him and told him what Ravana wanted. "Father, Ravana has sent me this message: Give me the city of Lanka which was previously occupied by the rakshasas. You are a person of good vows, tell me what I should do in this situation."

'Vishravas, a brahmin, bull among sages, said to the god of wealth, "Listen, son, to what I have to say. Mighty ten-headed Ravana has said the same thing to me. I rebuked that wicked creature and pleaded with him many times. I also told him angrily on several occasions that he would be destroyed. Listen, my son, to my words which are in keeping with dharma and will bring glory. That vile fellow is deluded by his boons and does not distinguish between those who should be respected and those who should not. Besides, it is because of the curse on me that he has a cruel nature. Therefore, go, mighty-armed one, to Mount Kailasha. Give up Lanka and settle there with your companions. The best of all rivers, the charming Mandakini, flows there and its waters are covered with lotuses as bright as the sun. God of wealth, you know that Ravana has obtained the best of boons, so do not make an enemy of him." To honour his father's word, Vaishravana took his wives and his family, his ministers and his chariots and set forth.

'Prahasta went to Ravana and reported everything. "The city of Lanka, thirty yojanas wide, is empty. Enter it with your people and practise your dharma there!" The moment he heard Prahasta's words, Ravana entered the city of Lanka with his brothers, his army and his companions. Crowned by the night-stalking rakshasas, ten-headed Ravana settled down in the city which was soon occupied by rakshasas and appeared like a dark blue rain cloud. The lord of wealth honoured his father's word and on the Kailasha mountain he built a city filled with ornately decorated mansions, just as Indra had built Amaravati.'

## Sarga 12: Ravana and His Brothers Get Married

'After his coronation, Ravana consulted his brothers about giving their sister away in marriage. Her name was Shurpanakha and he gave her in marriage to Vidyujjihva, lord of the danavas and the son of Kalakeya. After he had given his sister away, the king went hunting. There, he chanced upon Maya, the son of Diti, and seeing that he was with a young woman, Ravana, the night-ranger, asked, "Who are you, sir? Why are you in this forest that has neither humans nor animals?" Questioned thus by the rakshasa, Rama, he said, "Listen and I will tell you everything that happened to me. There was an apsara named Hema, you must have heard of her before. She was given to me by the gods, as Paulomi was given to Indra, he of a hundred sacrifices. I was very attached to her and lived with her for five hundred years. It has now been fourteen years since she went away to do the work of the gods. With my magic powers, I built Hema a city made entirely of gold and decorated with lapis. I lived there alone and was miserable without her.[7] And so I came with my daughter into

[7] This story resonates with an encounter that the south-bound monkeys have in the forest as they search for Sita. In the Kishkindha Kanda (see Sattar, *Valmiki's Ramayana*, chap. 43), the monkeys fall into a cave that is filled with fruit and flowers that are like jewels and cool lakes and magnificent mansions. It is guarded by a woman ascetic named Svyamprabha who says that she is a friend of the apsara Hema for

this forest. This is my daughter, your majesty, born from Hema's womb. I have come here to find her a husband. A daughter causes grief to her father as well as to those who seek respectability. A daughter places two families in difficulty. I also have two sons by my wife. The first one is named Mayavi and the one that comes after him is Dundubhi.[8] As you asked, I have told you everything about myself. Now, you tell me. I wish to know who you are."

'Addressed thus, the lord of the rakshasas replied humbly, "I am descended from Pulastya and my name is Ravana." Realizing that he was the son of a great sage, Maya was extremely happy. He decided to give him his daughter in marriage then and there. The lord of the daityas smiled and said to the lord of the rakshasas, "This is my daughter, born from the apsara Hema. Her name is Mandodari. Take her as your wife." Ravana agreed. He lit a fire there and took her hand in marriage. Even though he knew that Ravana was under a curse,[9] Maya gave his daughter to him because his family was rich in austerities. He also gave him the wondrous spear that never missed its mark which he had gained through the practise of severe austerities, the very spear that struck Lakshmana.

'After getting married, Lanka's powerful lord returned to the city to arrange the marriages of his brothers. Ravana arranged the marriage of Kumbhakarna with the daughter of Vairochana whose name was Vajrajvala. Dharma-knowing Vibhishana got Sarama, the daughter of the gandharva king Shailusha, as a wife. She was born on the shores of Lake Manasa at a time

---

whom this wondrous place had been created by Maya. In the Kishkindha story, Maya is killed by Indra.

8 Both Mayavi and Dundubhi challenge Vali, the monkey king, to fight in the Kishkindha Kanda. Sattar, *Valmiki's Ramayana*, chap. 35–44.

9 It is not clear what curse is being referred to since all the curses that Ravana carries, and there are many, occur after this point (see the essay on Ravana in this volume). The same problem occurs in Sarga 15, when Kubera/Vaishravana is fighting Ravana. A possible explanation for this could be that the Uttara Kanda was composed later than the rest of the Valmiki Ramayana and was composed over a long period in order to answer the questions that the main body of the text suggests. Here, the Uttara text stumbles against its own foreknowledge and assumes, in the larger and deterministic Ravana narrative it is creating, that the curses are already in place against him.

when the lake was rising due to the monsoon. The girl's mother cried out in affection, "Lake, do not rise!" and so the girl was named Sarama.[10]

'Now married, the rakshasas took their pleasures, each with his own wife, as the gandharvas do in Nandana. Mandodari gave birth to a son, Meghanada, the one that you all know by the name of Indrajit. This son of a rakshasa cried as soon as he was born and let out a terrible sound that was like the crash of thunder. All of Lanka was stunned by this sound and so his father named him Meghanada, the sound of thunder. As fire is kindled with wood, the child grew in Ravana's women's quarters, cared for by excellent women.'

## Sarga 13: Ravana Challenges Vaishravana

'After a while, Kumbhakarna was overwhelmed by a deep sleep as had been ordained by Brahma, lord of the worlds. And so, he came to his brother and said, "I am being obstructed by sleep, your majesty. Build me a mansion." The king appointed builders who were like Vishvakarma and they made a mansion for Kumbhakarna that was like Kailasha itself. It was bright and shining, one yojana long and twice as wide. It was beautiful and secure. It was lovely in all aspects, with pillars of crystal and gold. It was decorated with lapis and the window lattices had little gold bells. The doorways were made of ivory, the seats were of crystal and diamonds, it was pleasant in all seasons and was like a sacred cavern on Mount Meru. And there it was that the rakshasa Kumbhakarna lay, overcome by sleep, never waking for thousands of years.

'While Kumbhakarna was asleep, ten-headed Ravana constantly harassed the gods, the sages, the yakshas and the gandharvas without restraint. Violent Ravana went to many gardens, including Nandana, and laid them waste. He disrupted rivers like an elephant at play, scattered trees like a storm wind, crushed mountains like a flying lightning bolt. When the lord of wealth, Vaishravana, who was a knower of dharma and kept in mind the customs of his family, heard about Ravana's behaviour, he sent a messenger to Lanka out of brotherly concern and for Ravana's benefit. He went to the city of Lanka

---

[10] What her mother said in Sanskrit was '*Saro, ma vardhayat,*' meaning literally, 'Lake, do not grow bigger!', hence the name Sarama.

and approached Vibhishana, who asked him with all respect and formality about the reason for his arrival. He also asked about the welfare of the king and his family. Then, he took him to the assembly hall to see ten-headed Ravana on the throne.

'The messenger saw the king sitting there, shining with his own glory. He burst into words of praise and then fell silent. He said to Ravana, who was sitting on a couch covered with fine fabric, "I will tell you everything that your brother has said to you, your majesty. It is applicable both to your behaviour and to the family. All that you have done is fair enough. And if you can, please try and behave in accordance with dharma. I have seen your destruction of Nandana and I have heard about the sages you have killed. And, majesty, I have also heard about the plans the gods are making against you. You have pushed me away many times, king of the rakshasas. But one must protect one's family, even if their transgressions arise from childishness. I have been to the slopes of the Himalayas in the service of dharma. I have undertaken terrible vows. I have controlled my senses. I have seen the lord god Shiva along with the goddess Parvati. I looked at her by chance, just to make sure that it was really her. It was for no other reason. Parvati was frolicking there, showing off her incomparable beauty. My left eye was burned out by the goddess's power and the light of my other eye grew weak, as if blurred by dust. And so I went to another vast plateau on the mountain slopes and for a full eight hundred years, I undertook the great vow of silence. When my austerities were over, Shiva came there. He was pleased and spoke sweetly to me. 'I am pleased with you, you undertake good vows and you know dharma. I was the only one to have undertaken this vow and now you have, too, lord of wealth. There is no third person who can fulfil a vow like this one. Long ago, it was I who created this difficult vow. Accept my friendship, lord of wealth. I have been won over by your penance. Be my friend, flawless one. Since the power of the goddess burned out one of your eyes, you shall be now known as One Weak Eye for all time.' I secured this friendship with Shiva and with his permission, I returned and heard all about your wicked plans. You are a blot upon our family! You must stop this unrighteous behaviour. The gods and the sages are devising ways to kill you."

'Ravana was enraged when he heard this and his eyes grew bloodshot. He wrung his hands and ground his teeth and said, "Messenger, I understand these words that you have related to me. Neither you nor that brother who sent you to me will survive! What the lord of wealth has to say is not to my advantage. That fool boasts of his friendship with Shiva to me? I used to think I should not kill him because he is older than me. But now that I have heard these words from him, I have changed my mind. I will conquer the three worlds relying on the strength of my own arms. I shall send the guardians of the four quarters to Yama's abode because of what he has said to me!" Speaking thus, the lord of Lanka cut off the messenger's head with a sword and gave it to the wicked rakshasas to eat. Then, he asked for benediction. Finally, Ravana mounted his chariot and eager to conquer the three worlds, he set off to meet the lord of wealth.'

## Sarga 14: Ravana Takes on the Yakshas

'Glorious Ravana rode forth, as if to set the three worlds on fire, surrounded by his six ministers – Prahasta, Mahodara, Maricha, Shuka, Sarana and Dhumraksha – all drunk on their own strength and always ready to fight. Crossing cities, rivers, mountains, forests and woods, he reached Mount Kailasha in no time at all. When the yakshas there saw that the king of the rakshasas had reached the mountain, they recognized him as the brother of their king. They went to the lord of wealth and told him about Ravana's intentions. With the god of wealth's permission, they set out, prepared for battle. Like the ocean swelling, a vast excitement arose in the rakshasa king's army and it seemed to shake the mountain. A great battle ensued and it agitated the ministers of the rakshasa king. Ravana saw his forces in that state and he came forth in anger and shouted encouragement. Then, the ministers of the rakshasa king, all of them fierce in valour, each took on a thousand yakshas in battle. Hitting out with maces and clubs and swords and spears, ten-headed Ravana plunged into the enemy forces. Ravana could barely breathe, struck on all sides by arrows that fell like rain from a cloud. The wicked one raised his mace which was like Death's own staff and entered that fighting force, sending countless yakshas to Yama's abode. Like a fire driven by the wind, cruel Ravana tore through the yaksha army which spread out as if it were dry grass and dead trees. Like clouds scattered by the wind, more yakshas were scattered in battle by the ministers, Mahodara, Shuka and the others. Some of them fell on the battlefield, their bodies smashed. Others fell to the ground biting their lips with their own sharp teeth. Some clung to each other from fear. Others dropped their weapons even while in battle, like the banks of a river that collapse in a flood. There was no space in the sky between the slain ascending to heaven and the hosts of sages that stood there watching.

'At that time, Rama, a great yaksha named Samyodhakantaka arrived with a huge army and many chariots. Maricha was struck by him as if by Vishnu's discus and he fell to the ground like a star that has used up its store of merit. After he regained consciousness and had rested for a while, the rakshasa took on the yaksha again and defeated him and caused him to flee. Then, Rama, night-ranging Ravana entered the gateway that was decorated with gold, studded with lapis and silver and was the last bastion of the doorkeepers. There, a doorkeeper named Suryabhanu challenged him. When he did not stop, the yaksha hit him with a post that he broke off from the gate. Bleeding, Ravana looked like a mountain releasing rivers of molten metal. Then he hit the yaksha with the same post and the yaksha vanished as his body was smashed to dust. When the yakshas saw such valour, they all fled and hid in rivers and caves, their faces pale, tormented by fear.'

## Sarga 15: Ravana Defeats Vaishravana and Takes Pushpaka

'The lord of wealth himself came to the battlefield when he saw the yakshas fleeing in the hundreds of thousands. Then, the yaksha named Manibhadra, who was difficult to defeat, entered the battle surrounded by four thousand yakshas. They charged towards the rakshasas and attacked them with maces and clubs and spears and arrows and other weapons. Thousands were slain by Prahasta in battle and another thousand by Mahodara with his mace. Wicked Maricha was enraged and he felled two thousand yakshas in the blink of an eye. Manibhadra was engaged in battle by Dhumraksha and though he was hit on his chest by his mace, he did not move an inch. Then, Dhumraksha was hit on the head by Manibhadra's mace and he fell to the ground in great pain. Ravana was enraged and rushed towards Manibhadra when he saw that Dhumraksha had been wounded and had fallen to the ground covered in blood. When Manibhadra saw Ravana rushing towards him, enraged and like unto the doomsday fire, the best of yakshas hurled three spears at him. The yaksha's crown was knocked awry by a blow from Ravana's mace and from that time onwards, he was known to all as Crooked Crown. When the great Manibhadra turned his face away from battle, a huge roar arose on that mountain.

'Then, at a great distance, the lord of wealth appeared, surrounded by Shukra and Praushthapada and Shankha and Padma. He saw his brother on the battlefield, his glory tarnished by the curse. Wise Vaishravana spoke these words, appropriate to one born in the line of Grandfather Brahma. "Even though I warned you, you have not restrained your powers. You will understand the consequences of this later, when you end up in hell. The fool who drinks poison out of confusion does not understand the consequences until he has reaped the fruits of that action. The gods will not be pleased with you even if you act righteously. But you do not seem to understand that. He who insults his mother or father or his brother or his teacher only understands the consequences after death. He who does not use this impermanent body for the practise of austerities will see the results of that after he dies. Intelligence never arises in the minds of the wrong-headed. One eats the fruits of one's actions. A man attains wisdom, beauty, strength, riches, sons and greatness through his own deeds in this life and from those in previous lives. You will go to hell, which is the place for people with this temperament. I have nothing more to say to you, this is a judgement on your perverted behaviour!"

'Assaulted by his words, Ravana's ministers, led by Maricha, turned their faces away and ran. Then the king of the rakshasas was struck on the head by a blow from great-souled Vaishravana, but he did not move an inch from where he was standing. In that magnificent duel, Rama, they struck each other mighty blows but neither was hurt nor injured. Vaishravana employed Agni's weapon in battle and Ravana retaliated with Varuna's weapon. The lord of the rakshasas invoked his powers of illusion and struck the lord of wealth on the head and he bled profusely from that mace wound. He fell to the earth, covered in blood, like an ashoka tree cut at the root.

'Padma and Nidhi and the other deities who were with the god of wealth brought him to the forests of Nandana and laid him down to sleep. And then Ravana, who had defeated Vaishravana, took Pushpaka from him as a sign of his victory. The celestial chariot was enclosed by golden pillars, its entrances were studded with lapis, its windows were inlaid with pearls and it had every kind of fruiting tree you could desire. The king of the rakshasas mounted that vehicle which could go anywhere at pleasure and descended from Mount Kailasha.'

## Sarga 16: Ravana Encounters Shiva

'After defeating his brother, Ravana went to the forest of reeds where Kartikeya, the great army commander, had been born. He saw the forest shining golden, circled by rays of light, like a second sun. As he ascended the mountain covered in pleasant woodlands, he noticed that the celestial Pushpaka had come to a halt. When the chariot stopped, surrounded by his ministers, the rakshasa wondered, "How can this chariot, which moves according to the wishes of its owner, have stopped? Why is it not going any further? Why has it stopped against my will? What could be on this mountain that has stopped it?"

'Maricha, who was wise and knowledgeable, said to Ravana, "There must be a reason why Pushpaka is not going forward." Then, mighty Nandi, Shiva's retainer, approached them confidently from the side and said to the king of the rakshasas, "Turn back, Ravana! Shiva is frolicking on this mountain! Birds and serpents, yakshas, daityas, danavas or rakshasas – no living beings can access this place!" Enraged, his eyes coppery with anger, Ravana dismounted from Pushpaka and stood at the base of the mountain. "Who is this Shiva?" he said. He saw Nandi standing by the god's side, holding a shining spear and looking like a second Shiva. The rakshasa noticed that he had the face of a monkey and he mocked him and laughed like a thundering rain cloud. Blessed Nandi, who was not separate from Shiva's body, grew angry. He said, "Wicked rakshasa! You saw my monkey form and you had contempt for me. You laughed at me, in your folly. Because of that, monkeys will be born for the destruction of your clan. They shall have my form, my energy and my valour. I could kill you right now, but I will not, for you are already slain by your own deeds!"

'The rakshasa disregarded Nandi's remarks and approached the mountain and said, "You, husband of cows! I shall uproot this mountain which obstructed Pushpaka as I was travelling. What power allows this Shiva to frolic here, as if he were a king? He does not know what he should do, but the danger has now arrived." Saying that, Rama, he picked up the mountain in his arms and raised it, along with its animals of prey and predators and trees and plants.

'Shiva smiled when he saw Ravana's act and, playfully, he pressed down on the mountain with his big toe. As his ministers stood there in shock, the rakshasa's arms were trapped under the mountain. The pain from his crushed arms made him emit a roar that was so loud that it shook the three worlds. Humans heard that sound and thought it was the end of the world. Even the gods trembled and the mountains shook. Sitting on the mountain, Shiva was pleased and he released his arms. He said to ten-headed Ravana, "I am pleased with your courage and your arrogance, rakshasa. The screams you emitted when you were in pain were terrifying. You shall now be known as Ravana because you made the three worlds cry out! Gods and humans and yakshas and all those that live on this earth shall address you as Ravana because you made the worlds cry out. Go, now, without fear, descendant of Pulastya, by whichever path you choose. You have my permission to leave, king of the rakshasas!" Having seen Shiva and been named by him, Ravana honoured the great god and climbed back into his vehicle. Then, Ravana roamed the earth, obstructing heroic kshatriyas in various places.

## Sarga 17: Ravana Meets Vedavati

'And so, your majesty, mighty Ravana roamed the earth. When he arrived at the forests of the Himalayas, he wandered around. He saw a young woman who was wearing an antelope skin and had matted locks. She was practising austerities fit for the sages and she was shining like a goddess. He looked at that beautiful woman of great vows and he was overcome with desire. Laughing, he asked her, "What are you doing, my pretty lady, contradicting your youth in this manner? Your actions are in contrast to your beauty. Whose daughter are you, pretty one? You are flawless, who is your husband? I ask you and so tell me quickly, what is the purpose of these austerities?"

'Addressed by the ignoble rakshasa, that girl, rich in austerities, welcomed him appropriately and said, "My father is named Kushadhvaja and he is righteous, a brahmin sage. He is the son of Brihaspati and equal to him in wisdom. He is constantly engaged in the study of the Vedas and since I was born to him through them, I am called Vedavati. The gods, gandharvas, yakshas, rakshasas and pannagas have all been to my father to ask for me in marriage. But my father did not give me to any of them, lord of the rakshasas. I will tell you the reason for that. Listen, strong-armed one. My father wanted only Vishnu, best of the gods, lord of the three worlds, as a son-in-law. And so he would not give me to anyone else. A wicked daitya named Shambhu, who was arrogant because of his strength, heard about this and wanted me. He grew angry and one night, while my father slept, he killed him. My illustrious mother pathetically embraced my father's body and entered the fire with him. I have placed Vishnu in my heart since then so that I can carry out my father's wishes in that regard. I want to fulfil the wishes of my dear father and so I have embarked on this vow and have undertaken these austerities. I have told you everything, bull among rakshasas. I want to take shelter in Vishnu as my husband. Go now. I also know who you are, son of Pulastya. I know everything that happens in the three worlds because of my austerities."

'Struck by the arrows of the god of love, Ravana climbed down from his chariot and spoke to that girl of great vows. "Lady, you have lovely hips, but you are arrogant, indeed, to have made up your mind thus. Such austerities that create merit are for the elderly, doe-eyed girl. You are rich in all the virtues, it is not right for you to behave like this. You are the most beautiful woman in the three worlds. Your youth is slipping away, my timid one! Who is this Vishnu that you speak of? He cannot compare with me in valour or austerities or pleasures or strength, pretty lady. I want you."

'"Stop this, stop this!" said the girl to the night-ranging rakshasa. The rakshasa grabbed her harshly by the hair. Vedavati was enraged. She cut off her hair with her hand and created a fire in order to kill herself. She said, "Ignoble creature! I do not wish to live because of the way you have insulted me. Watch me, rakshasa, as I enter this fire! I shall be born again for your destruction because you have humiliated me, a woman without protection and in danger. A woman cannot kill a man, even if he is wicked. And if I curse you, I will use up the power I have gained from my austerities. If I have done anything good, given gifts, sacrificed to the fire, I shall be the daughter of a righteous man, but I shall not be born of a female womb." She entered the blazing fire and a rain of flowers fell from the heavens.

'You, Rama, were able to kill the enemy because of her anger,' said Agastya. 'You have taken refuge in the form of a heroic man. In the same way, this illustrious woman has appeared among men again. She has emerged from a field that is being ploughed, blazing like the fire on a sacrificial altar. Her name is Vedavati in the Krita Yuga. In the Treta Yuga, born for the destruction of that rakshasa, men have called her Sita because she was born from a furrow.'

## Sarga 18: The Gods Disguise Themselves as Birds

'After Vedavati had entered the fire, Ravana climbed back into Pushpaka and roamed across the earth again. When he reached Ushirabijam, he saw that a king named Marutta was performing a sacrifice along with the gods. A brahmin sage named Samvarta, who was Brihaspati's brother and was just like him, a knower of dharma, was conducting the sacrifice, surrounded by hosts of brahmins. The gods were frightened when they saw the rakshasa who was difficult to defeat because of the boons that had been given to him and they took on the forms of animals. Indra became a peacock, the god of death became a crow, the lord of wealth became a lizard and Varuna became a swan. Ravana, lord of the rakshasas, approached the king and said, "Fight with me. Or say, 'I am defeated!'"

'King Marutta said, "Who are you, good sir?"

'Ravana laughed and said to him, "I am pleased that despite your lack of curiosity, you have not insulted Ravana, the younger brother of the lord of wealth. Who is there in the three worlds that does not know my strength, or that I defeated my brother and took away his flying chariot?" King Marutta said to the rakshasa, "How wonderful, good sir, that you defeated your elder brother in battle. An unrighteous act is criticized by people and can never be worthy of praise. You have done a wicked thing by defeating your brother – how can you expect praise? What righteous act did you perform in the past that you obtained a boon? I have never ever heard anyone talk like this before."

'The enraged king grabbed his bow and quiver of arrows and came out to fight, but Samvarta blocked his way. The great sage spoke affectionately to the king and said, "Listen to what I have to say. Fighting is not to your advantage. If this sacrifice to Shiva remains incomplete, your family will be consumed by fire. How can one who has been purified for a sacrifice take to combat or become angry? Victory in battle is always uncertain." Marutta, the lord of the earth, listened to his teacher's words and turned back. He relinquished his arrows and bow and concentrated on completing the ritual.

'Ravana's minister, Shuka, thought he had been defeated and proclaimed this in all directions, letting out a huge shout, "Ravana has won!" He ate the sages who had come there for the sacrifice and then satisfied himself further by drinking their blood. And then, Ravana wandered around the earth again. When Ravana had left, Indra and the other heavenly beings returned to their original forms and thanked the animals. Joyfully, Indra said to the blue-bedecked peacock, "I am pleased with you, dear bird, knower of dharma, because of the favour you did me. My hundred eyes will appear on your tail and when I rain down, you shall rejoice as a sign of pleasure." Before this, peacocks' tails were simply blue. Once they had this boon from the king of the gods, they all went away, multicoloured. Yama said to the crow who was sitting on top of the sacrificial enclosure, "I am pleased with you, bird. Listen to what I have to say with pleasure. You will not be afflicted by any of the diseases that strike other living beings because of my favour. This will be certain. You shall not fear death because of my boon. You shall live as long as men do not kill you. When you have been fed, those who are under my power and suffer from hunger shall be completely satisfied, along with their relatives."

'Varuna said to the swan, who was swimming in the waters of the Ganga, "Lord of the birds, listen to my words which arise from pleasure. Your colour shall be enchanting, as pleasant as the full moon. Your upper body shall be held high and will be as white as foam. And when you approach my body, which is water, you shall always be beautiful and you will enjoy immense delight. This shall be a sign of my favour." In the old days, Rama, the plumage of swans was not entirely white. The tips of their wings were dark and their breasts were the colour of dried sacrificial grass. Then Vaishravana Kubera spoke to the lizard who was sitting on a rock. "I am pleased with you and so your colour shall be golden. Your head shall always be golden, never fading. Your golden colour shall be a sign of my favour." Once they had given these boons to the animals on the occasion of the sacrifice, the gods, along with their king, returned to their homes.'

## Sarga 19: Ravana Defeats Rama's Ancestor

'Even though he had defeated Marutta, ten-headed Ravana, king of the rakshasas, was still eager to fight and so he went to the capital cities of all the kings. He approached great kings, who were like Indra and Varuna, and said to them, "Give me battle! Or say, 'I have been defeated.' This is my decision. There is no other choice, there is no escape for you!" Those kings, who were wise and righteous, knew that the enemy had been made mighty by boons and so, they declared, "I am defeated." Dushyanta, Suratha, Gadhi, Gaya and Pururavas, all these kings, my child, said, "I am defeated."

'Ravana, king of the rakshasas, approached Ayodhya which was well protected by Aranyana the way Amaravati is by Indra. He went to the king and said, "Give me battle or declare, 'I have been defeated.' This is my command." Enraged, Aranyana said to the king of the rakshasas, "I'll give you single combat, you rakshasa king!" Since Aranyana had already heard about Ravana, he had prepared an enormous army. The king's army came forth, eager to kill the rakshasa. With many thousands of elephants and horses and chariot-warriors and foot soldiers, the army covered the earth in a moment. But when the king's army encountered Ravana's army, it was consumed like offerings in a sacrificial fire.

'The king watched his great army dissolve, like rivers rushing into an ocean. In anger, he twanged his bow, which was like Indra's, and he came close to Ravana. He released eight hundred arrows on to the head of the king of the rakshasas. But the arrows that struck bothered him not a whit and were like a shower of rain upon a mountain. Then, in anger, the king of the rakshasas struck the king on the head with his palm and the king toppled from his chariot. Stunned and trembling, he fell from his chariot like a great sala tree in the forest struck by lightning.

'The rakshasa laughed at the Ikshvaku monarch and said, "This is what you get for taking me on in combat! There is no one in the three worlds that can match me in a duel. Perhaps you did not hear of my strength because you were engaged in drunken pleasures." The king, his voice fading, said, "What can I do now? The march of time is inexorable. I was not defeated by you, rakshasa. You praise yourself. I have been felled by time, of which, good sir, you were only an instrument. What can I do now that my life is ebbing away? Because of what has happened to the Ikshvakus today, let me tell you something, rakshasa. If I have given gifts, if I have performed sacrifices, if I have done good deeds, if I have done penance, if I have ruled my people well, then let my words come true. In this very family of the great-souled Ikshvakus, there shall be born a king of great energy who will take your life." When that curse was uttered, flowers rained from the sky and drums sounded like the rumbling of thunder from the clouds. Then the king went to heaven and after he had departed, the rakshasa also went on his way.'

## Sarga 20: Narada Tells Ravana about Death

'The king of the rakshasas continued to harass people as he wandered over the earth. He encountered Narada, the best of sages, standing on a cloud. Effulgent Narada, a divine sage with immeasurable radiance, said to Ravana, who was standing in Pushpaka, "King of the rakshasas, son of Vishravas, gentle creature, stay a while. I am pleased with you and I know your feats of valour. Vishnu gave me satisfaction by killing the daityas, you have done the same by tormenting the gandharvas and the uragas. I am going to tell you something and you should listen, for it is worth hearing. Bull among rakshasas, you should listen with concentration. You cannot be killed even by the gods. Why are you destroying the worlds? The worlds are already dead, because they are subject to death. King of the rakshasas, look at the humans in the world pursuing various goals and yet unknowing of their fate. In some places, people delight themselves with music and dancing. There are others who cry all night long with tears streaming down their faces. Caught in the delusion of love for fathers and mothers and sons and attachments to family, they are lost and not aware of their troubles. Why are you tormenting this world that is already in the grip of delusion? My friend, you should conquer the world of the dead, without a doubt."

'Spoken to thus, the lord of Lanka, blazing with his own glory, honoured Narada. He laughed and said, "Great sage, you who enjoy the company of gods and gandharvas, you who enjoy war, I am ready to go to the underworld to fight! After conquering the three worlds and establishing my rule over the nagas and the gods, I shall churn the ocean of the underworld to secure nectar!" The blessed sage Narada said to ten-headed Ravana, "Why are you going by this path? This is a difficult way to get to the city of the lord of the dead. Tormentor of enemies, this is the inaccessible path!" Ravana unleashed a laugh that sounded like the rumble of an autumn cloud. "I've done that before," he said. Then he added, "Great brahmin, I am eager to kill the son of Vivashvat and so I am heading in a southerly direction. Where shall I find the king, the son of the sun? I am eager to fight, blessed one. I took a vow in anger that I would conquer the four guardians of the quarters. Now I shall set off for the city of the lord of the dead. I shall kill him, he who tortures all living beings." Ravana honoured the sage and set off for the south happily, in the company of his ministers.

'Effulgent Narada stood for a while in thought. That best of brahmins, who was like a smokeless fire, wondered, "How will this fellow kill Death? By virtue of his own dharma, Death has an impact on everyone in the three worlds whose time has come. Not even Indra, nor all the moving and unmoving things will be spared. So how will the lord of the rakshasas alone subdue Death, in fear of whom the whole of the three worlds flee? How will he defeat the one who is the foundation of the world, who judges good and bad deeds, who has himself conquered the three worlds? What other methods has he arranged? My curiosity has been aroused, I shall make my way to Yama's realm."'

## Sarga 21: Ravana Fights Yama, Lord of the Dead

'Thinking thus, fleet-footed Narada went quickly to Yama's realm to tell him what had happened. He saw Yama sitting before a sacrificial fire, judging all beings according to the nature of their actions. Yama noticed that the great sage had arrived. He offered him a comfortable seat and water, as was the custom. He said, "Is everything all right? Sage of the gods, is dharma still unharmed? You are worshipped by the gods and the gandharvas, why have you come here?" Narada, the blessed sage, said, "Listen, I will relate it all to you and then you must make the appropriate arrangements. Lord of the dead, there is a rakshasa named Dashagriva Ravana who is coming here to subdue you with his valour, you who are so difficult to defeat. He is the reason that I have come here in such a hurry, lord. You hold the rod of punishment, I wonder what he will do to you today."

'At that moment, shining like another sun, Pushpaka, Ravana's vehicle, appeared in the distance. Mighty Ravana's Pushpaka lit up the region with its brilliance, turning away the darkness. Great-armed Ravana saw creatures everywhere, reaping the fruits of their good and bad deeds. Ravana liberated all those who were being punished for their wicked actions with his enormous strength. The sentinels guarding the spirits who had been freed by Ravana's valour now rushed towards the king of the rakshasas. In hundreds and thousands, those brave warriors rained their arrows and spears and clubs and maces upon Pushpaka. Like a swarm of bees, in moments they had demolished Pushpaka's seats and enclosures and platforms and doorways. But because of Brahma's power, Pushpaka itself, a vehicle for the gods, remained unchanged in that battle.

'Ten-headed Ravana and his ministers, all heroic warriors, fought fiercely, each according to his strength and his will. Ravana's ministers put up a great fight even though they were drenched in blood and their bodies were injured by innumerable weapons. The ministers of Yama and Ravana, great warriors all, landed blows on each other with different kinds of weapons. Yama's ministers, who were energetic warriors, turned away from the rakshasas and charged together towards Ravana with a hail of spears. Sitting in Pushpaka, Ravana, best of the rakshasas, blood-smeared and injured by weapons, seemed like an ashoka tree in bloom. The mighty rakshasa unleashed various weapons with his great strength – trees and rocks and clubs and maces and spears and arrows and missiles. Warding off all the missiles that were hurled at them, in their hundreds and thousands, they struck Ravana who was fighting alone. They surrounded him as a cloud would a mountain and tried to suffocate him with their arrows and spears. Ravana was enraged. Streaming with blood, his armour torn and soaked, he came out of Pushpaka and stood on the ground. The king of the rakshasas quickly regained his senses. He took up his bow and arrows and stood there like Death himself. He strung the divine weapon Pashupata on to his bow and shouting "Stay, Stay!" he drew back his bow.

'Garlanded with flames, the missile was followed by beasts of prey as it tore through the battlefield, turning bushes and trees to ash. Yama's army was scorched by its power and fell to the ground, like a forest burning on a mountain. The brave rakshasa and his ministers sent up a huge roar which seemed to make the earth tremble.'

## Sarga 22: Brahma Protects Ravana

'Yama Vaivashvata, son of the sun, heard that huge roar. He thought that the enemy had won and that his own army had been destroyed. Believing his warriors to be dead, his eyes blazed with anger and he said to his charioteer, "Bring my chariot here quickly!" The charioteer brought the great chariot, blazing like a massive fire, and effulgent Yama stepped into it. Yama, god of death, who destroys the three worlds with their moving and unmoving beings, stood before his charioteer with his noose and club in hand. His weapon, the rod of punishment, stood by his side, manifest and blazing with its own glory. The three worlds were terribly afraid and the residents of heaven trembled when they saw that Death was angry.

'The rakshasa king's ministers were also terrified when they saw hair-raising Death, enraged and standing in his chariot. Faint of heart, they lost consciousness. "We cannot fight now," they said as they fled. But Ravana was neither afraid nor agitated when he saw dreadful Death in his chariot. Yama approached Ravana and assaulted the vulnerable parts of his body with lances and spears. Ravana stood strong and unleashed a shower of arrows at Yama which fell on him in his chariot, like rain upon a mountain. Yama attacked with all kinds of weapons and as hundreds of arrows hit his chest, the rakshasa was unable to respond because of the pain from his wounds. The battle went on for seven nights and even then, there was no victor.

'The great battle between Yama and the rakshasa went on, both were eager for victory, neither turned away from the fight. With Prajapati Brahma at their head, the gods, gandharvas, the siddhas and the great sages gathered to watch that battle. It seemed as if the world would end as the best of the rakshasas and the lord of the dead fought each other. The lord of the rakshasas pulled back his bow and unleashed a volley of arrows that seemed to fill up the entire sky. He hit Yama with four arrows and his charioteer with seven and then he attacked Yama's vital organs with thousands of arrows. The fire of Yama's anger issued forth from his mouth with a garland of flames for its breath. Gods, danavas and rakshasas watched in amazement as that blazing fire, born of anger, was determined to burn the enemy army. Death personified grew angry and said to Yama Vaivashvata, "Release me quickly, god. I will kill this enemy in battle! Naraka, Shambara, Vritra, Shambhu and Bali, Namuchi and Vairochana, and the brothers Madhu and Kaitabha, all these and so many other powerful creatures who were difficult to approach – I destroyed them all as soon as I saw them. Why worry about this night-stalking rakshasa, this Ravana! Release me quickly, knower of dharma, so that I can kill him. No one lives for even a moment after I have set eyes on them! This is not because of my might, it is the law of nature. There is no chance that he will live once I have touched him!"

'Mighty Yama then turned to his powerful staff, who was death incarnate, and said, "You stay here. I shall kill him!"

'Lord Vaivashvata, his eyes bloodshot with anger, lifted the rod of punishment which always found its mark. The unimpeachable nooses of time stood beside him, and his hammer, now embodied, blazed like a fire. Just the sight of this hammer interrupts a creature's life, to say nothing of being touched by it or knocked over by it. Held by Yama, who was both angry and violent, it was surrounded by flames, as if to consume the rakshasa. All living beings fled from the battlefield. Even the gods were alarmed when they saw Yama with his rod raised high.

'As he raised his rod to strike Ravana, Grandfather Brahma appeared and said to Yama, "Vaivashvata, mighty-armed one, you of immeasurable prowess, you must not kill this rakshasa with this rod. Bull of the three worlds, I have given him a boon. Do not act against the cosmic law by making my words worthless. This rod will find its mark among all living creatures and strike them down because it is accompanied by death. I created it a long time ago. So, my friend, do not let this weapon strike the rakshasa on the head. Wherever it falls, whoever it strikes will not survive for even an instant. It will be against the cosmic law whether or not ten-headed Ravana is killed by this weapon. Do not strike the king of the rakshasas with your upraised staff this time! Make my words true, if you have any consideration for the three worlds!"

'Spoken to thus by the great-souled one, Yama replied, "Blessed one, because you are our lord, this rod is now withdrawn. But what can I do on this field of battle, since I cannot kill this rakshasa, made so proud by his boons? I shall vanish from his sight!" He disappeared along with his horses and his chariot. Ten-headed Ravana declared his victory over Yama. Mightily pleased, he proclaimed his own name, climbed back into Pushpaka and left Yama's realm. Equally pleased, Vaivashvata and the gods, with Brahma at their head, went to heaven with the great sage Narada.'

## Sarga 23: Ravana Kills the Sons of Varuna

'Having defeated Yama, bull among the thirty gods, ten-headed Ravana was proud of his victory and he looked over at his companions. Led by Maricha, they praised him for his victory. Ravana invited them into the chariot and thrilled, they all climbed into Pushpaka. They entered the waters to reach the underworld which was protected by Varuna and inhabited by hosts of daityas and uragas. Ravana went to the city of Bhogavati, ruled by Vasuki. After he had brought the nagas under his control, he set forth for the city of Manimayi, where the daityas who had received boons and were called Nivatakavachas lived. The rakshasa approached them and challenged them to fight. The sons of Diti were all courageous and powerful, equipped with all kinds of weapons and intoxicated with war, so they were eager to fight. An entire year went by as they fought. Neither side was victorious and neither was conquered. Then, Grandfather Brahma, eternal refuge of the three worlds, came there, standing in the best of all flying chariots. Ancient Brahma prevented the Nivatakavachas from continuing the battle and said these significant words, "Ravana cannot be defeated in battle by the gods or the asuras. And you, good sirs, also cannot be defeated by the gods led by Indra or by the asuras. It would be to your advantage to make friends with this rakshasa. There is no doubt that friends enjoy everything together."

'And so, with fire as the witness, Ravana made a friendship with the Nivatakavachas and was very pleased. Appropriately honoured by them, ten-headed Ravana stayed there happily for a year and enjoyed pleasures that were no different from those in his own city.

'Having now mastered one hundred kinds of illusions, Ravana wandered around the underworld, searching for the city of Varuna, the lord of the waters. He came upon a city named Ashmanagar which was protected by the Kalakeyas. He conquered them and killed one hundred daityas in no time at all. Then, the king of the rakshasas saw Varuna's celestial palace. It was like white clouds and shone like Kailasha. He saw the magic cow who gives milk continuously, from whose flow the ocean of milk is formed, from which is born the cool-rayed moon, from which arises the foam upon which the great sages live, from which the gods created the nectar of immortality that is their food. Ravana circumambulated the wondrous cow, known in the world of men as Surabhi, and entered that remote and frightening palace which was protected by various forces. Inside, he saw hundreds of waterfalls like autumn clouds that seemed to always be filled with joy. Ravana killed the leaders of the army but he was also struck by them. He said, "Go quickly and inform your king that Ravana has come here, eager to do battle. Say to him, 'Confront him or, say with your palms joined in respect, "I have been defeated," and there will be no cause to fear him.'"

'The sons and grandsons of great-souled Varuna were enraged and they came forth along with Gau and Pushkara, surrounded by their armies and enveloped in their own courage and virtues. They yoked their chariots which shone like the sun and went wherever their drivers wanted. A violent and hair-raising battle began between the rakshasa Ravana and the sons of the lord of the waters. In no time at all, the extremely courageous ministers of the ten-headed rakshasa completely destroyed Varuna's forces. Varuna's sons retreated from battle when they saw that their armies had been annihilated and that they themselves were being tormented by a rain of arrows. From the ground, they saw Ravana in the sky, in Pushpaka, and rapidly, they rose into the air in their chariots. They reached the same level as Ravana and then, a great and tumultuous battle began in the sky, equal to the war between the gods and the danavas. They managed to get Ravana to turn away from the battle with their fiery arrows. They were very pleased and shouted various things.

'The rakshasa Mahodara was enraged when he saw that his king had been overcome. Ignoring the fear of death, he sallied forth, eager to do battle. Horses which were like the wind and could go where they willed fell dead to the ground when they were struck by Mahodara's mace. He released a huge roar when he killed the soldiers and the horses that belonged to Varuna's sons and destroyed their chariots. Struck by Mahodara, chariots and their horses along with their valiant charioteers fell to the earth. The heroic and great-souled sons of Varuna were unperturbed. They abandoned their chariots and stood in the sky with their own power. They pulled back their bowstrings and pierced Mahodara with their arrows. Angrily, they surrounded Ravana together on the battlefield. Ravana, who was also angry, seemed like the doomsday fire as he unleashed a rain of swift arrows aimed at the vulnerable parts of their bodies. He stood firm and hurled arrows and spears and lances and clubs and maces.

'The heroic infantry moved forward, despite being injured. Roaring loudly, the rakshasa killed Varuna's sons by showering them with all kinds of weapons, like rain upon trees. They all fell on to the ground, their faces turned away, until their servants came and took them away to their homes. Then the rakshasa said, "Tell Varuna about this!"

'One of Varuna's ministers named Prahasa said to Ravana, "The effulgent lord of the waters, whom you are challenging to fight, has gone to Brahma's realm to listen to the music of the gandharvas. And since he has already left, your majesty, what is the use of this effort? The heroic princes who were present here have been defeated." When he heard that, the rakshasa king loudly proclaimed his own name and shouting with joy, he left Varuna's abode. He went back along the path by which he had come, turned his face towards Lanka and rose into the sky.'

## Sarga 24: Ravana Sends His Sister to Dandaka

'As he returned home well pleased, wicked Ravana captured the daughters of the gods, sages and gandharvas along the way. In his vehicle, the rakshasa imprisoned women and virgin girls whom he found attractive, after killing their families. Ravana took the young women of the pannagas, yakshas, humans and rakshasas, of the danavas and the daityas. They had long hair and comely limbs, their faces were like full moons, their breasts heavy. All those young women were stricken with grief. They trembled and were overcome with sorrow. They shed tears which were like fire, born as they were from the fires of grief and fear. Pushpaka blazed on all sides with the fire of their sighs and appeared like a fire altar holding the sacrificial fires within it. Some of those virtuous, sorrow-laden women wondered if they would be eaten, others if they would be killed. They remembered their mothers and fathers and brothers and sons and their sisters and, overwhelmed with sorrow, they wailed together:

'"What must my son be doing without me? And what of my mother and brother, who are drowning in an ocean of sorrow?"

'"How will I live without my godlike husband! Ah, death, I beg you, take me to Yama's realm!"

'"What bad deeds did I commit before, in another body? I am a fallen woman, sunk into this ocean of grief!"

'"At the moment, I see no end to this sorrow. Damn this world of men, there is nothing lower than this!"

'"Our families are destroyed in front of Ravana's strength, weak like stars before the rising sun."

'"This mighty rakshasa who invents new methods of destruction! He behaves so badly but does not realize it."

'"He is as powerful as he is wicked. But taking the wives of others in this way is not appropriate."

'"This perverted fellow delights in the wives of others, he is sure to be killed because of a woman's actions."

'Ravana's lustre dimmed and his energy was depleted when he was cursed by the women who were devoted to their husbands and who were firm in their goodness. Even as they lamented, Ravana, the king of the rakshasas, entered the city of Lanka and was honoured by the night-stalking rakshasas.

'Ravana's sister was very upset and came to speak to him, falling at his feet. Ravana lifted her up to console her and said, "My dear, what is it that you wish to say to me so urgently?" Her eyes were red and filled with tears. The rakshasi said, "I am destroyed, great king. You have made me a widow with your strength. You killed the daityas known as the Kalakeyas, who are strong and brave, in battle with your valour. You are an enemy disguised as a brother, you killed my husband, dearer to me than life! I have been killed by you, your majesty, by my own relative. I will now suffer the sorrow of being called a widow because of you! Your brother-in-law should have been protected by you in battle. Instead, you killed him and you are not even ashamed!"

'The rakshasa consoled his wailing sister and replied to her with gentle words. "Don't cry, young one. You need not fear anyone. I will please you continuously with gifts and honours and favours. I hurled those arrows and did not distinguish between my own people and others in battle because I was filled with the madness of war and was eager for victory. That is how I killed your husband, my sister. Now, I will act for your benefit. Stay with your glorious brother Khara. He maintains fourteen thousand mighty rakshasas and he is their commander. Khara is your maternal cousin, he will do whatever you ask. Let brave Khara go quickly to the Dandaka forest which he shall now protect. Mighty Dushana shall be the commander of his forces. That forest was cursed long ago, but the rakshasas will occupy it now. There can be no doubt about that!"

'Ten-headed Ravana ordered fourteen thousand rakshasas who could change form at will to form an army. Khara, who had no reason for fear, left immediately for the Dandaka forest, surrounded by the grim-faced rakshasas. He established his rule there without obstruction and Shurpanakha also lived happily in the Dandaka forest.'[11]

## Sarga 25: Ravana Saves Madhu

'Ten-headed Ravana was pleased and felt at ease now that he had given the dense Dandaka forest to Khara and consoled his sister. The great-souled king

[11] In the middle books, where the Ramayana resembles an Indo-European epic more than it does a Hindu Purana, the rakshasas are simply another set of dangers that the warrior/king who leaves the city must encounter in the untamed places that he will traverse. Here, the Uttara Kanda provides an explanation for why Khara, Dushana and Shurpanakha are in the forests around Janasthana, a fact that goes unremarked in Valmiki's Aranya Kanda. Further, the rakshasas' relationship to Ravana also changes as the Uttara Kanda makes Khara Ravana's cousin and Dushana his commander. In the Aranya Kanda, they are both Ravana's brothers but the Uttara Kanda has set up an elaborate scheme of how Ravana and his three other siblings are born and how each one of them gets their rakshasa natures and their boons which determine and restrict their actions and behaviour (see Sarga 9 for how Ravana and his siblings were born and acquired their particular natures).

of the rakshasas went with his companions to a vast grove in Lanka called Nikumbhila. He saw a sacrificial enclosure with a hundred shining posts in which a sacrifice that blazed with its own splendour was being conducted. He saw his own son, Meghanada, scorcher of his enemies, clad in the skin of a black antelope, his head shaved, with a water pot and a staff. The lord of the rakshasas went up to him, embraced him and said, "Tell me, my son, what are you doing?"

'Shukra, best among the twice-born, he of great austerities, was in charge of the sacrifice. He said to Ravana, "I will tell you, your majesty. Listen to everything. Your son has performed seven huge sacrifices: the agnishtoma, the ashvamedha, the bahusuvarnaka, the rajasuya, the gomedha and the vaishnava. When he was performing the maheshvara, which is very difficult for men, your son received boons from Pashupati Shiva in manifest form as well as a chariot that traverses through the air and goes wherever its charioteer wills. He also received the power of illusion called tamasi which can produce darkness. Lord of the rakshasas, when these powers of illusion are employed in battle, not even gods and asuras can see your movements. He received an inexhaustible quiver of invincible arrows and a weapon that can destroy enemies in battle. These are the boons that your son has received, Ravana! When the sacrifice is completed today, he shall stand ready to receive you, as shall I."

'Ten-headed Ravana said, "What you have done is not good. You are worshipping my enemies, the gods who are led by Indra, with various offerings. What has been done now cannot be undone. Come, my dear, let us go to our own house." And so Ravana left with his son and Vibhishana. He released the women, all of whom were choked with tears. They all had auspicious marks and were jewels among the gods, danavas and rakshasas. They were richly decorated with ornaments and they shone with their own glory. Great-souled Vibhishana saw the sorrowing women and he understood what was in Ravana's mind. He said, "You continue to do exactly as you please, knowing that it hurts living beings and can destroy your fame, your wealth and your family. You took these beautiful women after overpowering their families. But Madhu has ignored you, king, and has taken Kumbhinasi."

'Ravana said, "I do not understand. Who is this creature that you say is named Madhu?"

'Angrily, Vibhishana said to his brother, "Listen, this is all the result of your own misdeeds. Our maternal grandfather, Sumali, has an elder brother named Malyavan. He is old and wise. He is our mother's elder uncle and therefore, he deserves our respect. His daughter had a daughter called Kumbhinasi. Anala is the daughter of our mother's sister, and so by right, she is a sister to us brothers. While your son was conducting his sacrifice and I was practising austerities under water, she was taken by Madhu, the stronger rakshasa. She was overpowered and taken from your inner apartments when some of your best and strongest ministers were killed. We forgave Madhu and did not kill him when we heard about this, your majesty, for a girl is given in marriage by her brothers. You should know that we have come to this because of you!"

'Ravana's eyes were bloodshot. Enraged, he said, "Summon my chariot at once! Tell the heroic warriors to be prepared. Let my brother and the other important night-ranging rakshasas mount their vehicles and arm themselves with various weapons. After I slay in battle that Madhu who has no fear of Ravana today, I shall go to Indra's world, surrounded by my friends and eager to fight. I will conquer the three worlds and bring Indra, destroyer of cities, under my control. I shall return covered in the glory of the three worlds and I shall wander wherever I please!" Four thousand akshauhinis of magnificent rakshasas set out, armed with all kinds of weapons and eager to do battle. Leading the troops was Indrajit, Ravana was in the middle and Kumbhakarna brought up the rear. Great-souled Vibhishana stayed in Lanka and walked the path of righteousness. And all the others marched towards Madhu's city.

'The rakshasas covered the sky as they went forth in their chariots drawn by camels and mules and horses and great, shining serpents. Thousands of daityas, who are hostile to the gods, saw Ravana and followed behind him. Ravana reached Madhu's city and entered it. He did not see Madhu there, but he did see his sister. Kumbhinasi joined her palms and touched her head to his feet because she was afraid of the rakshasa king. Ravana, best of the rakshasas, raised her up and said, "Do not be afraid. What can I do for you?" She said, "Mighty king, you who grant respect, if you are pleased with me, do not kill my husband. Be true to your word, majesty! Look at me, pleading with you. You yourself said, 'Do not be afraid!'"

'Ravana was pleased when he was spoken to in this manner by his sister as she stood before him. He said, "Tell me, quickly, where is your husband? I will go with him to conquer the realm of the gods. I am filled with compassion and good feeling for you. I will not kill Madhu!" The rakshasi was pleased and she went and woke her sleeping husband. She said, "Ten-headed Ravana, my powerful brother, is here and he is eager to conquer the world of the gods. He asks for your help. You and your friends should go and help him. You should partake equally in the efforts of those who love you." Madhu replied, "It shall be so!" and he watched Ravana approaching him. He honoured the king of the rakshasas appropriately. Treated thus in Madhu's house, heroic Ravana stayed there for one night and then prepared to leave. Ravana, who was like the king of the gods, reached Mount Kailasha, which is Vaishravana Kubera's home, and settled his army there.'

## Sarga 26: Ravana Rapes Rambha

'Ten-headed Ravana settled there with his army which was prepared for battle. As the sun set and the moon rose, white as the mountain itself, Ravana saw the mountain made radiant in the moonlight with its trees, its divine groves of karnikara and thickets of kadamba, its pools of water from the river Mandakini which were filled with blooming lotuses. He heard a beautiful sound, like a bell – it was the sound of apsaras singing in the house of the lord of wealth. Stirred by the wind, the trees rained their flowers upon the mountain, perfuming it with the fragrances of springtime. The pleasant breeze, carrier of the fragrance of honey and pollen from the flowers, increased Ravana's desire. The singing, the abundance of flowers, the cool breeze, the beauty of the mountain and the rising moon all increased his lust. Mighty Ravana was spellbound by the arrows of love. He gazed at the moon and sighed again and again.

'At that very moment, Rambha arrived there. She was the best of all the apsaras. Her face was like the full moon and she was adorned with celestial flowers. Decorated with special designs of fresh flowers from all six seasons, she was veiled in a cloth as blue-black as a rain cloud. Her face was like the moon, her brows like beautiful bows, her thighs like an elephant's trunk, her hands like blooming lotuses. Ravana saw her as she passed through the army camp. The rakshasa king, overwhelmed by the arrows of love, rose and grabbed her by the hand as she walked shyly by. He smiled and said, "Where are you going, my lovely? What have you planned for yourself? Whose lucky time has come, that he gets to enjoy you? Who are you going to satisfy tonight, who shall drink the nectar of your lips fragrant with lotus and lily? Who shall touch these breasts of yours, my pretty one, like golden urns and so tightly pressed together? Your hips are lovely, wide as a golden circle themselves and encircled by a golden belt. Who shall mount into these heavens tonight? There is no one more virile than me – not Indra, not Vishnu and not the ashvins. It is not good, pretty one, that you try to go past me! Rest here, on this beautiful rock, wide-hipped lady. I alone am the lord of the three worlds, there is no one that compares with me. Ten-headed Ravana, lord of the three worlds, pleads with you like this, with his palms joined. Accept me!"

'Rambha trembled and clasped her hands together. She replied, "I beg you, do not speak to me in this way. You are my elder! You should protect me from others if I am sexually assaulted, for by rights, I am your daughter-in-law. What I am saying is the truth!" As she stood there with her head bowed low, Ravana said to her, "You are my daughter-in-law only if you are my son's wife."

'"It is true," Rambha replied to Ravana. "Bull among rakshasas, I am legally the wife of your son. The son of Vaishravana, your brother, is dearer to him than his own life. He is known in the three worlds as Nalakubara. He is like a brahmin in his righteousness, but he is like a kshatriya in valour. He is like the fire when he is angry but like the earth in his patience. I have made an appointment with the son of Vaishravana Kubera, the guardian of the quarters. I have adorned myself in this way with him in mind. He is attached to no one but me and likewise, I am to him. For this truth alone, king, you should release me, scorcher of enemies! Righteous Nalakubara is eagerly waiting for me. Do not come in the way of your son. Let me go! Bull among rakshasas, walk the path trodden by good men. You are worthy of my respect, and I am worthy of your protection!"

'Overcome with lust, the mighty rakshasa mocked Rambha's righteous words. Inflamed by passion and desire, he violated her. When he let her go, Rambha's flower decorations were torn and she was agitated, like a river in which an elephant has played. Trembling, shamed and terrified, she went to

Nalakubara. She fell at his feet with her palms joined. Great Nalakubara saw the state that she was in and he said to her, "What is this, my lovely? Why have you fallen at my feet?" Sighing and trembling, she told him everything exactly as it had happened. "Lord, ten-headed Ravana is on his tour of the three worlds. He has camped here along with his army. He saw me passing by as I was coming to you. He grabbed me and asked me whom I belonged to, scorcher of enemies. I told him everything exactly as it was but because he was overcome with passion, he did not hear anything I had said. My lord, I pleaded with him saying "I am your daughter-in-law" but he put that aside and he raped me violently. You must forgive me for this transgression, destroyer of pride. A woman's strength does not match up to a man's!"

'Vaishravana's son was enraged when he heard that. He put himself into a trance and meditated on what she had told him. In a moment, he saw what had happened. His eyes red with anger, he took some water in his hand. He sprinkled it around, according to custom, and then he unleashed a terrible curse upon the king of the rakshasas.

'"My dear, because he took you violently against your will, he can never approach another young woman against her will. His head will split into seven pieces if he ever sexually violates another woman!" When this terrible curse, which was like a blazing fire, was uttered, celestial drums sounded and flowers rained from the sky. All the gods, with Prajapati Brahma at their head, rejoiced, recognizing the destiny of the worlds and the death of the rakshasa. Ravana lost interest in having sex with women who did not desire him when he heard that hair-raising curse.'

## Sarga 27: Sumali Is Killed in Battle

'Ravana went past Kailasha and approached Indra's realm with his mighty rakshasas. The sound of the rakshasa forces approaching the realm of the gods from all sides reverberated like the ocean. Indra shook on his throne as he listened to Ravana's arrival and he said to all the gods that had gathered there – the adityas, the vasus, the rudras, the sadhyas and the troops of maruts – "Get ready to fight wicked Ravana!" The effulgent gods, who were Indra's equal in battle, prepared enthusiastically for war by arming themselves. But Indra, made pathetic by Ravana, was agitated. He went to Vishnu and said, "Vishnu, you have great courage and valour, what should I do about this powerful rakshasa who has come here to fight? He is mighty for no reason other than his boons. We have to honour the words of Prajapati Brahma, lord! You supported me when I killed Namuchi and Vritra and both Naraka and Shambara. You must do the same now to get rid of these creatures. Lord, you are the final refuge among all the gods, there is no other, mighty one. You are Narayana, glorious, lotus-navelled, eternal. The worlds are established in you as am I, the king of the gods. Tell me, god of gods, will I fight this enemy alone or will you, with your sword and your discus, help me?"

'Spoken to thus by Indra, Vishnu Narayana said, "Do not be agitated. Listen to what I have to say. Ravana is hard to defeat and because of his boons, he cannot be killed by either the danavas or the daityas in battle. He shall accomplish great deeds along with his son, because of his strength. I have seen this with my supernatural powers. I cannot do what you have asked of me. I cannot take on the king of the rakshasas in battle. Vishnu never retreats from battle without having killed the enemy – and that pledge will be difficult to fulfil with this rakshasa who has been empowered by boons. Lord of the gods, performer of a hundred sacrifices, I swear in your presence that I shall be the cause of this rakshasa's death. When I see that the moment has arrived, I shall kill this rakshasa and his son in battle and I shall please the gods!"

'At that moment, a huge roar tore through the night and was heard everywhere. It was the sound of Ravana's army marching to war. A great battle with a terrible noise ensued as the gods and rakshasas attacked each other with all kinds of weapons. Ravana's companions, heroic rakshasas with grim faces – Maricha, Prahasta, Mahaparshva, Mahodara, Akampana and Nikumbha, Shuka and Sarana, Samhrada, Dhumaketu, Mahadanshtra, Mahamukha, Jambumali, Mahamali and Virupaksha – charged into battle at his command. Sumali, Ravana's grandfather, that bull among rakshasas, entered the fray surrounded by these mighty heroes. In anger and with all kinds of sharp weapons, he attacked Indra's troops like the wind scattering the clouds. At that moment, Savitra, the heroic eighth vasu, joined that great battle. The gods were angry about the rakshasas' reputation of never retreating from battle, which went on and on.

'Heroic rakshasas attacked the gods, who were standing firm, with hundreds of thousands of weapons that were designed to kill. And the gods retaliated by assaulting the rakshasas with different kinds of weapons. Sumali, brave and angry, charged into the battle, attacking the army of the gods with sharp weapons. Injured by those sharp arrows and spears and maces, the gods had to retreat. But even as Sumali scattered the army of the gods in all directions, Savitra, the eighth vasu, stood firm. Surrounded by his own people, he assaulted the rakshasa with great courage.

'A violent duel ensued between Sumali and Savitra who would not retreat in battle. Sumali's chariot, drawn by massive serpents, was struck by a hail of mighty arrows from the great-souled vasu and fell over. After destroying the chariot with hundreds of arrows, Savitra grabbed a mace with both hands in order to kill Sumali. He held that shining mace, as glorious as death's rod, and smashed it on Sumali's head. The mace crashed on to his head like a meteor and thundered like a bolt thrown at a mountain by Indra. The blow crushed Sumali to dust so that neither his head nor his flesh nor his bones could be seen on the battlefield. The rakshasas ran in all directions when they saw Sumali dead, crying loudly to each other.'

## Sarga 28: Ravana Fights Indra

Distraught, the rakshasas attacked their own army with arrows. Then Meghanada, Ravana's son, a hero in battle, grew angry. He turned the rakshasas around and took a stand. The great chariot-warrior, with a chariot that could go where he willed, charged the army like a fire raging towards a forest. The gods scattered in all directions as soon as they saw him holding his many weapons. Eager as he was to fight, no one could hold their ground against Meghanada on the battlefield. Indra saw that the gods were pierced with arrows and that they were greatly agitated. He said, "Do not be afraid. Do not retreat from the battle. My undefeated son is joining the war!" Indra's son, the god known as Jayanta, came forth and entered the battle in a marvellously wrought chariot, surrounded by the thirty gods. Ravana's son confronted him and the battle that took place between the son of Indra and the son of the rakshasa was like that between all the gods and all the rakshasas. The rakshasa's son showered arrows decorated with gold upon Gomukha, the son of Matali, who was Indra's charioteer. Indra's son was enraged and retaliated with arrows that struck Ravana's son and his charioteer. The mighty rakshasa, his eyes wide with anger, showered Indra's son with arrows. Ravana's son grabbed all kinds of weapons – arrows, spears, javelins, maces and swords – and battered the gods, causing a great darkness to fall upon the world as he attacked. The army of the gods that had gathered around Indra's son ran hither and thither. They could not distinguish between the enemy and the gods and they ran around frantically in confusion.

'At that moment, the heroic warrior Puloma, a leader of the daityas, picked up Indra's son and carried him away. Puloma was the father of Indra's wife and he took his grandson and dived into the depths of the ocean. The gods thought Jayanta was dead. They were disheartened and depressed and they fled in all directions. Ravana's son, surrounded by his own army, was delighted and he charged towards the gods, roaring loudly. When he saw that his son had been felled by Indrajit's valour, Indra, the king of the gods, said to Matali, "Bring my chariot!" Matali brought that mighty chariot which moved as swiftly as thought, formidable and well equipped. Great clouds driven by the wind rolled out before the chariot, rumbling like thunder and flashing with bolts of lightning. Gandharvas played musical instruments and groups of apsaras danced as Indra set out to do battle. The king of the gods went forth with many weapons and he was surrounded by the rudras and the vasus, the adityas and the sadhyas and troops of maruts. Great meteors fell, a dreadful wind blew and the sun's light was dimmed as Indra emerged. Then, Ravana, the powerful warrior, mounted his divine chariot which had been fashioned by Vishvakarma. It was covered with great serpents who made one's hair stand on end and whose hissing seemed to set the battlefield aflame. Surrounded by daitya warriors and night-stalking rakshasas, the chariot came face to face with Indra on the battlefield. Ravana restrained his son and took a stand himself. His son left the battlefield and waited nearby. A great battle began between the gods and the rakshasas, dense with showers of arrows, like rain clouds colliding.

'Wicked Kumbhakarna arrived, equipped with all kinds of weapons, but he did not know whom he was fighting. He struck the gods furiously with his teeth and his arms and his feet and with various weapons. The mighty rudras and the adityas began to fight the rakshasas with an endless stream of missiles.

The entire rakshasa army fled from the battle when they were attacked by the gods and the troops of maruts. Some were killed, others were pierced by weapons and lay on the ground, others stood where they were struck on their mounts – in their chariots, on their nagas, on mules, on camels, on many kinds of serpents, on their sea monsters and boars and other creatures with fiendish faces. They stood there, stunned, holding on to them with their arms. The rakshasas who rose up were slashed by the gods and died.

'With all the dead and unconscious rakshasas lying on the ground, the deluge on the battlefield resembled a river with blood for water, thronged by vultures and crows and with weapons as water creatures. Mighty Ravana was enraged when he saw that his entire army had been slaughtered by the gods. He re-entered the ocean of soldiers and, killing gods along the way, he charged towards Indra. Indra twanged his great bow and the sound of it reverberated in the ten directions. Indra drew his bow and aimed for Ravana's head with arrows that blazed like fire, like the sun. Mighty-armed Ravana also covered Indra in a shower of arrows. As the two of them fought on in a rainstorm of arrows, darkness fell and nothing could be distinguished.'

## Sarga 29: Meghanada Defeats Indra

'As darkness fell, the gods and the rakshasas continued to fight and to kill each other, maddened by their strength. The gods had left only a tenth of the huge rakshasa army on the battlefield, having killed the rest. As they fought each other in the dark, they could not tell god from rakshasa. The only three who were immune to the spellbinding web of darkness were Indra, Ravana and Ravana's son. Ravana saw that his huge army had been destroyed. He was enraged and let out a huge roar. Dangerous in his anger, Ravana said to his charioteer who was standing in the chariot, "Take me through the middle of the enemy army to the other side. I shall banish all the gods from the heavens today, relying on my own valour and using all kinds of weapons! I shall kill Indra and Varuna and the god of wealth and Yama. And after I have speedily dispatched the gods, I shall place myself above them. Have no fear. Do what is necessary. Drive my chariot. This is the second time I am telling you, take me to the other side of the army! We are now in the groves of Nandana. Take me to the mountain where the sun rises!"

'The charioteer heard his words and guided the horses, who were as swift as thought, through the middle of the enemy army. Indra, the king of the gods, standing in his chariot, realized Ravana's intentions and said to the gods who were on the battlefield, "Listen to what I want. It would be good to capture ten-headed Ravana alive. He is so strong that he rides through our forces on his chariot with the speed of the wind, like a rising wave in the ocean when the moon is full. We cannot kill him and because of his boons, he is fearless. We should capture him on the battlefield. I enjoy the three worlds because I conquered Bali. I think it is right to capture this wicked creature in the same way." Indra turned away from Ravana and went to establish himself in another area, fighting and killing rakshasas in battle. Ravana, who never turned from battle, entered from the northern side and Indra, the performer of a hundred sacrifices, penetrated the southern flank. When the king of the rakshasas had moved one hundred yojanas in, he covered the army of the gods completely with a rain of arrows. Indra saw that his military formation had been breached but he was not disturbed. He forced Ravana to turn back by having him surrounded. The danavas and rakshasas saw Indra taking Ravana and they shouted aloud, "Alas! We are destroyed!"

'Standing in his chariot, Ravana's son was numb with anger. He entered that awesome army in a terrible rage. He used the powers of illusion that he had been given by Shiva in the past and became invisible to all beings. He penetrated the ranks of the gods and scattered them. He charged directly towards Indra, ignoring the other gods. But mighty Indra could not see his enemy's son who had attacked Matali and his horses with superb arrows. Indrajit covered Indra with a shower of arrows, his hands flying fast. Indra relinquished his chariot and dismissed Matali. He mounted Airavata and went in search of Ravana's son who was invisible in battle because of his powers of illusion. When Ravana's son realized that Indra was exhausted, he bound him with a spell and carried him off to his own forces. The gods saw that Indra had been taken away from the battlefield. They said, "What is this? He has been taken away by that master of illusion who cannot be seen!" The gods were enraged and they went after Ravana and covered him with a hail of weapons.

'Although he was injured, Ravana confronted the vasus, adityas and maruts. He could not fight any more nor even stand. Ravana's son, although he was invisible in battle, saw that his father was tired and injured and he said to him, "Come, father, let us go. Our work on the battlefield is done. You should know that we are victorious, so feel at ease, do not be anxious. I have captured Indra, the lord of the three worlds and the leader of the gods' army. The pride of the gods has been shattered. Enjoy the three worlds! You have overcome your enemy by your power. There is no need to do anything more, your fighting is useless." The gods turned away from the battlefield and when Ravana heard his son's words, he was restored.

'The lord of the rakshasas, free from the fatigue of battle, went towards his home along with his son. Pleased, he said to him, "You have added to the glory of my clan with your great might and your valour. You have defeated the king of the gods and the gods themselves. Take Indra to the city immediately, surrounded by your own forces. I shall bring up the rear and follow soon after with my people!" Having captured the king of the gods, Ravana's son reached his own home with his soldiers and vehicles. And then he dismissed the rejoicing rakshasas.'

## Sarga 30: The Reason for Indra's Defeat

'When mighty Indra had been conquered by Ravana's son, all the gods, with Prajapati Brahma at their head, went to Lanka. They approached Ravana, who was seated and surrounded by his sons and his brothers. Brahma stood in the sky and said, "Ravana, my son! I am pleased with your son in battle. Indeed, his strength and prowess are equal to yours, perhaps even greater! You have fulfilled your pledge and conquered the three worlds with your own power. I am pleased with you and your son. Your son is very powerful, Ravana. He shall be known in the three worlds as Indrajit, the conqueror of Indra. This rakshasa will be strong and remain undefeated by his enemies. You have brought the gods under your control with his efforts. Mighty-armed one, you should release Indra, the punisher of Paka. What would you ask from the gods for his release?"

'Victorious Indrajit, the mighty one, said, "I demand immortality in exchange for his freedom!" Brahma said to Ravana's son, "There is no creature on earth that has complete immortality." Indrajit replied to lotus-born Brahma, "Listen, then, to what will secure the release of Indra. When

I offer oblations and worship the fire to secure victory and invincibility in war, I ask that should I complete those rituals, I will be invulnerable in battle. All men ask for immortality by performing austerities, but I will obtain immortality through my prowess!"

'"It shall be so," said Brahma. Indra was released and returned to heaven.

'Meanwhile, Indra was pathetic. His lustre had dimmed and he began to worry about all that had happened.

'Prajapati Brahma noticed him in that sad state and said, "Performer of a hundred sacrifices, why this uneasiness? Remember, you had once done something wrong. Long ago, lord of the immortals, I had created beings that were all the same on the outside – the same colour, speaking the same language, of the same form. There was nothing different in their appearance or in their characteristics. Then, with a concentrated mind, I began to think about those living beings and in order to make some distinction, I created a woman. I put into her everything that was special among those living beings. I formed a blameless woman with beauty and virtue. I gave her the name Ahalya, by which she was known. After I had created that woman, lord of the gods, I began to think about whom she should belong to. But you, Indra, destroyer of cities, you fixed your mind on that woman and thought of her as your wife because you were superior to her! I entrusted her to the great-souled Gautama and after many years of looking after her, he gave her back. Now that I was sure of the great sage's patience and knew that his austerities were complete, I gave her to him as a wife. The righteous sage enjoyed her but the gods were disappointed that I had given her to Gautama. You were angry and in the mood for love. You went to the sage's hermitage and saw the woman, shining like a flame. Filled with lust and anger, you violated her, Indra. Gautama saw you in his hermitage and enraged, he cursed you. That led to a change in your circumstances, lord of the gods.

'"'You shall fall into your enemies' hands in battle, king Vasava, because you fearlessly violated my wife!" said Gautama. "Idiot! This passion that you have unleashed will stay among all men, have no doubt about that! Whoever commits this same transgression shall bear one half of its consequences. The other half will fall on you. Your position will never be secure, destroyer of cities, because of your unrighteous deed. Whoever becomes the king of the gods shall be unsteady in his position – this is the curse I declare and cast upon you!" Gautama, a man of great austerities, then berated his wife, "Disappear from the vicinity of my hermitage, you badly behaved woman! You were rich in youth and beauty and that made you restless. You will no longer be the only beautiful woman in the world. This beauty, which was so hard to obtain, shall now belong to all beings. All of this will come to pass because of your blunder."

'"From then onwards, most living beings were beautiful and shared in the sage's curse. So remember this transgression, mighty-armed one. This is why you were captured by your enemies. Quickly, concentrate your energies and undertake the vaishnava sacrifice. It will purify you and you shall go to heaven. Your son was not killed in that battle, he was taken to the depths of the ocean by his grandfather."

'Indra quickly performed the sacrifice and went back to the realm of the gods and ruled as their king.

'Such is Indrajit's might, Rama. I have told you all about it. He overcame the king of the gods, what is there to say about other living beings?'

## Sarga 31: Ravana Relaxes on the Banks of the Narmada

Mighty Rama was surprised and he spoke humbly to Agastya, the best of sages. 'Blessed one, best among the twice-born, was there no one in the world with any courage at the time when Ravana, king of the rakshasas, was being so cruel? Did all the kings of the earth lack courage or were they all defeated by his marvellous weapons when they tried to oppose him?'

The blessed sage Agastya smiled and spoke to him as Grandfather Brahma would speak to Shiva. 'Rama, bull among monarchs, Ravana wandered over the earth harassing kings. He reached Mahishmati, which was like the heavenly city where the god of fire lives. There, where the sacrificial fire is kept burning, was a king named Arjuna, Agni's equal in valour. That day, the mighty king of the Haihayas had gone to the river Narmada to enjoy himself with his wives. Ravana, king of the rakshasas, asked Arjuna's ministers, "Where is King Arjuna now? Answer me quickly! I, Ravana, have come here today because I want to fight him. Inform him of my arrival at once!"

'The wise ministers told him that the king was not there. Ravana, son of Vishravas, left and went to the Vindhya mountain when he heard that from the citizens. He gazed at the Vindhya which touched the sky. It seemed to have burst out of the earth and penetrated the clouds. It had a thousand peaks and lions lived in its caves. Its many cool waterfalls made it seem as if it were laughing out loud. Gods, danavas, gandharvas and groups of apsaras, kinnaras and their women amused themselves there and the great mountain seemed like heaven. Flowing with rivers that were as clear as crystal, the mountain stood like the cosmic serpent with his many tongues lolling out of his mouth.

'Ravana saw the mountain that resembled the Himalaya with its fiery caves and went onwards to the Narmada whose sacred waters flowed over rocks towards the western ocean. Her waters were made turbulent by buffalo and deer and lions and tigers, bears and the best of elephants who were thirsty and tormented by the heat. She was covered with geese and ducks and swans and cranes that called out loudly as if they were always in mating season. The river had flowering trees as her crest jewel, a pair of geese as her breasts, the wide sands as her hips and a line of swans as her girdle. Her limbs were covered with pollen from flowers and foam from the waters was her spotless garment. Waves were her gentle touch and blooming lotuses were her eyes.

'Ten-headed Ravana dismounted from Pushpaka and bathed in the best of beautiful rivers, which was like a desirable woman. The bull among the rakshasas sat on her pleasant banks adorned with many kinds of flowers. Along with his ministers, he enjoyed the pleasure that came from observing her beauty. Then, Ravana laughed and playfully said to Maricha, Shuka and Sarana, "The sun, which stands in the middle of the sky, which turns the world to gold with its thousand rays and scorches it, knows that I am sitting here and has turned as cool as the moon. The breeze, which removes our fatigue, is chilled and made fragrant by the waters of the Narmada. It blows gently from fear of me. This best of rivers, which increases our pleasure and carries fish and crocodiles and birds on her waves, looks like a terrified woman. Gentlemen, you have all been injured by the weapons of kings who are Indra's equal in battle. You are covered in blood as if soaked in the sap of sandalwood trees. You should bathe in the Narmada which confers happiness, like the lotus-mouthed elephants, mightily rutting, bathe in the Ganga. You shall be cleansed of all your sins by bathing in this river. And

I, too, shall slowly make an offering of flowers to Shiva on these banks that shine like the autumn moon."

'Urged by Ravana, Maricha, Shuka, Sarana, Mahodara and Dhumraksha bathed in the Narmada. The river was disturbed by the massive rakshasa leaders as the Ganga is by Vamana, Anjana, Padma and other great elephants. The rakshasas came out of the Narmada and gathered flowers for Ravana. In no time at all, they had created a mound of blossoms on the bright, cloud-white banks of the Narmada. Ravana accepted the flowers and climbed down to the river to bathe himself like a mighty elephant at the Ganga. He recited the best of incantations and came out of the water. The seven rakshasas honoured Ravana with joined palms. A golden lingam was carried wherever Ravana, king of the rakshasas, went. Ravana established the lingam on a mound of sand and worshipped it with perfumes and flowers whose fragrance was immortal. After he had completed his worship of Shiva, the great lord, the giver of boons, the one whose head is adorned with the moon, Ravana spread his arms and sang and danced.'

## Sarga 32: Ravana Is Captured by Arjuna of the Haihayas

'Not far from where Ravana was offering flowers on the banks of the Narmada, Arjuna, best of the victorious, lord of Mahishmati, was playing in her waters along with his wives. Arjuna seemed like a great tusker surrounded by a thousand female elephants as he stood in their midst. Arjuna blocked the flow of the Narmada simply because he was curious about the strength of his thousand arms. Obstructed by those powerful arms, the clear waters flooded their banks and began to flow in the opposite direction. Filled with fish and dolphins and crocodiles and with flowers and grasses, the Narmada's waters had a monsoon force.

'The torrential waters sent downstream by Arjuna swept away Ravana's flower offering. Ravana abandoned his half-finished ritual and looked at the Narmada as one would at a beloved wife who was acting against her nature. Ravana watched the waters coming from the west like a riptide and flowing towards the east but he noticed that in the distance, the water-birds were undisturbed and that the waters were in their natural state, calm, like a woman. Curious about what had caused the surge, Ravana pointed it out to Shuka and Sarana with a finger of his right hand. The heroic rakshasa brothers, Shuka and Sarana, rose into the air and looked towards the west. About half a yojana away, they saw a man frolicking in the water with his women. He was as huge as a sala tree, his hair streamed wildly in the water, his eyes were red from drinking and he was altogether intoxicated. That subduer of his enemies obstructed the flow of the waters with his one thousand arms as a mountain might block the earth with its one thousand feet. He was surrounded by thousands of beautiful women the way a tusker is surrounded by thousands of rutting female elephants.

'Shuka and Sarana saw that amazing sight and they went back to Ravana and said, "There is someone who is as large as a sala tree, your majesty. He is blocking the Narmada and enjoying himself with his women. The river rises in huge waves, like a tide in the ocean, because she is obstructed by his thousand arms." When they had reported this, Shuka and Sarana fell silent.

'"That is Arjuna," said Ravana, eager to fight. Clouds rumbled and rained blood when the king of the rakshasas set off to confront Arjuna. Mighty Ravana shone dark like collyrium and quickly reached that terrifying place in the middle of the Narmada along with Mahodara, Mahaparshva, Dhumraksha, Shuka and Sarana. There, he saw King Arjuna surrounded by his women.

'The king of the rakshasas was proud of his strength. His eyes red with anger, he said to the king's ministers in a deep voice, "Go at once and tell the king of the Haihayas that Ravana has come here to fight him!" Arjuna's ministers stood up and said to heavily armed Ravana, "Good wishes, Ravana, good wishes! You know the right time to fight. You wish to fight our king who is drunk and engaged with his women in the same way that a tiger would attack an elephant who is surrounded by his female herd. Calm down, Ravana, and spend the night here. If you still want to fight Arjuna, you can do that tomorrow. But if you want to fight in a hurry, then you will have to kill us all before you can get close to him!"

'Then, Ravana's ministers, who were hungry, killed the king's ministers in combat and ate them. Arjuna's companions and Ravana's ministers created a huge uproar on the banks of the Narmada. Arjuna's ministers ran here and there and assaulted Ravana and his companions with arrows and spears and other weapons which were sharp and like thunderbolts. The noise of the attacking Haihaya warriors was fierce, like an ocean filled with fish and crocodiles and alligators. Ravana's ministers, Prahasta, Shuka and Sarana, were enraged and they slew Arjuna's warriors with their fiery energy.

'The men reported the actions of Ravana and his ministers to Arjuna while he was enjoying himself. Arjuna said to the women, "Do not be afraid!" and rose out of the waters like Anjana, the great elephant. His eyes were red with anger and he blazed like the terrible fire at the end of time. He quickly picked up his mace made of gold and scattered the rakshasas the way the sun does the darkness. Arjuna raised that great club, which he could toss between his hands, and fell upon the rakshasas with the speed of Garuda. Prahasta, the mace warrior, blocked his path and stood before him, unmoving, as the Vindhya mountain stands before the sun. Driven by war-lust, Prahasta picked up a mace bound with iron and roared in anger like the ocean. A fire the colour of ashoka flowers crowned the mace that was released from Prahasta's hand and it flew as if it were burning. Arjuna, who had the valour of an elephant, blocked the oncoming mace, which was deadly accurate. The king of the Haihayas lifted his own mace with his five hundred arms and whirled it aloft as he charged towards Prahasta. His weapon hit Prahasta with great force and he fell to the ground like a mountain struck by Indra's thunderbolt.

'Seeing that Prahasta had fallen, Maricha, Shuka and Sarana, along with Mahodara and Dhumraksha, slipped away from the battlefield. Ravana charged towards Arjuna, that best of kings, when Prahasta fell and his ministers ran away.

'The combat between the thousand-armed king and the twenty-armed rakshasa was truly hair-raising. Like two agitated oceans, like two moving mountains, like two splendid suns, like two blazing fires, like two arrogant elephants, like two bulls with their rutting cows, like two thundering clouds, like two proud lions, both enraged like Shiva at the end of time, the rakshasa and Arjuna attacked each other mightily with their maces. As mountains endure being struck by thunderbolts, so the rakshasa and his opponent bore the terrible blows. As thunder is born from flashes of lightning, so the directions resounded with the clashing of their maces. When Arjuna's mace fell upon his enemy's chest, it seemed golden, as if struck by lightning. And when Ravana's mace struck Arjuna again and again, it was like a meteor falling on a huge mountain. Neither Arjuna nor the king of the rakshasas grew tired and their combat resembled that between Indra and Bali, long ago. The best of men and the best of rakshasas attacked each other like two bulls with their horns, like two elephants with their tusks.

'Arjuna struck Ravana on the chest angrily with all his might in that battle. Ravana's chest was protected by boons and so the mace broke into two pieces and fell to the ground, useless. But Ravana was pushed back a bow-length by the blow from Arjuna's mace and he fell, crying. Arjuna saw ten-headed Ravana in distress and he pounced on him suddenly, as Garuda would upon a snake. Grabbing him with the strength of his thousand arms, the valiant king tied him up as Narayana had tied Bali. The gods, the siddhas and the charanas shouted "Bravo!" and rained flowers upon Arjuna's head. Like a tiger with a deer or a lion with an elephant, the king of the Haihayas roared like a thundercloud.

'Prahasta had recovered his senses and he was angry when he saw Ravana tied up. He rushed towards the king. The force of the charging rakshasa was like the rising of the ocean during the monsoon. "Release your weapons, release!" he shouted and "Stand! Stay!" as he unleashed clubs and arrows upon Arjuna. Unperturbed by the attack, Arjuna, the subduer of his enemies, grabbed the weapons of the rakshasas, enemies of the gods, before they struck. He wounded them with their own excellent weapons and set them to flight, as the wind does the clouds. Having tormented the rakshasas, Kartavirya Arjuna took Ravana and entered his city surrounded by his friends. Arjuna entered the city like the thousand-eyed Indra had with Bali bound, while flowers and rice were showered upon him by the citizens and the brahmins.'

## Sarga 33: Arjuna Frees Ravana

'In the heavens, the sage Pulastya heard the gods talking about Ravana's capture, which was like the capture of the wind. Though steadfast, the great sage was moved by love for his grandson and he went to see the king of Mahishmati. That brahmin, who had the speed of the wind and the force of the mind, arrived in the city of Mahishmati through the air.

'Like Brahma entering Indra's city Amaravati, he entered that city of prosperous people who recognized the sage who was difficult to see. He was like the sun god walking on foot and they went to inform Arjuna. Hearing the words "It is Pulastya!" the king of the Haihayas joined his palms and placed them on his head as he went to greet the best of brahmins. The chief priest walked ahead like Brihaspati before Indra, carrying the materials for the welcome ritual.

Arjuna saw the sage, who was like the rising sun, coming forward and he bowed to him as Indra would to Shiva. He offered him water to wash his feet and something sweet to eat. The king spoke to Pulastya in a voice filled with joy. "Today Mahishmati has become the equal of Amaravati because I behold you, best of the twice-born, you who are difficult to see! I am happy that my family prospers because today I have been able to worship your feet, which have been worshipped by the hosts of gods. This my kingdom, these my sons, these my wives, we all are yours. What shall we do? Tell us what we can do for you, brahmin!"

'After enquiring about his rituals, his sons and his conduct, Pulastya said to Arjuna, the king of the Haihayas, "Your majesty, you with eyes like the petals of a lotus, with a face like the full moon, you have conquered ten-headed Ravana with your incomparable strength. You have tied up my grandson who is extremely difficult to defeat and from fear of whom the ocean and the wind stand still. You have eclipsed my grandson's glory and enhanced your own. Listen to my words today, my son, and release ten-headed Ravana!"

'Arjuna heard Pulastya's command and, without a word, he happily set the king of the rakshasas free. He released the enemy of the gods and honoured him with celestial ornaments and clothes. With fire as witness, he made a pact of friendship and non-violence with him. Having honoured Brahma's son, he went home.

'The mighty lord of the rakshasas was embarrassed because he had gained his release through Pulastya's intervention and had been embraced and welcomed. Pulastya, best of sages and son of Grandfather Brahma, went back to Brahma's realm after he had secured ten-headed Ravana's freedom.

'In this way, Ravana was captured by Kartavirya Arjuna and was released because of Pulastya's word. And, so, joy of the Raghus, there is always someone stronger than the strong. One who wishes for his own glory should not ignore others.

'Once he had obtained the friendship of the thousand-armed Arjuna, Ravana again wandered the earth harassing kings.'

## Sarga 34: Ravana Challenges Vali

'Ravana, king of the rakshasas, wandered the earth, free of all cares. He would approach whoever he heard was powerful, whether human or rakshasa, and ask them to fight him.

'In time, he came to the city of Kishkindha and challenged gold-garlanded Vali, who ruled there. Tara, the minister of the monkeys, who was also the father of Tara, Vali's wife, said to Ravana who was eager to fight, "King of the rakshasas, Vali, the only one who can match you in strength, is not here. Who else is there among the best of monkeys who has the capacity to stand up to you in battle? Vali will return shortly, Ravana, after performing the evening rituals at the confluence of the four oceans. You can wait for him. Look! There are the skeletons, white as conch shells, of those who came here wanting to fight the effulgent king of the monkeys. Ravana, even if you have drunk the elixir of immortality, you will meet the end of your life when you encounter Vali. If you are in a hurry to die, go to the southern ocean and see Vali, who stands there like the sun on the earth."

'Ravana ignored Tara. He climbed into Pushpaka and made for the southern ocean where he saw Vali, bright as a mountain of gold, his face like the rising sun, absorbed in the evening ritual. Dark and large as a mountain of collyrium, Ravana dismounted from Pushpaka, full of wicked intentions, and crept silently towards Vali so that he could grab him. Like a lion glimpsing a hare or Garuda a snake, it happened that Vali saw Ravana. But Vali was not at all worried about Ravana's intentions. "Wicked Ravana wants to seize me, but I will take him under my arm and travel to the vast oceans. Everyone will see my enemy Ravana, stuck under my arm, with his legs and arms and clothes dangling, like a snake in the mouth of Garuda."

'Vali made up his mind to do that and he stood there like the king of the mountains, reciting sacred mantras to himself. And so the two of them, the king of the rakshasas and the king of the monkeys, each proud of his strength, each eager to grab hold of the other, decided to act. Though Vali was facing the other way, he heard the sound of Ravana's footsteps and realized that Ravana was about to seize him. He pounced on Ravana as a bird would on a snake. As the king of the rakshasas was about to attack, the monkey grabbed him, tucked him under his arm and rose powerfully into the air. Vali carried

Ravana away as the wind carries the clouds, even though Ravana assaulted him with his nails and teeth over and over again.

'The rakshasa ministers saw Ravana being carried away. They leapt into the sky in order to set him free. Vali looked like the sun being followed by clouds when they chased him across the sky. Even those incomparable rakshasas could not catch Vali and they fell away, exhausted by the speed of his arms. The best of mountains moved out of Vali's way as he went along. The lord of the monkeys, he of great speed, flew where even birds cannot reach and he was able to complete the evening rituals at all the oceans. Vali, lord of the sky-flyers, was worshipped by all the creatures of the air. He reached the western ocean with Ravana. He completed the evening rituals there and bathed and recited prayers and then, carrying Ravana, he went to the northern ocean. After performing the evening rituals there, Vali, still carrying Ravana, went onwards to the eastern ocean. There, too, Indra's son, the king of the monkeys, completed the evening rituals. Then he turned his face towards Kishkindha and picked up Ravana again.

'The monkey had performed the evening rituals at all four oceans and now, tired from carrying Ravana, he landed in the groves of Kishkindha. The best of monkeys released Ravana from under his arm. Laughing, he asked Ravana, "Where are you from?"

'Amazed at having seen the entire world, the lord of the rakshasas said, "Lord of the monkeys, you are like Indra. I am Ravana, the lord of the rakshasas. I came here to fight. But you have defeated me. What strength, what courage, what gravity you have! You bore me to all the four oceans as if I were a sacrificial animal. Monkey hero, you carried me so swiftly and without any fatigue. What other hero could possibly have done this! Leaping monkey, there is no doubt that there are only three other beings with this kind of speed apart from you – the mind, the wind and Garuda. Bull among monkeys, now that I have seen your strength, I wish to establish a close and lasting friendship with you with fire as the witness. Wives, sons, cities, kingdoms, pleasures, clothes and food – we shall share these from now on, lord of the monkeys!"

'And then, the two of them, the monkey and the rakshasa, lit a fire and pledged brotherhood as they embraced each other. With their arms around each other, the monkey and the rakshasa entered Kishkindha like two lions entering a mountain cave. Ravana stayed there for a month as if he were Sugriva and then, his ministers, who wished to conquer the three worlds, came and took him away.[12]

'This is what happened long ago between Vali and Ravana, who was first defeated by Vali and then taken as a brother by him before the fire. Vali's strength was great and unmatched, but he was destroyed by you, like a moth in a flame.'

## Sarga 35: The Story of Hanuman's Birth

His palms joined in respect, Rama spoke these significant words and asked Agastya, the sage who lived in the southern regions, 'The strength of both Ravana and Vali is beyond measure. But in my opinion, they cannot equal Hanuman's heroism. Valour, skill, strength, steadfastness, wisdom, the capacity to think clearly about strategy, courage and power – all these reside in Hanuman. When the monkey army despaired upon seeing the great ocean, Hanuman gave them hope by leaping one hundred yojanas. He penetrated the city of Lanka and entered Ravana's inner apartments where he saw Sita. He spoke to her and reassured her. Single-handed, Hanuman defeated the leader of the army, a minister's son, a warrior and Ravana's own son. He confronted Ravana and then he freed himself from his bonds and burned Lanka to ashes like the fire that consumes the earth itself. I have never heard that Yama or Indra or Vishnu or Kubera performed deeds such as Hanuman's in battle. It is by the strength of his arms that I obtained Lanka, Sita, Lakshmana, victory, my friends and my family. If Hanuman had not been the friend of the monkey king, who would have had the capacity to bring news of all that had happened to Sita, daughter of Janaka?

[12] This is another case where the Uttara Kanda provides a post-facto explanation for something that has happened in the earlier books. There is no apparent reason for Rama choosing Sugriva, in all ways the lesser of the monkey brothers, as his ally. The Uttara Kanda, displaying some anxiety about this, lets us know that Vali and Ravana had a friendship that had been sealed years before. Rama could not have chosen Ravana's friend as an ally in his quest for Sita, hence his unlikely alliance with Sugriva. This explanation appears to be for us, the audience of the Ramayana, because Rama hears about this friendship long after he has defeated Ravana with the help of Sugriva.

'But why did Hanuman, who wanted the best for Sugriva, not burn Vali like a log of wood when they became enemies? I think Hanuman must not have been aware of his strength for him to have stood by and watched Sugriva, who was as dear to him as his own life, suffer. You who are worshipped by the immortals, tell me everything about Hanuman, tell me in great detail!'

Hearing Rama's pointed question, the sage said to him in the presence of Hanuman, 'What you say about Hanuman is all true, best of the Raghus. No one compares with him in strength and intelligence, there is none superior to him in speed or in thought. Long ago, oppressor of enemies, Hanuman was cursed by sages whose curses are unerring. Although he was strong, he did not know the extent of his own strength. Mighty Rama, it is not possible to describe all the things he did when he was a mischievous child. But if you really want to hear about them, then listen with a concentrated mind as I speak.

'There is a mountain called Sumeru, golden because of the sun. Hanuman's father, Kesari, ruled there. His beloved wife was known as Anjana and it was upon her that Vayu engendered an excellent son. Anjana gave birth to a son the colour of young wheat and then she wandered off into the forest because she wanted some fruit to eat. Tormented by hunger and by the separation from his mother, the infant cried out, as the baby Kartikeya in the rushes had done. He saw the sun rising, the colour of a china rose, and he leapt towards it, thinking it was a fruit. Facing the sun, the little fellow, who was like a young sun himself, flew through the air wanting to grab it.

'The gods and danavas and siddhas were filled with a great wonder when the infant Hanuman leapt in that fashion. "The way this son of Vayu is coursing through the sky, not even the wind or Garuda or the mind have speed like this! If he has this kind of speed and strength as an infant, what will they be like when he is a youth!" Afraid the sun would burn him, Vayu flew behind his flying son, cool as a mound of snow. Hanuman flew many thousands of yojanas into the sky. Because of his father's strength and his own childishness, he drew closer to the sun. But the sun did not burn him because he knew that he was an infant, free of all faults, and that his great deeds lay ahead of him.

'Rahu wanted to seize the sun on the very day that Hanuman leapt towards it. Hanuman grabbed Rahu who was sitting in the sun's chariot and Rahu, that oppressor of the sun and the moon, grew agitated and fled. Rahu, son of Simhika,[13] was angry and he went to Indra's palace. Frowning, he spoke to the god who was surrounded by the troops of gods. "Vasava, you gave me the sun and the moon to eat. Why have you now given them to someone else, killer of Bala and Vritra? I was coming to seize the sun today, the first day of the lunar fortnight, and suddenly there was another Rahu approaching the sun to grab it."

'Indra was confused when he heard Rahu's words and he jumped up from his throne, holding his gold necklace tightly. He mounted his great elephant, as large as Kailasha, four-tusked and dripping with ichor, beautifully adorned, the tinkling of his golden bells making him seem as if he was laughing. Indra mounted the elephant and placing Rahu in front of him, he went to where the sun and Hanuman were.

'Rahu moved quickly and left Indra behind. Hanuman saw Rahu, large as a mountain peak, running towards him. Hanuman thought that he, too, was a fruit and so he let go of the sun and moved through the air towards Rahu, the son of Simhika, so that he could grab him. Rahu saw that the monkey had dropped the sun and was coming towards him, Rama. He turned and fled in the direction from which he had come. Simhika's son was terrified and he took refuge with Indra, crying, "Indra! Indra!" over and over again.

'Indra realized how agitated Rahu was from his voice and he said, "Don't be afraid. I will kill him!" Hanuman, son of Vayu, looked at Airavata, king of the elephants, and mistook him, too, for an enormous fruit. He charged towards him and for an instant, he seemed like Agni and Indra together. Although Indra was not terribly angry, he tossed his thunderbolt and struck the charging Hanuman. When the thunderbolt hit him, Hanuman fell upon a mountain and broke his left jaw.

'Vayu became angry with Indra when his son was struck by the thunderbolt and injured, and that spelled discomfort for all living beings. Vayu, the lord who lives within all beings, made it impossible for them to urinate and defecate. He obstructed all creatures as Indra does the rains. Living creatures could not breathe and their joints became as stiff as wood

---

13 It is interesting that the Uttara Kanda makes Rahu Simhika's son and further makes him Hanuman's rival in this episode of attacking the sun. Simhika is one of the obstacles that Hanuman has to overcome on his flight across the sea to Lanka.

because of Vayu's anger. The three worlds were like hell, without the study of the sacred books and their extensions, without rituals and without dharma.

'The unhappy living beings, along with the gandharvas and gods, the asuras and humans, went to Prajapati Brahma, desperate for ease. Their bellies swollen with gas, the gods spoke with their palms joined in respect. "Blessed one, protector of all living beings, you have created four kinds of beings. And you have given us the wind as the lord of our life's breath. Why is he behaving like this today, obstructing our breath, like a king who holds his women back in his inner apartments? We have come to you to take refuge from Vayu's torments. Slayer of enemies, relieve us of this distress caused by Vayu!"

'Prajapati Brahma, the protector of all beings, heard what the creatures were saying and he said, "There is a reason for this!" and then he spoke further. "There is a reason why Vayu is angry and has caused these obstructions. All of you should listen, as it is worth hearing. Be calm. Vayu is angry today because Indra, the king of the gods, was instigated by Rahu and struck his son. Although he is bodiless, Vayu, god of the wind, moves to maintain all embodied beings. Bodies become equal to dust without Vayu. Wind is breath, wind is happiness, wind is the whole universe. There can be no happiness in the universe without wind. Living beings cannot breathe and are like blocks of wood because Vayu has turned away from the universe today. Let us go to where the wind, the maker of our discomfort, is. We cannot be destroyed just because we have displeased this son of Aditi."

'With living beings and with the gods, with the gandharvas, the serpents and the guhyakas, Prajapati Brahma went to where the wind was sitting with his son who had been struck down by the king of the gods. Four-faced Brahma, along with the gods, the siddhas, the sages, the serpents and the rakshasas, looked at the infant in Vayu's lap, bright as the sun, shining like gold, and he was filled with compassion.'

## Sarga 36: Hanuman's Childhood

'Vayu, who was devastated by the injury to his son, noticed Brahma. He stood in front of the foremost of all beings, holding his child. Adorned with dangling earrings, a crown and flower garlands, Vayu bowed at Brahma's feet three times. Brahma, knower of the Vedas, lifted Vayu and touched the infant with his outstretched hand that was adorned with ornaments. Like a plant sprinkled with water, the infant came back to consciousness as soon as he was touched lightly by lotus-born Brahma's hand. Vayu, who is breath himself, saw him breathing and was pleased and began to circulate freely among all creatures again, without obstruction. Like a lotus pond freed from cold winds, living beings were delighted, now that they had been relieved from the illness caused by Vayu.

'To placate Vayu, Brahma, who had the six great qualities and was worshipped by the thirty gods, said to them, "Indra, Agni, Varuna, Kubera, Shiva! Even though you know everything, I will tell you something of benefit. Listen! This child will perform great deeds in the future. To that end and to make Vayu happy, all of you should give him boons."

'Thousand-eyed Indra, filled with affection, his face bright, took off his garland of flowers and placed it on Hanuman. "Because his jaw broke when it was struck by my thunderbolt, this tiger among monkeys shall be named Hanuman! And I shall give him the best of boons – from now on, he shall be invulnerable to this thunderbolt." Then the sun, the blessed one that drives away darkness, spoke. "I shall give him one-hundredth of my effulgence. And when he starts to study the sacred texts, I will give him the capacity to become a scholar." Varuna gave him a long life, invulnerability to water and to his noose for a hundred years. Yama made him invulnerable to his staff, gave him freedom from sickness for all time, and the boon that he would stay well and be tireless in battle. Kubera said, "No one shall be able to kill him with a mace in battle." Shiva gave him the best boon of all. "He shall be invulnerable to my weapons in battle." Brahma said, "He shall have a long life and become a great being. He shall be invulnerable to punishments from brahmins." Wise Vishvakarma, best of all builders, looked at the infant who was like the sun and said, "In times of war, he shall not be slain by any of the weapons that I have crafted for the gods."

'Pleased that the little one had been marked by the boons from the gods, four-faced Brahma, the eldest in the world, said to Vayu, "Your son will strike fear into his enemies and make his friends free from fear. He shall be invincible. He shall perform hair-raising deeds in battle for Rama's benefit and to Ravana's detriment."

'Having finished their conversation with Vayu, all the gods, with Brahma at their head, went back the way they had come. Vayu, bearer of perfumes, picked up his son and took him home. He told Anjana all about the boons and went away. With these boons, Rama, Hanuman became strong and depending on that strength, he was like the swelling ocean. That bull among monkeys was fearless because of his strength and he violated the hermitages of the great sages. He broke their sacrificial pots and ripped apart their bark garments and obstructed their offerings to the fire and other such things. The sages knew that he was invulnerable to punishments from brahmins and they remained silent because of his powers. Hanuman continued to transgress all bounds of decency, although he was forbidden to do so by Vayu and Kesari and Anjana. Those great sages, born in the line of Bhrigu and Angiras, were not usually given to anger. But they were angry now, Rama, and they cursed Hanuman. "You shall be confused by our curse and you shall not know the strength with which you have tormented us for such a long time!" And so, Hanuman was deprived of his powers by the sages' words.

'Later, there was a king of all the monkeys, effulgent as the sun. He was named Riksharaja and he was the father of Vali and Sugriva. After ruling over the monkeys for a long time, the lord of the monkeys made his tryst with death. Vali was appointed in his father's place by wise ministers and later, Sugriva was elevated to Vali's position.[14] Hanuman allied with Sugriva in a friendship that was as firm and unshakeable as that between fire and wind. Hanuman did not know his own strength because of the sages' curse and so when hostilities arose between Vali and Sugriva, neither the wandering Sugriva nor Vali knew about his powers.

---

[14] A wonderfully neutral elision of the ghastly fight between the brothers Sugriva and Vali for the throne of Kishkindha that we read about in the Kishkindha Kanda. By this erasure, the Uttara Kanda plumps for Sugriva as Rama's natural and appropriate monkey ally. Also, this version of Hanuman's birth and childhood accounts for why Hanuman speaks Sanskrit, and good Sanskrit at that – he was taught grammar by the sun. Any of us might ask: How is it that a monkey speaks in human language? How is it that he speaks flawless Sanskrit? But the Uttara Kanda has already answered that question.

'Who is there in the world that is greater than Hanuman in valour, enthusiasm, wisdom and splendour, good conduct, sweetness, discrimination, gravity, cleverness, heroism and firmness?

'Long ago, Hanuman faced the sun and followed him from the mountains where he rises to the mountains where he sets in order to learn grammar. Incomparable Hanuman mastered the great books. Who is there that can stand up to Hanuman, who swallows the earth like the ocean, who consumes the worlds like fire, who destroys the worlds like time? And like this great monkey, the gods created others for your purpose, Rama – Sugriva, Mainda, Dwivida, Nila, Tara, Tareya, Nala, Rambha.

'I have told you everything that you asked about – I have related Hanuman's childhood deeds to you. Now that we have talked together, we shall leave, Rama.'

So saying, the great sages went back the way they had come.

## Sarga 37: Praise for Rama

After Rama had been crowned according to the prescribed rituals, he passed his first night in the city, much to the joy of the citizens. When the night was over and the morning came, the singers appointed to wake the king assembled in the palace rooms. In voices as sweet as those of the kinnaras, they joyfully praised the king's valour as they had been taught. 'Dear hero, you increase Kaushalya's happiness. Gentle one, wake up! Your majesty, the world sleeps while you sleep! You are as brave as Vishnu, as beautiful as the ashvins, you are as wise as Brihaspati, you are the equal of Prajapati. You are like the earth in endurance, you are as brilliant as the sun, you are as swift as the wind, you are as deep as the ocean! You stand as firm as Shiva, you are as charming as the moon. There has never been a king like you before and there will not be in the future. You are hard to defeat, you are dedicated to dharma and the welfare of your people. Bull among men, neither your fame nor your fortune will ever desert you. Royal splendour and righteousness are established in you!'

The bards praised him with these and other sweet words and with divine songs of praise. Rama awoke while they were still singing. He rose from his bed which was covered with white sheets and he seemed like Vishnu rising from his bed of serpent coils. Thousands of servants arrived with shining pitchers of water and stood with their heads bowed before the king who had just risen. Rama purified himself with the water and at the appropriate time, he placed oblations in the fire. Then, he went to the temple that was under the patronage of the devout Ikshvakus. After he had worshipped the gods, the ancestors and the brahmins according to custom, he came to the outer chambers, surrounded by people.

All the great ministers stood there along with the priests with Agastya at their head, all of them blazing like fires. Great warriors, who were rulers of many different lands, sat by Rama's side as the immortals sit with Indra. Glorious Bharata, Lakshmana and Shatrughna joyfully attended to Rama, like the three Vedas present at a sacrifice. A number of servants, their palms joined and their faces happy, either stood or sat near Rama. With Sugriva at their head, twenty heroic monkeys, able to change shape at will and filled with great energy, stood near Rama. Accompanied by four rakshasas, Vibhishana served Rama the way the guhyakas serve Kubera. Wise men from good families, who knew the Vedas, also served the king with their heads bowed. The king was surrounded by glorious sages, excellent kings and heroic monkeys and rakshasas. And Rama shone more brightly than thousand-eyed Indra, king of the gods, who is constantly worshipped by sages. When they were all seated, those great-souled ones who knew the ancient stories began to narrate the sweet tales that were filled with righteousness.

## Sarga 38: Rama Gives the Kings Leave to Depart

Mighty-armed Rama performed the daily tasks for the people, both city and country dwellers. And then, after many days, Rama joined his palms and said to the king of Mithila, 'Sir, you are our protector. Thanks to your fierce energy I was able to defeat Ravana. Your majesty, there is great affection between the Ikshvakus and everyone in Mithila because of our marriage ties. Proceed, honoured sir, to your own kingdom with these valuable gifts. Bharata will follow behind as an escort.'

'I shall,' he said to Rama and spoke further. 'I am pleased, king, with your vision and your views. I shall give my daughter all these jewels that you have chosen for me.'

When Janaka had left, Rama joined his palms and spoke humbly to the king of the Kekayas, his maternal uncle. 'This kingdom, myself, Bharata and Lakshmana, we are all available to you, for you are our refuge, bull among men! The elderly king, your father, must be worried on your account. Therefore, I think it would be best if you left this very day, your majesty! Lakshmana will travel behind you, bringing these riches and jewels of many kinds.'

Yuddhajit prepared to leave, saying, 'It shall be so. But I shall leave this wealth and these jewels with you for all time!' Yuddhajit circumambulated Rama who had done the same to him while honouring him. The king of the Kekayas departed with Lakshmana as Indra had with Vishnu after killing the asura Vritra.

After seeing him off, Rama embraced his friend Pratardanam, the fearless king of Kashi, and said to him, 'You have shown me great friendship and sympathy. And your efforts have created a great city. Go now, dear sir, to your city of Kashi which is decorated with gateways and mansions.' Rama rose from his magnificent throne and hugged him close to his chest. When he was given leave by Rama, the king of Kashi departed for his city at once. Having bade the king of Kashi on his way, Rama addressed the thirty princes who were still there. Smiling, he spoke these sweet words, 'Your affection for me is protected by your effulgence! Dharma and truth are always firm in you. It was your energy and affection that killed wicked Ravana in the city of the rakshasas. I was but the instrument of that killing. Ravana and his troops, his sons, ministers and family were killed in battle because Bharata brought you all together when he heard that Janaka's daughter had been abducted. You great-souled ones have devoted yourself to my welfare for a long time now. I think it is time for you to depart.'

Happily, the kings replied, 'What good fortune that you were victorious and are established in your kingdom. What good fortune that you got Sita back and that you defeated your enemy. This was our dearest wish and it gives us the greatest satisfaction to see you victorious over your enemy. You are right to praise us but we have no way to praise you. We ask permission to leave but you will always be in our hearts, dear sir. We leave you, great-armed one, with much affection. And may you feel warmly towards us!'

Rama agreed that they should leave and the kings were filled with joy. With their palms joined, they said, 'We are happy to depart!' and honoured by Rama, they set off for their own lands.

## Sarga 39: The Kings Depart

The great-souled princes left happily, their army divisions of elephants and horses shaking the earth. The many divisions of vehicles that had come there to serve Rama's purpose moved easily, steadied by Bharata. Those protectors of the earth, proud of their armed strength, said, 'We were not able to see the battle between Rama and Ravana ourselves. We were of no use because Bharata summoned us so late. We would have certainly killed the rakshasas quickly. Protected by Rama and Lakshmana's valiant arms, we would have fought tirelessly and easily on the far side of the ocean!'

Talking like this and saying a thousand other things, the princes went back to their own kingdoms, filled with joy. They reached their own capital cities which were prosperous and happy, wealthy and overflowing with abundance. Because they wanted Rama's favour, the kings made presents of all kinds of jewels and decorated horses and chariots and rutting elephants and silver and ornaments that sparkled and gems, pearls and coral and beautiful slave girls and goats and vehicles and all kinds of other things. Mighty Lakshmana and Bharata and Shatrughna took those valuable things and returned to their own beautiful city. When they arrived there, they surrendered that great wealth to Rama. Rama accepted the gifts with joy and then gave them to the great-souled Sugriva for all that he had done, as well as to Vibhishana and all the other rakshasas and monkeys who had helped him be victorious. The mighty rakshasas and monkeys wore the jewels given by Rama on their heads and on their arms.

Rama, king of the Ikshvakus, that heroic mighty-armed warrior, his eyes shaped like lotus petals, took Hanuman and Angada on to his lap and said to Sugriva, 'Angada and your minister, this marvellous son of the wind, who were giving you advice when they were devoted to my purpose, deserve all kinds of honours for what they have done for you, king of the monkeys!' Glorious Rama removed the ornaments from his own body and placed them on worthy Angada and Hanuman.

Then Rama spoke to the heroic forest dwellers – Nila, Nala, Kesari, Kumuda, Gandhamadana, Sushena, Panasa, Vira, Mainda, Dwivida, Jambavan, Gavaksha, Vinata and Dhumra, Valimukha, Prajangha, Samnada, Mahabalam, Darimukha, Dadhimukha and Indrajanu. Speaking sweetly in a soft voice and as if drinking them in with his eyes, he said, 'Good sirs, you are like my brothers, like my body. You are friends of my heart. Dear forest dwellers, you saved me from disaster. King Sugriva is lucky to have you all as friends.' He embraced them warmly and gave them all jewels as they deserved, as well as diamonds and other ornaments. The honey-hued monkeys drank fragrant honey and ate roots and fruits and well-cooked meats. They stayed there for over a month but because of their devotion to Rama, it seemed to them no more than a moment. Rama also enjoyed his time with those monkeys who could change form at will and with the heroic rakshasas and the mighty bears. And so the second month of winter passed pleasantly. All the monkeys and the rakshasas were happy. They enjoyed the greatest pleasures in the beautiful city of the Ikshvakus and they passed their time happily as Rama's guests.

## Sarga 40: Rama Dismisses the Monkeys and the Rakshasas

Effulgent Rama spoke to Sugriva about the monkeys, bears and rakshasas who were staying there. 'Go, my friend, to Kishkindha, hard to breach by the gods and the asuras. Rule your kingdom along with your advisers, without any obstacles. Look upon mighty-armed Angada with favour, and also upon Hanuman and the mighty Nala. And on your father-in-law Sushena and heroic Tara, best among the strong. And Kumuda and Durdharsha and mighty Nila, heroic Shatabali and Mainda and Dwivida, too. And Gaja, Gavaksha, Gavaya and mighty Sharabha. And the king of the bears, mighty Jambavan, who is hard to defeat. Look with affection upon Gandhamadana, too. And courageous Rishabha and ruddy Plavamgam. And Kesari and Sharabha and Shumbha and mighty Shankachuda. These are all the great monkeys who would give up their lives for me. Look upon them favourably, do not make me unhappy.' Having said this, he embraced Sugriva again and again.

Then he spoke sweetly to Vibhishana. 'Rule Lanka well, for I, the rakshasa citizens and your brother Kubera, we all know you to be a man of righteousness. Never, at any time, turn your mind towards unrighteousness, for it is wise kings who rule the earth firmly. Think of me and Sugriva fondly at all times. Go now, be free from anxiety.'

The bears and monkeys and rakshasas shouted 'Bravo! Bravo!' when they heard Rama's words and they praised him over and over again.

'Mighty one, your wisdom and courage are amazing. Your sweetness is equal only to that of the self-born Brahma.' Even as the monkeys and the rakshasas were speaking, Hanuman bowed low and said to Rama, 'May the great love that I have for you be everlasting. Hero! May I remain devoted to you and no other. It is certain that there shall be breath in my body as long as your story is current on earth! Let the marvellous story of your life be related to me by apsaras, bull among men! When I listen to the nectar of your deeds, they will dispel my anxieties as the wind dispels the clouds.'

Rama rose from his splendid throne as Hanuman was speaking. He embraced him and said sweetly, 'It shall certainly be so, great monkey. You shall exist on earth as long as my story is told, as will your fame and your embodied self. My story will last as long as the worlds themselves. I would give my life for every favour that you have done me, monkey! We remain in your debt for every single thing you have done for us. All that you have done finds its end in my body! For it is only the man in adverse circumstances who does not repay in equal measure.' Rama took a necklace of pearls that was bright as the moon from his own neck. He tied it on to Hanuman's great chest and the monkey seemed like a snow-covered mountain with the moon upon its peak.

Listening to what Rama had said, the mighty monkeys rose one by one and touched his feet with their heads and left. And when Rama held Sugriva and Vibhishana close against his chest, they were overcome with tears. As they left Rama, they wept, their voices were choked and they were filled with a numbing sadness. Though they had received Rama's grace, they went to their own homes as if they were giving up their bodies. Weeping at the separation from Rama, the bears and monkeys went back to where they lived.

Mighty-armed Rama dismissed the bears and monkeys and rakshasas, and then he enjoyed great happiness with his brothers. After many days with them, Rama heard a sweet voice speaking from the air. 'Dear Rama, look upon me with kindness. I am Pushpaka, the celestial vehicle from Kubera's palace. I obeyed your command, best of men, and went back there. But Kubera said to me, "Rama, the greatest of all monarchs, has won you by killing Ravana, the invincible king of the rakshasas, in battle. I am delighted that wicked Ravana and his troops and his sons and all his family have been killed. Great-souled Rama won you in Lanka. I command you now to go to him. Carry him. It is my greatest wish that you should carry Rama who supports the world. Go now, without anxiety!" And ordered thus by the lord of wealth, I have come to you. Do not hesitate to accept me. I am invincible to all creatures by my own power and, by the lord of wealth's decree, I shall carry you and obey your commands.'

Rama gazed at the vehicle again and said, 'If that is the case, then welcome to you, Pushpaka, greatest of all vehicles. Kubera's favour ensures that we do no wrong.' Rama worshipped the vehicle with fragrant flowers and incense and grains of rice and then he said, 'Go now and come back when I think of you. Go to the siddhas, my dear, do not be downcast. May you encounter no obstructions as you travel where you please!'

'So be it,' said Pushpaka. And honoured by Rama, it went on its way.

When the finely crafted Pushpaka had departed in the direction of its choice, Bharata joined his palms and said to Rama, 'Since you began your reign, even non-human creatures are talking about it. It hasn't been a month and already people are free of disease, the old do not die, women have no complications in childbirth and everyone experiences great happiness. All the citizens are happy and the clouds shower rain that is like ambrosia at the right time. The breeze is gentle and soft to the touch. "May we have a king like this forever," say the people from the city and from the countryside.'

Rama was thrilled when he heard these words from Bharata.

## Sarga 41: Sita Is Pregnant

Rama dismissed gold-decorated Pushpaka and then he entered the small ashoka grove which was like a grove of celestial trees. It was adorned with rows of mango and coconut and sandal and other fragrant woods and surrounded by other flowering trees like the kadamba and the amaranth and the jambu. Always flowering and fruiting, the buds on the trees were circled by swarms of intoxicated bees. Cuckoos and shrikes and other birds of many colours landed on the tops of the mango trees, creating a beautiful scene.

Some trees appeared golden, others were like flames of fire, still others like blue-black collyrium. Lakes of various shapes were filled with clear water. The steps leading into them were jewelled and their floors were crystal mosaics. The lakes were made more beautiful by lotus flowers and buds and the gardens were adorned with walls and rock formations of different shapes. Here and there, the grove was decorated with cat's eyes and beryls, swathes of green grass and more flowering trees. Rama's grove, the one he entered, was like Indra's garden, Nandana, or Brahma's garden, Chaitraratha.

Rama, joy of the Raghus, entered the thick grove which had many small shelters and places to sit, all shaded by creepers. Rama took his seat on a beautiful couch which was decorated with flowers and covered with a gorgeous cloth. Rama took Sita by the hand and gave her exotic wine from the region of Mira to drink, as Indra gives Shachi nectar. Servants swiftly brought different kinds of meats and various fruits for Rama to eat. Beautiful young women, skilled in music and dance and song, now under the influence of alcohol, danced for the king. And so, like a god, Rama enjoyed many pleasures with radiant Sita day after day, for a long time. Great-souled King Rama's lovely winter passed thus, in pleasure.

Rama, knower of dharma, would spend the early part of the day performing his duties and then he would spend the remainder of the day attending to matters in his court. Sita, too, would spend the early part of the day performing sacred rituals. Then, she would serve all her mothers-in-law, standing before them with her palms joined in respect. After that, Sita, beautifully clothed and adorned with many jewels, would come to Rama as Shachi would to thousand-eyed Indra in the heavens.

Rama was filled with an immense happiness when he noticed that his wife was pregnant. 'Excellent, excellent!' he said. 'Sita, you stand in front of me carrying a child. What do you wish for? Tell me! What desire of yours can I satisfy?'

Sita smiled and said to Rama, 'I wish to see the sacred groves again, Rama, to visit the great sages of holy deeds, to live under the trees on the banks of the Ganga, to eat roots and fruits. This is my greatest wish, Rama, to spend one night with the sages who live like ascetics.'

'It shall be so,' promised Rama of energetic deeds. 'Trust me, Sita. I promise that you shall go there tomorrow.'

Saying this to Sita, princess of Mithila, daughter of Janaka, Rama went into the middle chambers of the palace along with his companions.

## Sarga 42: Rama Hears the Townspeople's Gossip

Many experienced men surrounded the seated king and they were telling various amusing stories. Vijaya and Madhumatta, Kashyapa, Pingala, Kusha, Suraji, Kaliya, Bhadra, Dantavakra and Samagadha happily related all kinds of funny stories in the presence of great-souled Rama.

After one of them had finished a story, Rama addressed them all. 'What do they talk about in the city, Bhadra? The city dwellers and those who live in the country, what do they say? About me? About Sita? And Bharata and Lakshmana? What about Shatrughna and my mother Kaikeyi? For kings are criticized when they are new rulers.'

Bhadra joined his palms and said, 'The citizens speak highly of you, king. Dear sir, bull among men, both the people of the city and those of the country talk a lot about your victory over ten-headed Ravana.'

Rama said to Bhadra, 'Tell me everything as it is, without omitting anything. Tell me the good and the bad things that are being said by the citizens. There are those who want to hear only the good and not the bad. Speak to me with confidence, without fear or anxiety. Tell me exactly what the city dwellers and the country folk are saying.'

Bhadra joined his palms and with a steady mind, he said to radiant Rama, 'Listen, king, to what the citizens are saying, the good and the bad, on the streets and in the markets, in the forests and in gardens. "Rama did a difficult thing when he built the bridge over the ocean, such a thing had never been done before, not even by the gods and the danavas. He destroyed invincible Ravana along with his army and his chariots. And he brought the monkeys and bears under his control, along with the rakshasas. He killed Ravana in battle and he brought Sita back. He turned his back on anger and led her into his own house. How could he take Sita back into his heart? How could he enjoy pleasures with her when she had been snatched from him by Ravana and had even sat on his lap? Ravana had taken her to Lanka and kept her in the ashoka grove – she was at the mercy of the rakshasas. How can Rama not be repulsed? We shall have to treat our wives in the same way – for whatever a king does, his subjects must do the same." This, and various other things, are what the citizens are saying, king, in the city and everywhere in the country.'

Rama grew agitated when he heard this. He said to his friends, 'What is this? Tell me!'

They hung their heads and bowed to him and replied, 'It is sad, but it is true!'

## Sarga 43: Rama Summons His Brothers

Rama, scorcher of his enemies, dismissed them all when he heard what they had said. After he had sent his friends away, he began to worry about what he should do. He called the doorkeeper who was standing nearby and said, 'Go quickly and bring Lakshmana, the auspicious son of Sumitra, and bring mighty-armed Bharata and unvanquished Shatrughna.'

At Rama's command, the doorkeeper placed his joined palms on his head with respect. He went to Lakshmana's house and entered there without being stopped. He honoured him with his palms joined and said, 'The king wishes to see you. You must go to him without delay!'

'Yes!' said Lakshmana when he heard the words that Rama had sent him. He climbed into his chariot and went quickly to Rama's palace.

Knowing that Lakshmana was on his way, the doorkeeper went into Bharata's presence and honouring him, he said, 'The king wishes to see you.' When Bharata heard Rama's order from the doorkeeper, he left his seat and rushed away on foot.

With his palms joined in respect, the doorkeeper watched Bharata's hurried departure and he went to Shatrughna's palace and said, 'Come, best of the Raghus. The king wishes to see you. Lakshmana has already gone there as has illustrious Bharata.' Shatrughna touched his forehead to the ground when he heard this command and went to Rama.

Rama, agitated and anxious, heard that the princes had arrived. His head hanging low, he said sadly to the doorkeeper, 'Allow the princes to enter and let them come to me quickly. This is about my life and they are more to me than my life!' The princes were dressed in white, their minds were calm. They joined their palms and entered with the king's permission. They saw that his face was like an eclipsed moon, like a setting sun that had lost its light, that wise Rama's eyes were filled with tears and that his lotus face had lost its glory. Quickly, they greeted him and touched his feet with their heads. They stood there calmly as Rama wept.

Mighty Rama raised them up and embraced them with both arms. He asked them to sit down and then he said, 'You are everything to me, you are my life. I rule this kingdom because of your deeds! You are learned in the great books, you are intelligent and you are accomplished. Great kings, I present you with a matter to consider.'

## Sarga 44: Rama Decides to Banish Sita

They sat with heavy hearts and then Rama said to them, his face thin and drawn, 'Listen, all of you, my dear ones, and do not go against what I want. I will tell you the kinds of things the citizens have being saying about Sita. And about me. Prominent citizens as well as common people speak ill of me. They loathe me and this cuts at my vitals. I have been born in the line of the great-souled Ikshvakus. How can they speak like this about Sita's misdeeds in the past? You know, my dear ones, how Sita was alone in the deserted Dandaka forest and how she was abducted by Ravana and how I destroyed him. In front of you, Lakshmana, Agni, the carrier of oblations, and Vayu, the sky-traveller, declared Sita sinless before the gods. The moon, the sun, the gods and the sages, all of them, attested that Janaka's daughter was without sin. On the island of Lanka and in the presence of the gods and the gandharvas, Indra himself placed her, innocent and virtuous, in my arms. In my heart, I knew that illustrious Sita had conducted herself appropriately. So I accepted her and brought her back to Ayodhya.

'But the terrible things that people are saying break my heart. Those who are infamous in this world descend to the realms of ghosts and stay there as long as their infamy is discussed. The gods do not like people of ill repute, they admire those who are famous. All great-souled people are motivated by compliments. Bulls among men, I would give up my life and you from fear of a scandal. How can I do less in the case of Janaka's daughter? It is because of this that you see me drowning in an ocean of sorrow. I have never experienced a sorrow greater than this.

'Tomorrow morning, Lakshmana, let Sumantra have the chariot ready. Climb into it with Sita and leave her on the borders of the kingdom. The hermitage of the great-souled sage Valmiki, which is like heaven, lies on the far shore of the Ganga. Leave her in that desolate place, joy of the Raghus, and come back quickly. Do as I say, Lakshmana! Do not speak to me ever again about the matter of Sita. I will be greatly displeased if you try to obstruct me. I swear by my arms and by my life that I will not abide anyone speaking against my wishes. If you have any respect for me and are obedient to my commands, do as I say and take Sita away from here at once. Sita has already told me that she wishes to visit the sages' dwellings on the banks of the Ganga. Her wishes will now be fulfilled!'

Having said this, Rama, the soul of dharma, his eyes filled with tears, departed, surrounded by his brothers.

## Sarga 45: Lakshmana Takes Sita to the Forest

When the night ended and the dawn came, a dispirited Lakshmana, his mouth dry, said to Sumantra, 'Charioteer, quickly harness horses to the best of chariots. And bring a fine seat for Sita from the palace. I will take Sita from here to the hermitage of great sages, those men who practise acts of piety. Bring the chariot quickly.'

'It shall be done,' said Sumantra and he yoked the best of horses to the chariot with a seat covered with a bright and cheerful cloth. 'The chariot is ready,' he said happily to Lakshmana, his friend. 'You can now carry out your assigned task.'

Lakshmana entered the palace and stood before Sita. The bull among men said, 'By the king's command, good lady, I have come to take you immediately to the banks of the Ganga, to the auspicious settlements of the great sages in the forest.'

Sita was filled with immense joy and she made preparations to leave. She quickly picked up all kinds of clothes and ornaments and jewels and was ready to depart. 'I will give these ornaments to the sages' wives,' she said as Lakshmana helped her climb into the chariot. Remembering Rama's instructions, he drove away quickly.

Sita said to Lakshmana, the increaser of prosperity, 'Joy of the Raghus, I see a number of bad omens today. My right eye twitches and my limbs tremble. Son of Sumitra, even my heart seems ill at ease. I feel a great anxiety and an immense unsteadiness. I see a vast emptiness in the world, large-eyed one. I hope all is well with your brother and with his brothers, and I hope all is well especially with my mothers-in-law, hero, and with all living beings in the city as well as in the countryside.' Thus, she entreated the gods with her palms placed together.

Lakshmana bowed his head when he heard Sita's prayer. 'Everything is well,' he said, though his heart contracted.

They reached the banks of the river Gomati and stayed in a hermitage there. In the morning, Lakshmana rose and said to the charioteer, 'Harness the chariot quickly. Today, I will touch the waters of the Ganga with my head, as did Shiva, the pervader of the three worlds!' Sumantra yoked the horses swift as thought to the chariot and said to Sita with his palms joined, 'Step in, madam!' At his words, Sita mounted the chariot along with Lakshmana and the wise Sumantra. At midday, they reached the waters of the Bhagirathi and Lakshmana, who was in poor spirits, began to cry audibly when he saw them.

Sita, who knew dharma, saw Lakshmana's great distress and asked cautiously, 'Why are you crying? We have reached the banks of the Ganga, my long-standing wish has been fulfilled. This is a time of happiness, why do you grieve, Lakshmana? Bull among men, you are always in Rama's presence. Why are you overcome with unhappiness after only two days away from him? Rama is dear to me, too, dear as my own life. But I am not grieving like you. Don't be a child. Take me across the Ganga so that I can see the sages. I will give them these clothes and ornaments and jewels. I will honour those great sages as they deserve. We shall spend one night here and then return to the city.'

Lakshmana listened to Sita. He wiped his beautiful eyes, called for the boats and crossed the river.

## Sarga 46: Lakshmana Abandons Sita

The boat had been made comfortable by the Nishadas and Lakshmana, Rama's younger brother, stepped into it after he had helped the princess of Mithila aboard. 'Wait here with the chariot,' Lakshmana said to Sumantra and then, burning with grief, he told the boatman to set forth. When they reached the far shore of the Ganga, Lakshmana joined his palms and spoke to Sita, his voice thick with tears. 'A massive spear has pierced my heart, Sita, for the wise and noble Rama has asked me to do something that will make me notorious in the worlds for all time! It would be better to be dead. Death would be far better than the act I must perform today, an act that will never be forgiven by the world. Forgive me, virtuous lady. Do not be angry with me!' Joining his palms, Lakshmana fell to the ground.

Seeing Lakshmana thus, with his palms joined and crying and asking for his own death, Sita was very disturbed. She said to him, 'What is this? I don't understand. Speak to me, Lakshmana! I see that you are not at ease. Is the king well? I asked the king to grant me a wish and that has made you so unhappy. Look me in the eye and speak to me. You are under an oath!' Prodded by Sita, Lakshmana, his heart heavy, turned his face away. In a choked voice, he said, 'Daughter of Janaka, the council heard cruel and insulting things about you that were being spoken in the city and in the countryside. The king has taken those words spoken behind your back seriously and they have caused him great distress. I cannot say those words in front of you, my lady. Although you were proved innocent in my presence, the king has rejected you from fear of common people's gossip. You have to accept this, my lady, there is no other way. I must leave you in this hermitage, albeit with a heavy heart, in keeping with the king's orders. The sacred and pleasant meditation groves of the brahmin ascetics lie here, on the banks of the Ganga. Do not grieve, lovely one. The best of brahmins, the illustrious Valmiki, bull among sages, is a friend of my father, King Dasharatha. Approach the pleasant shade of the great sage's feet, daughter of Janaka, and live there simply with your mind focused. Keep Rama in your heart at all times, adopt the vows of a wife. There is much benefit for you in this, my lady!'

## Sarga 47: Lakshmana Turns Away

Sita, Janaka's daughter, was overcome with intense sorrow and fell to the ground when she heard Lakshmana's harsh words. She lost consciousness for a moment and then, her agitated eyes filled with tears, she said pathetically to Lakshmana, 'This body of mine must have been created for suffering, Lakshmana, for today, without a doubt I am the very embodiment of sorrow. What sin did I commit in the past, what woman did I abandon that now I, who am pure and virtuous, am rejected by the king? In the past, when I followed Rama's footsteps, I lived in a hermitage under adverse circumstances. Then, I was soothed in my sorrow. How will I live in a hermitage in solitude, dear one? Whom will I talk to about my suffering when I am overcome with despair? What will I say when the sages ask me about my transgression, why great-souled Rama rejected me? I should throw my life into the waters of the Ganga this very day. But then, my husband's royal lineage will be mocked. Do as you have been ordered, son of Sumitra, and leave me, unfortunate as I am, here. Carry out your instructions with steadfastness. But listen to my words.

'Specifically to my mothers-in-law, I bow my head at their feet and honour them with my palms joined. Say to the king that I ask about his welfare. Say to him, "Your majesty, you are as concerned about your citizens as you are about your brothers. This is your highest duty and it will bring you unparalleled fame. And that, your majesty, can only be obtained by doing your duty towards your citizens. Bull among men, I am not lamenting my own situation. Do what you must to counteract the malicious words of your citizens."'

Lakshmana grew even more disheartened as he listened to Sita. He laid his head on the ground, unable to speak. He circumambulated her, sobbing aloud, and then he boarded the boat again, urging the boatman on. When he got to the far shore, he was overwhelmed by the burden of his grief. He quickly mounted the chariot, almost senseless with sorrow. Lakshmana went onwards, turning again and again to look at Sita who had been abandoned on that far shore, weeping in despair. Sita gazed after Lakshmana as he drew away into the distance and when she could no longer see him, she fell to the ground, overpowered by grief. Weighed down by her sorrow, that glorious woman, chaste and pious, could see no protector. Enveloped in sadness, the good woman cried out like a peacock in the forest.

## Sarga 48: Valmiki Rescues Sita

The young boys from the sage's hermitage saw Sita crying and they went running to the blessed Valmiki, he of incisive intelligence. The boys honoured him by touching his feet and then together, they told him about the crying woman. 'Blessed one, there is a woman here whom we have never seen before. She seems to be the wife of a great-souled man. She looks like Shri but in her sorrow, she is crying in a cracked voice. You should see her, blessed one. She seems like a divine being fallen from the skies. She doesn't seem like a mortal woman. You should offer her hospitality.'

After hearing what they said, the sage who knew dharma, verified this with his own mind, for he had attained an all-seeing eye through his austerities. He rushed to where Sita was. The great sage approached on foot and collected some water from the banks of the Ganga as an offering. He saw Sita, Rama's beloved wife, in a state of utter vulnerability. Valmiki, bull among sages, whose effulgence is refreshing, saw Sita overcome with grief and said to her sweetly, 'You are Dasharatha's daughter-in-law and Rama's virtuous queen. Daughter of King Janaka, virtuous wife, you are welcome! In my meditative trance, I knew that you were coming. And in my heart, I have discerned the reason. Sita, I know you are blameless, I saw this with the divine eye I obtained from my austerities. Be calm, Sita. You are with me now. My hermitage is not far from here. Ascetic women are busy in the practise of austerities there and they will surely look after you as if you were their own child. Take this water and refresh yourself. Be calm. You are as if in your own home, do not despair.'

Sita heard these wondrous words from the sage and joined her palms. She bowed her head at his feet and said, 'It shall be so.' Palms joined, Sita followed the sage to where women ascetics were continuously engaged in the practise of dharma. The women from the hermitage saw the sage approaching followed by Sita. They ran to him and said happily, 'Welcome, great sage. It has been a while since you were last here, lord. We all honour you. Tell us what you would like us to do!'

Valmiki said to them, 'This is Sita, she has come with me. She is the wife of wise Rama. This good woman is the daughter-in-law of Dasharatha and the daughter of Janaka. She has been renounced even though she is a good wife. And so it is I who must take care of her, always. Good ladies, you must look upon her with the greatest affection. My words must be especially honoured because of their gravity.' Reassuring Sita again and again, the sage of great austerities left for his own hermitage surrounded by his disciples.

## Sarga 49: Lakshmana Criticizes Rama's Decision

With a heavy heart, Lakshmana watched Sita, the daughter of Mithila, enter the hermitage and he was overwhelmed by a burning grief. Effulgent Lakshmana said to Sumantra, his adviser and his charioteer, 'Look at wise Rama's sorrow, born of Sita's torment! What greater sorrow could Rama possibly have than rejecting his wife, Janaka's daughter, whose conduct has been pure? I think it is destiny that has caused Rama's separation from Sita, for it is only destiny that cannot be avoided. Angry Rama abides by destiny in order to kill the gods, gandharvas, asuras and rakshasas. In the past, he lived in the desolate forests of the Dandaka for nine years and then another five because of my father's words. At that time, too, he suffered immense grief because of his separation from Sita. But now, I think he has committed a very cruel act after listening to citizens' idle talk. Which person who takes refuge in dharma, charioteer, would act in such a dishonourable way towards Sita based on the low and vulgar talk of common people?'

After listening to this and much else that Lakshmana said, Sumantra joined his palms in respect and spoke. 'Son of Sumitra, you should not be upset by what has been done to Sita. This was predicted by brahmins in the presence of your father – that Rama would experience enormous unhappiness and very little joy and that after a long time, righteous Rama would renounce Sita and you and Bharata and Shatrughna. When the king heard what the sage Durvasas had said, he declared that neither you, nor Shatrughna, the son of Sumitra, nor even Bharata should be told about this. Bull among men, I was with the king and with Vasishtha when the sages predicted this. When the king, that bull among men, heard the sage's words, he said to me, "Do not mention this to anyone else or speak of it in the presence of people." Then, dear one, I decided that I would never do anything to betray the king's word. I could have never spoken about this in front of you, but now, if you want to hear it, listen, joy of the Raghus. This is the king's secret that I heard long ago and I will give you an example of how destiny is hard to escape.'

When Lakshmana, son of Sumitra, heard this, he said solemnly to the charioteer, 'What you say is true.'

## Sarga 50: Sumantra Shares a Secret

Urged by great-souled Lakshmana, the bard began to relate what the sage had said exactly as he had said it. 'Long ago, the great sage Durvasas, son of Atri, stayed for the entire rainy season in the sacred hermitage of Vasishtha. Your father, glorious and effulgent, went himself to visit the great-souled Agastya, who was his chief priest. He saw another sage, blazing with effulgence, like unto the sun itself, seated on Vasishtha's left. He humbly greeted them, who were the best among those that practise austerities. They honoured the king in turn and welcomed him with a seat, water to wash his feet, and fruit and roots. He sat with them and they told pleasant stories as the afternoon wore on. As they were talking, the king joined his palms and said to the great sage, who was the son of Atri and rich in austerities, "Blessed one, how long will my dynasty last, how long will Rama live and how long will my other sons live? And what will be the lifespan of Rama's sons? Speak as you will, blessed one, about the destiny of my family."

'Effulgent Durvasas related everything to Dasharatha in chronological order. He declared, "Rama will be the ruler of Ayodhya for a long, long time. And his brothers will be happy and prosperous. But it is also certain that this righteous man will, for some reason, forsake Maithili for a long period. For ten thousand years and then another one thousand, Rama will rule and then he will depart for Brahma's realm. Rama, conqueror of enemy cities, will establish his dynasty firmly by performing many horse sacrifices." Having narrated everything about his dynasty to the king, the wise, effulgent sage fell silent. When both the sages had finished speaking, Dasharatha honoured the great-souled ones and returned to his own incomparable city.

'I heard all that the sage had declared so long ago and I kept it in my heart. Things cannot be any other way. And so, Lakshmana, you should not grieve on account of Sita or of Rama. Be resolute, best of men!'

Listening to the charioteer's wondrous words, Lakshmana experienced immeasurable happiness. 'It is good, it is good!' he said.

The sun set as the two of them, the charioteer and Lakshmana, chatted along their journey and they spent the night on the banks of the Gomati.

## Sarga 51: Lakshmana Consoles Rama

Lakshmana, joy of the Raghus, spent the night by the river Gomati and in the morning, he rose and went onwards. At about noon, the mighty warrior entered the city of Ayodhya which was rich in jewels and filled with healthy and happy people. Wise Lakshmana was despondent as he thought, 'What will I say when I approach Rama?' He was worrying thus when he saw Rama's large palace, as beautiful as the moon itself, in front of him. Lakshmana, best of men, entered unopposed and passed through the king's doors, his mind downcast, his head hanging low. He saw his elder brother Rama sitting sadly on the great throne, his eyes filled with tears. With a heavy heart, Lakshmana touched his feet. He joined his palms in respect and said sadly, 'I have carried out your noble order and left Sita by the banks of the Ganga, near Valmiki's auspicious hermitage. I have returned to serve at your feet. Do not be sad, tiger among men, for this is how time works. A wise and principled man like you should not grieve at things like this. All that we have gathered together is destroyed, all that rises falls. Reunions end in separations and the end of life itself is death. You are able to control your self by your self, Rama, you can conquer your own mind, to say nothing of other people's. Why, then, this sadness? Bull among men, you cannot be confused in this manner. Otherwise, what you fear, which is criticism for having renounced the princess of Mithila, will arise again. Pull yourself together. Embrace fortitude, tiger among men! Give up this weakness of the spirit. Stop grieving!'

Overcome with positive feelings, Rama spoke affectionately to Lakshmana. 'It is as you say, Lakshmana, best of men. Besides, I am pleased that you have carried out my command, my hero. My grief has diminished, my torment has been forgotten because of your sweet words, my dear one. I am calm.'

## Sarga 52: The Sages Appeal to Rama for Help

Sumantra arrived and said to Rama, 'The ascetics who live on the banks of the Yamuna have arrived, your majesty. They stand waiting at the door, led by the great sage Chyavana who is eager to have audience with you. They are very pleased with you, tiger among men!' Wise Rama replied, 'Let the great brahmin sages led by the son of Bhrigu enter!' Acknowledging the king's command, the doorkeeper bowed his head in respect and let all the great ascetics enter. More than one hundred great-souled ascetics, shining with their own effulgence, came into the royal palace. They offered Rama many kinds of roots and fruits, and water from all the sacred sites in pots made of leaves. Mighty-armed Rama accepted them with much delight and said to all the great sages, 'These are the places of honour. Please seat yourselves in order of your status.' At Rama's words, all the great sages took their places on those beautiful seats, cushioned and made of gold. When they were settled, Rama, conqueror of enemies, joined his palms and said, 'What is the reason for your visit? What can I do for you, for I must do as you command. I will happily do all that you ask. This kingdom, my entire life, my heart – they are all for the brahmins. I say this truthfully.'

The great sages of fierce austerities, dwellers on the shores of the Yamuna, broke out in loud shouts of delight when they heard Rama's words. They were exceedingly pleased and they said, 'There is no one on earth who can do what you can, best of men. We approached many mighty rulers, king, but when they heard the gravity of our situation, they could not promise to help us. You, on the other hand, have made this glorious promise to the brahmins. There is no doubt that you will be the one to carry out the task. You must save the sages from the great danger that they are in!'

## Sarga 53: Lavana the Invincible

When the great sages had spoken, Rama said, 'Tell me what has to be done. Speak without fear!'

The son of Bhrigu said, 'Listen, then, to the reason for our fear, leader of men. Earlier, in the Krita Yuga, there was a mighty daitya, the eldest son of Lola. His name was Madhu. He had a resolute mind and he protected the brahmins. He had an abiding friendship with the generous gods. Madhu was rich in valour and stood steadfast in dharma. Shiva gave him a most wonderful boon because he held him in such high esteem, a spear that was powerful and bright, born from Shiva's own spear. Shiva said, "I am pleased with you because you are so resolute in dharma. And so it is with great love that I give you this wondrous weapon. This spear shall be yours, mighty asura, as long as you do not oppose the gods and the brahmins. However, in any other event, it will vanish. This spear will reduce to ashes anyone who stands fearlessly before you in battle and then it shall return to your hand."

'When the mighty asura received this boon from Shiva, he bowed to him and said, "You are the lord of all the gods. Let this unparalleled spear always remain in my family!" Shiva, lord of all living things, said to Madhu even as he was speaking, "It shall be so. Your words will not be in vain because I am pleased with you. This spear shall be like a son to you as long as it is in your hand. No living being will be able to kill you as long as you hold this spear."

'With that wondrous boon from Shiva, the great asura built himself a splendid palace. His beloved wife was the fortunate and luminous Kumbhinasi who was descended from Vishvavasu and Anala. Her son was brave and violent and he was named Lavana. He had a tendency towards wickedness and bad behaviour from when he was a child. Madhu was upset to see his son's foul nature but despite his sadness, he did not say anything to him. He left this world and entered the realm of Varuna, having given Lavana the spear and told him about the boon. Because of the spear's power and his own wicked nature, Lavana began to torment the three worlds, most especially the ascetics.

'Now that you have heard about Lavana's might and about the nature of the spear that he has, Rama, you are our only refuge! He has terrified a great number of kings and sages in the past. We ask for protection, hero. We know no one else who will help us. We heard how you destroyed Ravana along with his forces and his vehicles, we know that there is no other king on earth who can save us. We want your protection from Lavana, who makes us fearful.'

## Sarga 54: Rama Appoints Shatrughna to Fight Lavana

Spoken to thus by the sages, Rama honoured them and replied, 'What does Lavana eat, where does he wander, how does he behave?'

The sages began to talk about how Lavana had grown. 'All living creatures are his food, especially ascetics. His behaviour is savage and he lives in Madhuvana all the time. Each day, he kills tens of thousands of tigers and lions and deer and birds and human beings and he eats them all. That mighty creature is like death itself, destroying living beings as if it were the end of time.'

Rama said to the great sages, 'I will kill that rakshasa! Your fears will vanish!'

When Rama, joy of the Raghus, had made this promise to the sages of fierce austerities, he turned to his brothers and said, 'Which of you heroes will kill Lavana? Whose fate will this be – mighty Bharata's or perhaps Shatrughna's?'

Bharata said, 'I will kill him! This falls to my lot!' Hearing Bharata's glorious words which were filled with courage, Lakshmana and Shatrughna rose from their spotless golden seats. Bowing to the king, Shatrughna spoke. 'Our mighty middle brother has many tasks. In the past, when you left the city of Ayodhya, it was Bharata who protected it until you came back, even though he endured difficult times. Afflicted with troubles of all kinds, your majesty, this great-souled one lay on a bed of grief in Nandigrama. He ate only roots and fruits, his hair was matted and he wore clothes of bark. He suffered greatly and I served him there. He does not deserve any more challenges.'

When Shatrughna finished speaking, Rama said, 'Let it be so. You can carry out my command. I shall crown you king of Madhu's beautiful city, mighty-armed one. If you feel Bharata should not be troubled, let him be. You are brave and well educated. You are capable of looking after Madhu's lovely city and its people. The one who destroys the lineage of a king and does not establish another ruler in his place goes to hell. Kill wicked Lavana, the son of Madhu. If you will consider what I want, then rule that kingdom with righteousness. Do not reply to my words, for a younger brother must always do what an older brother asks. Prepare for your coronation, in accordance with my wishes! It shall be performed by Vasishtha and other brahmins with all the appropriate mantras.'

## Sarga 55: Rama Gives Shatrughna Vishnu's Arrow

Spoken to thus by Rama, courageous Shatrughna was embarrassed and he said, softly, 'Bull among men, fortunate one, of course your orders will be carried out. It is difficult to deny your commands. I will fulfil your wishes.' Rama was very pleased. He addressed Lakshmana and Bharata, 'Gather all the materials for the coronation. Today I shall crown this tiger among men, who is difficult to defeat! Bring the family priests and the specialists in the Vedas and the other priests and all the ministers here by my order.'

In accordance with the king's wishes, the coronation of the great warrior began. With the family priest walking ahead of him, he entered the royal palace like Indra entering his home. Shatrughna's coronation delighted Rama and all the citizens. After the coronation was over, Rama made Shatrughna sit on his lap and said sweetly to him, 'Destroyer of enemy cities, this divine arrow never misses its mark and you shall kill Lavana with it, my dear. This arrow was created when Vishnu lay in the waters of the great ocean, when neither the self-born Brahma nor any of the other gods nor demons could see him. He was invisible to all creatures and he created this arrow out of his anger, to kill the two heroic demons, Madhu and Kaitabha. He killed both the demons with this unique arrow and then he went on to create the worlds as he had wanted to do.

'Shatrughna, I did not use this arrow earlier to kill Ravana because it would have caused great discomfort to all beings. Three-eyed Shiva gave the best of weapons, a marvellous spear, to Madhu so that he could destroy his enemies. Lavana worships that spear over and over again in his palace and he takes it with him wherever he goes in the worlds. And whenever someone eager to fight approaches him, he lifts the spear and reduces them to ashes. Tiger among men, wait at the eastern gate with your weapon when Lavana is outside the city and without his spear. You will kill that rakshasa if you challenge him to fight before he enters the city. If you do it any other way, he will be invincible. But if you do it this way, you will succeed in destroying him. I have told you all this about the spear because it is difficult to reverse the deeds of blue-throated Shiva.'

## Sarga 56: Sharughna Sets off to Confront Lavana

Rama, joy of the Raghus, praised Shatrughna over and over. And then he said these wonderful words, 'Bull among men, these four thousand horses, these two thousand chariots and these one hundred elephants and all the provisions you need from all the shops – take them with you along with these actors and dancers. And these innumerable gold coins. Go forth, Shatrughna, endowed with wealth and vehicles! This army is well maintained. It is healthy and prosperous. Enjoy these worlds and these gifts, best of men. The servants standing here have no riches, no wives nor relatives. They are happy and satisfied. Set out with this crowd of happy servants and this massive army. Go to Madhu's forest armed with a single bow. Go there in such a way that Lavana, son of Madhu, does not realize that you have come to do battle. There is no other way to kill him, bull among men, for Lavana will slay whoever attacks him in plain sight. You will kill him when the summer has passed and the rains arrive, my dear, for that is the time of his death. Set forth with these soldiers, letting the great sages lead you. The river Ganga will be easy to cross in the summer. Halt your army on the banks of the river and go forward alone, with only your bow.'

When Rama had spoken, Shatrughna summoned the mighty commanders of his army and said to them, 'Think about where you want to halt. Stay there without any impediment so that there are no obstacles.' Shatrughna commanded his army thus as he prepared to depart and then he honoured Kaushalya, Sumitra and Kaikeyi. Shatrughna, scorcher of his enemies, circumambulated Rama with his head bowed and he took permission to leave from the others. He bowed to Bharata and Lakshmana with his palms joined and circumambulated Vasishtha, the family priest. And then, the mighty one set forth.

## Sarga 57: Shatrughna Visits Valmiki

Having sent off his entire army, Shatrughna stayed a whole month with Rama and then went on his way armed only with his bow.

After two nights on the road, heroic Shatrughna, joy of the Raghus, reached the hermitage of Valmiki, a holy place which was the best of all places to stay. He honoured great-souled Valmiki, best of all sages, with his palms joined and then he said, 'I have come on a matter that is of concern to my elder brother. Tomorrow morning, early, I will leave in an easterly direction.' The bull among sages smiled and he said to that great-souled one, 'You are welcome here, illustrious one! My hermitage, dear fellow, belongs to the Raghu dynasty. Fearless Shatrughna, please have a seat and accept this water to wash your feet.' Shatrughna accepted the honour and roots and fruits as a meal. When the mighty-armed one had finished eating, he was completely sated. He asked the great sage, 'In the past, who made these preparations for a sacrifice that are near the hermitage?'

Valmiki said, 'Listen, Shatrughna, to whose resting place this was long ago. Your ancestor was a great-souled king named Sudasa. His son, named Mitrasaha, was courageous and exceedingly righteous. When he was a boy, Sudasa's brave son went hunting and saw two rakshasas wandering around. Those terrifying rakshasas had taken on the form of tigers and they devoured forest animals by the thousands without being satisfied. They could not quell their hunger. He saw the pair of tigers emptying the forest of animals and he was overcome with a mighty rage. He attacked the tigers, loosing a single arrow. Sudasa's son struck down one of the rakshasas. As he stared at the dead rakshasa, he became free from fear and fatigue. But, the other rakshasa was seized with anger and he said to Sudasa's mighty son, "Wicked man, you have attacked my innocent companion! I'll give you a fitting response!" disappearing as he spoke.

'In time, Sudasa's son, Mitrasaha, became king and came to the vicinity of this hermitage to perform a horse sacrifice presided over by the great sage Vasishtha. The huge sacrifice went on for many years, accompanied by all the good qualities. It was as opulent as the sacrifice of the gods themselves. When it was over, the rakshasa remembered his enmity with the king. He took on the form of Vasishtha and went to the king and said, "Now that the sacrifice has been completed, give me meat to eat. Quickly. There's nothing to think about!" Hearing the words of that rakshasa who could change form at will, the lord of the earth said to his skilled cooks, "Prepare a delicious meal with fats and meats at once so that our teacher can be satisfied!" The cooks were confused when they heard the king's command. Then, the rakshasa took on the form of a cook and brought a portion of human flesh to the king. He said, "This delicious food has both fats and meat." The king, tiger among men, along with his wife Madayanti, presented the meat that the rakshasa had given him to Vasishtha for his meal. The brahmin was overcome with immense rage because he knew that he had been served human flesh. "You wished to give me this as food, king. Let there be no doubt that this same thing shall become your food!"

'The king and his wife bowed at his feet again and again. The king said to Vasishtha, "Someone who had taken the form of a brahmin told me to do this!" When he heard that this was the work of a rakshasa, Vasishtha said to the king, bull among men, "I said these words when I was overcome with rage, but they cannot be in vain. However, I shall give you a boon. The curse will last for a period of twelve years. Then, by my grace, best of kings, you will not remember what happened." And so, the king, tormentor of his enemies, bore the curse and then he regained his kingdom and ruled over his people. That is the sacrifice you asked about. It was performed near this hermitage.' After hearing the ghastly story of King Mitrasaha, Shatrughna honoured the great sage and entered the thatched hut.

## Sarga 58: Sita's Sons Are Born

Sita gave birth to two sons on the very night that Shatrughna entered the thatched hut. In the middle of the night, some of the sage's young sons came to Valmiki with the good news about Sita's having given birth. 'Perform the rituals that will protect them from bad things!' they said. As soon as he heard this, the great sage went there and performed the rituals that would keep the two boys safe from dangers. He took a fistful of kusha grass and a little less for the second born and he offered it to ward off evil. 'This first-born one shall be cleaned with kusha grass purified with mantras and so his name shall be Kusha. Older women will clean the other one with a little less and so he shall be named Lava![15] In this way, I have named them Kusha and Lava. And it is by these names that they shall become famous.'

The faultless women took the grass from the hands of the sage and performed the rituals that would ward off danger. As they performed the rituals, they praised Rama and Sita's lovely boys and recited the names of their forefathers.

Shatrughna heard this in the middle of the night and was thrilled. He went to the thatched hut, saying, 'This is fortunate, indeed!' again and again. Great-souled Shatrughna was so pleased that he spent the night there. In the morning, the mighty warrior performed the appropriate rituals and honouring the sage, he set off in an easterly direction. After seven days on the road, he reached the banks of the Yamuna and stayed there in the hermitages of sages who were known for their good deeds. While he was with those foremost of sages descended from Bhrigu, he listened to the many stories they had to tell.

## Sarga 59: Shatrughna Learns about Lavana's Spear

The next night, Shatrughna asked Chyavana, the delight of the Bhrigus, about Lavana and his spear, his strengths and weaknesses. 'What is that spear's strength, brahmin? Who else has been killed with it in duels in the past?'

Effulgent Chyavana replied to the joy of the Raghus, 'Bull among men, his deeds are many. Listen as I tell you what happened with a member of the Ikshvaku dynasty.

'Long ago, in Ayodhya, there was a brave king named Mandhata who was the son of Yuvanashva, and he was famous in all the three worlds. That lord of the earth had brought the whole world under his control, all the way up to the realm of the gods, and he made efforts to conquer even that. Indra and the great-souled gods were terribly frightened of Mandhata's plans to conquer their realm. The king rose towards the realm of the gods, vowing to take half of Indra's throne and half of his kingdom.

'Indra, subduer of Paka, realized the king's wicked intentions and he said these conciliatory words to Yuvanashva's son, "King, bull among men, you

[15] One of the Sanskrit words for 'less' is 'lava'.

haven't yet completely conquered the world of men. How can you conquer the world of the gods? When you have conquered the entire earth, hero, you and your servants and your army and its vehicles can take over heaven."

'Spoken to thus by Indra, Mandhata said to him, "Where on earth, Indra, is my rule not accepted?"

'Thousand-eyed Indra said, "There is a rakshasa named Lavana, the son of Madhu. He is in Madhuvana, and sinless one, he does not obey you!"

'Hearing these displeasing and unpleasant words from Indra, the king was disheartened and he hung his head, unable to speak. The king of men said farewell to Indra and, his head still hanging low, returned to this world. But in his heart, he was angry and so with his retainers and his army and his vehicles, that blameless man set off to bring Madhu's son under his control.

'That bull among men was eager to fight Lavana and so he sent a messenger to him who went and said many unpleasant things to Madhu's son. But the rakshasa ate up the messenger even as he was speaking. When the messenger did not return for a long time, the king was overcome with anger and he assailed the rakshasa with a shower of arrows on all sides. Lavana laughed and grabbed his spear and hurled it at that best of warriors and his retainers in order to kill them. The blazing spear turned the king and his retainers and the army and all its vehicles to ash and returned to Lavana's hand. And so it was that that great king was killed, along with his army and his retainers, for, hero, the power of that spear is unmatched and supreme. Tomorrow morning, you will be victorious, there is no doubt about that. Victory will be yours if you attack him when he is without his weapon.'

## Sarga 60: Shatrughna and Lavana Confront Each Other

For Shatrughna, the great warrior who wanted victory, that night passed quickly, telling and listening to stories.

The clear morning broke and the heroic rakshasa came out of his city to kill the animals that he would eat that day. Valiant Shatrughna had already crossed the river Yamuna and was at the gates of Madhupuri with his bow in hand. At about midday, the cruel rakshasa arrived, carrying several thousand dead animals. He saw Shatrughna standing at the city gate with his weapon at the ready and said to him, 'What will you do with that? Lowest of men, I have killed thousands of warriors like you in anger. Do you want to die, worst of men? My meal for today is not complete. Idiot! Why have you come here to throw yourself into my mouth?'

He laughed again and again as he spoke and heroic Shatrughna's eyes filled with tears of rage. Shatrughna's anger was so great that all his limbs seemed to glow and become more lustrous. Irate Shatrughna said to the night-ranging rakshasa, 'I want to fight, you fool! I want a duel with you! I am the son of Dasharatha and the brother of wise Rama. My name is Shatrughna and I kill my enemies. I have come here to kill you! Come on! Fight me, for I am eager to fight. You are the enemy of all living creatures. You will not escape with your life.'

The rakshasa seemed to smile as Shatrughna spoke and he replied, 'Best of men, it is my good fortune that you have come to me. Idiot! My uncle is the rakshasa Ravana. He was killed by foolish Rama because of a woman, worst of men! I have endured the destruction of Ravana's entire clan. And I have tolerated your earlier insults to me. I have conquered others in the past as if they were straw. And I will do the same in the future! I'll give you the fight you are looking for! I shall go and prepare my weapon!'

At once, Shatrughna replied, 'How will you leave here alive? Unlike a coward, a disciplined man does not let his enemy go!'

## Sarga 61: Shatrughna Kills Lavana

Hearing Shatrughna's words, Lavana became exceedingly angry and said, 'Stay there! Stay right there!'

Rubbing his hands together and gnashing his teeth, Lavana challenged Shatrughna, that tiger among men. When he heard that rakshasa of terrifying valour speak, Shatrughna, killer of the enemies of the gods, said, 'All these people were defeated by you before I, Shatrughna, was born. Struck by my arrows which are like thunderbolts, you shall go to the realm of Yama today! The sages will watch me slay you in battle, evil-minded one, just as the gods and the learned brahmins watched Ravana being slain. You will fall, scorched by my arrows, night-ranger! And then this city and these people will be at ease! My whirling arms will send arrows bright as lightning into your heart, like sunbeams that enter a lotus!'

Lavana was overcome with rage when he was spoken to like this and he hurled a huge tree at Shatrughna's chest but he shattered it into a hundred pieces with his arrows. Seeing his effort come to naught, the mighty rakshasa threw even more trees at Shatrughna. Effulgent Shatrughna pierced those trees with his smooth arrows that had three and four shafts. Then Shatrughna, rich in valour, released a rain of arrows aimed at the rakshasa's chest but the rakshasa was not in the least troubled. Lavana laughed. As if in play, he threw a huge tree at the head of Shatrughna, who lost consciousness.

When heroic Shatrughna fell, there was a huge commotion among the sages, the troops of gods, the apsaras and the gandharvas. Taking Shatrughna for dead, Lavana did not enter his city, even though he could have. Nor did he pick up his spear when Shatrughna was lying on the ground. Assuming that he was dead, the rakshasa began to eat. After a while, Shatrughna, the determined warrior, regained consciousness and stood up. The sages praised him when they saw him standing at the city gate. Shatrughna picked a divine arrow, unsurpassed and unerring, whose blazing splendour filled the ten directions. As bright and as swift as lightning, as glorious as Mount Meru and Mandara, its shaft was smooth on all sides and it was invincible in battle. Smeared with red sandal paste, its fletch was finely feathered and it was terrifying to the danavas, the mountains and the gods.

All creatures were overcome with terror when they saw it blazing like the doomsday fire at the end of time. The entire world – along with the gods and the asuras, the gandharvas, sages and apsaras – was uneasy and so, Grandfather Brahma appeared. They said to him, 'Grandfather, are the worlds going to be destroyed? Has the time for the worlds to end arrived? We have never seen nor heard of anything like this before. The gods and all the world's creatures are afraid, lord!' Brahma, protector of the worlds, heard these words and understood the fear of the gods. He made an attempt to dispel that fear. 'The arrow that Shatrughna is holding, the one whose splendour has bewildered even the best of the gods, is for killing Lavana. This arrow which has terrified all of you, dear children, used to belong to the eternal creator of the worlds. This wondrous arrow was created by the great-souled one for killing the two daityas: Kaitabha and Madhu. Only Vishnu understands the splendour of this arrow. In fact, long ago, the arrow was made from his body. Now go and watch Rama's heroic and great-souled younger brother kill Lavana, the supreme rakshasa.'

Listening to that sweet voice, the gods went together to where Shatrughna and Lavana were fighting. All creatures saw that arcing arrow, blazing like the doomsday fire, which Shatrughna held in his hand. Shatrughna, joy of the Raghus, noticed that the sky was filled with gods and he let out a lion roar as he glared at Lavana once more. Lavana was incensed at the challenge and stepped forward to fight. Pulling his bowstring back to his ear, Shatrughna loosed the wondrous arrow against Lavana. It pierced his chest and entered the underworld and then, that divine arrow, worshipped by the gods, returned quickly to Shatrughna, joy of the Ikshvakus. The night-ranger fell to the ground, like a mountain struck by a thunderbolt. All living beings watched as the divine spear returned to Shiva's control after Lavana had been killed.

With a single arrow, the hero of the Raghus destroyed the fear that haunted the three worlds, just as the thousand-rayed sun dispels the darkness.

## Sarga 62: Shatrughna Is Crowned

When Lavana had been killed, the gods along with Indra and with Agni at their head, spoke in their sweet voices to Shatrughna, scorcher of his enemies. 'By good fortune you are victorious, by good fortune, Lavana, the rakshasa, has been killed. Tiger among men, choose a boon! Mighty-armed one, we, who wanted your victory, have come here together to give you a boon. Our presence cannot be in vain.'

Hearing the gods, the hero raised his joined palms to his head. Mighty-armed Shatrughna, the dutiful, replied, 'The boon I want is to enter this beautiful city of Madhupuri that has been so wonderfully constructed by the gods.' The gods were pleased and said to Shatrughna, 'It shall be so! This pleasant city will no doubt have an army of heroes!'

The great-souled ones rose up into the heavens and the effulgent Shatrughna summoned his army which arrived there quickly. For twelve years, Shatrughna lived peacefully in Shurasena's beautiful city, a city like that of the gods. Crops came from the fields, Indra sent the rains on time and the healthy and courageous people were protected by Shatrughna's arms. The city, made beautiful by fine mansions and crossroads and shops, sat on the banks of the Yamuna, shaped like a crescent moon. In the past, Lavana had built shining white buildings which heroic Shatrughna now decorated with many colours. Shatrughna gazed upon that prosperous city, so filled with bounty, and experienced the greatest possible happiness.

While living in the city of Madhupuri, his mind turned to the fact that it had been twelve years since he had seen Rama.

## Sarga 63: Shatrughna Misses Rama

With a few retainers and soldiers, Shatrughna decided to go to Ayodhya, which was protected by Rama. Placing his ministers and his army chiefs at the head, he set off in the best of chariots drawn by horses as bright as the sun. He stopped for only seven or eight nights along the way because he wanted to reach Ayodhya quickly, eager as he was to see Rama. Shatrughna, wise and heroic, entered that beautiful city and went straight to Rama. He honoured the great-souled one who blazed with his own splendour. He joined his palms and said to Rama, whose valour lay in truth, 'Great king, I have done all that you asked me to do. I have killed wicked Lavana and I have lived in his city, Madhupuri. I have been away from you for twelve years, joy of the Raghus. And I can no longer bear to live without you, your majesty. Show me your grace, mighty Rama, as if I were a child without a mother. I cannot live away any more.'

Rama embraced Shatrughna and said, 'Do not grieve, hero. This does not become a warrior. It is not a matter of sadness for a king to live away. He needs to protect his people according to the dharma of the kshatriyas. You can come and visit me in Ayodhya now and then, best of men. But you must return to your own city. There is no doubt that you are as dear to me as life itself. But a king must protect his kingdom. Stay with me for five nights, Shatrughna. After that, you can return to your own city with your retainers, your soldiers and your vehicles.' Rama's words were righteous and appealed to reason. Shatrughna said in a sad voice, 'It shall be so!' As commanded, he stayed five nights with Rama and then made preparations to leave. He bade farewell to mighty Rama and Lakshmana and Bharata and mounted a large chariot. Lakshmana and Bharata followed him for a good distance and then he went onwards to his own city.

## Sarga 64: The Death of the Brahmin's Son

Rama ruled the kingdom with his brothers and experienced happiness and felicity. One day, an elderly brahmin from the countryside came to the king's door, carrying his son's corpse. Overwhelmed by an immeasurable grief, he babbled as he wailed. 'My son, my son!' he cried and then he said, 'What misdeeds did I commit in my previous life that I now have to see my only son dead! Little boy, you were only five years old, you did not even become a young man. Your untimely death leaves me bereft. Grieving for you, there is no doubt that your mother and I shall soon die as well! I don't remember ever having spoken unlawfully, nor do I remember causing any harm. For what misdeed, little one, did you, my own son, go to Yama's realm today, even before performing the funeral rites for your father? Never before in Rama's realm have I heard or seen anything as awful as this, this untimely death! There can be no doubt that Rama himself has done something terribly wrong.

'You, king, you are the reason for the death of this living creature. You, along with your brothers, shall have a long life, king. Mighty one, we have lived happily in your kingdom. But now, the realm of the great-souled Ikshvakus is without a protector. Rama has become responsible for his people and children are dying. In this perverted reign, the king's faults bring misfortune to his subjects. Common people suffer untimely deaths when it is the king who acts wrongly. When city dwellers and country dwellers are not controlled and are not corrected, the fear of death abounds. Without a doubt, this child has died because of the king's failures, whether in the city or in the country.'

And so the brahmin continued to criticize the king in different ways. Burning with grief, he embraced the body of his son.

## Sarga 65: Narada's Counsel

Rama heard the brahmin's piteous wailing and he and others were overcome with sadness. Scorched by this sadness, he sent for his brothers and his ministers and the citizens. Eight brahmins – Markandeya and Maudgalya, Vamadeva and Kashyapa, Katyayana and Jabali, Gautama and Narada –

entered along with Vasishtha, saying 'May you prosper!' to the king who was like a god. All of them, bulls among brahmin sages, took their seats and the ministers and the citizens were greeted according to custom. When those men who blazed with effulgence were all seated, Rama said to them, 'A brahmin is crying.'

Hearing the disconsolate king, Narada said these auspicious words to him in the presence of all the brahmins. 'Listen to the reason for this boy's untimely death, king! Joy of the Raghus, do your duty when you have heard this! In the Krita Yuga, Rama, only brahmins became ascetics. Your majesty, non-brahmins never became ascetics under any circumstances. In that yuga, the shining brahmins were dominant, they were immortal and they could see the future. Then came the Treta Yuga, where the men of glory were kshatriyas, and they ruled as the brahmins had done before. The great-souled men of this age were not superior in their heroism and practise of austerities to those in the previous yuga. Brahmins had been superior to the kshatriyas, but in this yuga, both were equal in power. Because there was no perceptible difference between the brahmins and the kshatriyas, the system of the four castes was established everywhere. Adharma stood on one foot on the surface of the earth and the twice-born became apathetic because of their attachment to adharma. Lifespans diminished. Only those who were dedicated to truth and righteousness performed auspicious activities.

'In the Treta Yuga, both brahmins and kshatriyas performed austerities and all the other people served them – this was the highest dharma for vaishyas and shudras. Shudras, especially, had to worship everyone. Then, the second foot of adharma descends, so that becomes known as the Dwapara Yuga. In this Dwapara Yuga, decay will prevail and, bull among men, adharma and lawlessness will increase. In the Dwapara Yuga, vaishyas will take to ascetic practices. But, bull among men, shudras cannot access this, the dharma of fierce asceticism. In the future, in the Kali Yuga, best of kings, men without caste shall take on great austerities and those born of shudra wombs will also perform penances. But it is the greatest unrighteousness, Rama, for a shudra to appropriate this in the Dwapara Yuga.

'Somewhere in your realm, your majesty, a shudra of corrupted intelligence has undertaken terrific ascetic practices and that is why this boy is dead. Tiger among kings, there is no doubt that it is the king who goes to hell if someone of perverted intelligence performs unrighteous deeds within the kingdom or in the city. You yourself should, therefore, seek out where in your kingdom unrighteousness is being practised, tiger among men. And when you see it, you should correct it. Then dharma shall prosper and men will live longer. And, best of men, this boy will come back to life.'

## Sarga 66: Rama Addresses the Problem

Hearing Narada's words, which were like nectar, Rama was flooded with great happiness and he said to Lakshmana, 'Go, my dear Lakshmana, and console that best of brahmins. Place the boy's body in a vat of oil. Let it be perfumed with the best of fragrant oils so that the body does not decay in any way. Act such that the boy's body is preserved, that it is not disturbed and suffers neither injury nor destruction.' Having instructed Lakshmana of the auspicious marks thus, Rama thought of Pushpaka and called it to himself. Divining Rama's intentions, gold-decorated Pushpaka arrived in his presence in an instant. Bowing, it said, 'I am here, best of kings. Strong-armed one, your obedient servant is present!' Hearing Pushpaka's sweet words, the best of kings honoured the great sages and climbed into the vehicle. Taking his bow and quiver and a gleaming sword, he left the city in the care of Bharata and Lakshmana.

Rama searched here and there and then set off towards the west. Then, he went to the northern regions which are enclosed by the Himalayas. Not seeing even the smallest misdemeanour there, he went east and the best of men looked everywhere in that region. Rama, joy of the royal sages, then headed south and on the northern slopes of Mount Shaivala, he saw a huge lake. At the lake, glorious Rama saw a great ascetic, with his head hanging down, practising the most difficult austerities. Approaching the man who was performing the best of penances, Rama said to him, 'You are blessed, man of good vows! Man of great resolve, may your austerities increase. What womb are you from? I am Rama, son of Dasharatha and I ask out of curiosity. Great ascetic, do you wish to go to heaven or is it something else that you desire? I want to hear the purpose of your ascetic practice. If you are a brahmin, it is fortunate, if you are a kshatriya, you are hard to defeat. But you must tell me truthfully if you are a vaishya or a shudra!'

## Sarga 67: Rama Kills Shambuka

When he heard the spirited Rama's words, the ascetic lifted his head and said, 'I, who stand here in fierce asceticism, am born of a shudra womb. I want to be like a god, Rama, and earn great fame by going to heaven in this very body. I am not lying, king, I desire heaven. Know me to be a shudra, Rama! My name is Shambuka.' Even as the shudra was speaking, Rama drew his beautiful gleaming sword from its sheath and cut off his head. At that very moment, the boy came back to life.

Then lotus-eyed Rama went to the hermitage of Agastya. He bowed to him with humility and was filled with happiness. He honoured the great sage who blazed with his own effulgence and the great king, having accepted the appropriate rituals of hospitality, sat down. Then, that great ascetic, Kumbhayoni Agastya, supremely effulgent, said to him, 'Welcome, best of kings. It is my good fortune that you are here, Raghava. I have great regard for you, Rama, because of your many excellent virtues. As a guest, you are worthy of my worship and you are always in my heart. The gods told me you were coming here after killing the shudra. And that a brahmin's son had been brought back to life by your righteous actions. Stay the night here with me, Rama, and in the morning you can return to your own city in Pushpaka.

'This ornament, my dear, has been fashioned by Vishvakarma. It is extraordinarily beautiful and it shines with its own lustre. Take it, Rama, and make me happy. It is said that one who gives away what has been gifted to him gains an even greater result. Therefore, I give you this with due ceremony, best of men. Please accept it.'

Rama took the ornament, which was unique and beautiful and shone like the sun, from the great-souled sage and asked about its divine origins. 'Where or how did you get this wondrous ornament, so beautifully wrought, brahmin? I ask out of curiosity because you are the repository of many marvellous things.'

The sage replied, 'Listen, Rama, to all that happened in the Treta Yuga.'

## Sarga 68: The Story of the Corpse Eater

'In the past, in the Treta Yuga, there was a vast forest. It covered an entire one hundred yojanas in all directions and had no birds or animals. I went to that uninhabited forest, my dear, in order to practise the highest of austerities. I am not able to describe the beauty of that forest, with its pleasant and delicious roots and fruits and its many trees. There was a lake in the middle of the forest which was one yojana long. It was filled with blooming lotuses and it was free of moss. Its waters were delicious. It was always clean and calm and it was frequented by flocks of birds. There was a truly wondrous hermitage on its banks. Old and sacred, it had been abandoned by the ascetics. One night, during the summer, I stayed there, bull among men. In the morning, I went to the lake to perform rituals and bathe. I saw a corpse that seemed in good condition and had not spoiled in any way. Resplendent, it lay by the shores of the lake. I stood there, Rama, and thought for a while, wondering, "What could this be?"

'Soon, I saw a marvellous celestial vehicle. It was huge and yoked with swans and it moved as quickly as thought. Joy of the Raghus, a heavenly creature was in that vehicle. He was covered in divine ornaments and he was surrounded by apsaras who were singing and dancing and playing sweet musical instruments. Even as I watched, Rama, the divine being dismounted from the vehicle and devoured the corpse. After he had eaten his fill of meat and fat, he went down to the lake and began to wash himself. When he had cleansed himself in the prescribed way, he climbed back into the celestial vehicle. Best of men, I saw that man who seemed like a god, ascending and I said to him, "Who are you, sir? You resemble the gods, but your food is disgusting. Tell me, why did you eat this dead body? It is amazing that you look like the gods but you eat this forbidden food. I want to hear more about this."'

## Sarga 69: Shveta's Hunger

'Appreciating my eloquence, the heavenly being joined his palms and said to me, "Because you asked, brahmin, listen to what happened – to that transgressive incident which caused both joy and sorrow. Long ago, the king of Vidarbha was my illustrious father. His name was Sudeva and that heroic man was renowned in the three worlds. He engendered two sons on his two wives, brahmin. I am known as Shveta and my younger brother is called Suratha. When my father died, the people crowned me king and I ruled in accordance with dharma. In this way, man of good vows, a full thousand years passed. I ruled and I protected my people according to dharma. And then, in the course of things, I learned something about my life. In my heart, I saw the time of my death and so I came to this dense forest, devoid of animals and birds. I anointed my brother king and embarked on the practise of austerities on the shores of this beautiful lake.

'"For three thousand years, great sage, I engaged in this practise and then, I was able to reach Brahma's realm, which is the best of them all and hard to attain. But when I got to heaven, twice-born one, I was overcome with extreme hunger and thirst, so much that all my senses were greatly agitated. I went to Grandfather Brahma, lord of the three worlds, and I said to him, 'Lord, your realm is free of hunger and thirst. I am still overcome by both. Of what acts is this a consequence? What is my food, Brahma, you need to tell me.' The grandfather said to me, 'Son of Sudeva, your food will forever be your own sweet-tasting flesh. When you were performing those exemplary austerities, you nourished only your own body. Wise Shveta, nothing rises from a seed that has not been sown. You attained heaven, but you gave nothing to the denizens of the forest. Child, of course you will be plagued by hunger and thirst. You will be sated when you eat the elixir of immortality that is your body, which was sustained by wholesome foods. When the great sage Agastya comes to the forest, you will be able to liberate yourself from this difficulty, Shveta. Dear one, he has the strength to save even troops of gods. Your hunger and thirst, mighty-armed one, will be as nothing to him.'

'"Best of the twice-born, when I heard the words of that god of gods, I decided to eat my own body, however repulsive. For many years, brahmin, I have been eating this body. It never diminishes and I am satisfied. None but Agastya could have come to this forest, so release me from these troubles, twice-born one! Accept this ornament for saving me. Sage among brahmins, please be gracious to me."

'When I heard that sorry tale from the heavenly being, I accepted this best of ornaments from him as recompense for saving him. The moment I took the beautiful ornament, the previous human body was destroyed and the king was overjoyed. Satisfied and happy, he returned to heaven. This is the reason, Rama, that this ornament of wondrous beauty was given to me by that king who was Indra's equal.'

## Sarga 70: Rama's Ancestor

Rama was filled with amazement when he heard that wondrous tale from Agastya and he continued to question the sage. 'Blessed one, how come the forest in which Shveta, the king of Vidarbha, practised austerities was devoid of animals and birds? Why did he come to that uninhabited forest with no living beings to practise austerities? I wish to hear about that fully.' Hearing Rama's words which were filled with curiosity, the exceedingly effulgent sage proceeded to speak.

'Long ago, in the Krita Yuga, Rama, Lord Manu ruled the world. He had a mighty son named Ikshvaku, who was the nourisher of his clan. He made his invincible son king of the earth and he said to him, "Establish a royal line on this earth!" "It shall be so," the son promised his father and Manu, who was delighted, spoke further. "I am pleased with you. There is no doubt that you will accomplish this. Protect your people with this staff of punishment but do not punish them without reason. A king should punish those who commit crimes in accordance with the law. That will take him to heaven. This is the justice that you should strive for, my mighty-armed son, for then you will attain the highest dharma in the world." Having instructed his son thus, Manu concentrated his mind and happily went to heaven, to Brahma's realm.

'When he had gone to heaven, Ikshvaku of limitless splendour began to think about how he would produce sons. Using a variety of means, the righteous son of Manu engendered a hundred who were like the sons of the gods. But the youngest of them all, joy of the Raghus, was dull-witted and ignorant and he did nothing for his older brothers. And so his father named that son of little effulgence Danda, because he knew that he would have to suffer punishment upon his body. Recognizing that his son had deep flaws, Rama, he gave him the kingdom of Shaivala, in the middle of the Vindhyas.

He ruled that pleasant land on the slopes of the mountain and he named his incomparable city Madhumanta. He appointed Shukracharya, of good vows, as his family priest and he reigned over his contented subjects like Indra in heaven.'

## Sarga 71: Danda Rapes Araja

When the great sage Agastya had narrated this to Rama, he went on to relate the rest of the story. 'And so, Rama, dull-witted Danda ruled for many years with no difficulties at all. One day, in the month of Chaitra, for some reason, the king went to the pleasant and beautiful hermitage of the sage Shukra, who was descended from Bhrigu. There, Danda saw the sage's incomparable daughter, the most beautiful girl on earth, wandering through the forested region. The unwise king was overcome by the arrows of love when he saw her and he said to the girl, "Lady with the lovely hips, where have you come from? Whose daughter are you, lovely one? Slim-waisted girl, I ask because I am pierced by the arrows of love!" Spoken to like this by the king who was befuddled with desire, the sage's daughter said to him, "Know that I am the oldest daughter of the Bhargava sage who is as pure in his actions as the gods. My name is Araja and I live in a hermitage. My father is a teacher, your majesty, and you are his disciple. That great ascetic could harm you if he were angered. If you want to marry me, take the path of truth. Act according to dharma and take the consent of my illustrious father. The consequences could be harsh for you if it is otherwise. My father can burn up the three worlds in his anger."

'Danda was overpowered by desire when Araja spoke and thus intoxicated, he bowed his head, joined his palms and said, "Be kind to me, lady with the lovely hips! There is no time to waste. I live only for you. I can accept death or the worst of all sins once you are mine. I am your devotee, my lovely, accept me as your slave." He grabbed her with both his powerful arms as he spoke and though she trembled, he proceeded to violate her as he pleased. After this terrible and unrighteous deed, Danda came back to his wonderful city, Madhumanta.

'Araja was agitated and she began to weep as she saw her godlike father approaching the hermitage from a distance.'

## Sarga 72: The Origins of Dandakaranya

'The godlike sage, his glory unlimited, was surrounded by his disciples as he returned to his hermitage to eat a meal. After some time, he listened to what had happened. He looked at Araja, weeping and pathetic, covered with dust.[16] Like the moon eclipsed at dawn, she no longer shone. The sage's anger was sufficient to burn the three worlds because he was especially hungry. He said to his disciples, "Watch! A fiery catastrophe will arise from my anger against this foolish Danda who has committed a terrible deed. The destruction of that wicked fellow and his followers has arrived and it blazes like flames that wish to be touched. He will now face the consequences of his deeds because he did a terrible thing. That wicked king along with his retainers, his army and his vehicles will be dead seven nights from now. Indra, the subduer of Agni, will send a huge rain of dust which will cover that fool's kingdom for one hundred yojanas in all directions. All living things, everywhere, both moving and unmoving, will be destroyed by that mighty rain of dust. Danda's kingdom shall be covered with dust and shall become as if invisible."

'Still enraged, he said to the people who lived in the hermitage, "Go to his country and settle among the people!" They set off at his command and settled on the borders of the kingdom. Then he said to Araja, "Stay right here, you silly child, and concentrate your mind. Enjoy yourself without fatigue at this lovely lake which is one yojana long. Wait for time to ripen. The creatures that come to stay with you at night will not be destroyed by the rain of dust." Having said that, the Bhargava sage went off to live in another kingdom and seven days later, all creatures were burned just as the brahmin had declared.

'Thus was Danda's kingdom, which lay between the Vindhya and the Shaivala mountains, cursed long ago, in the Krita Yuga by that brahmin. After that, Rama, it was known as Dandakaranya.[17] When the ascetics settled there, it came to be known as Janasthana. I have told you everything that you asked about, Rama. It is now time for the evening worship so the sages here

---

[16] Her name, Araja, means 'free of dust'.

[17] Another later explanation for the name of the wilderness that Rama, Sita and Lakshmana lived in during their forest exile (Dandakaranya) as well as for the region in which the sages had their settlements, Janasthana, 'the place of living beings'.

will bathe and then worship the sun with these sacred pots of water. The sun will set after receiving the prayers of those great sages who are the best of brahmins. Now go and purify yourself by touching the water.'

## Sarga 73: Rama Takes Leave of Agastya

Following the sage's instructions, Rama went to the shores of the beautiful lake which was frequented by apsaras. Facing west, he performed the evening worship with water. Then Rama entered the hermitage of the great sage Kumbhayoni Agastya who had created an exceptional meal for Rama from excellent roots and vegetables and herbs that had medicinal properties. Rama was pleased with the meal, which was like the food of the immortals. Content, he spent the night there. Rama, subduer of his foes, woke in the morning and performed the morning rituals. Then, he approached the sage for leave to depart. He greeted the sage who had been born from a pot and said, 'I wish to leave, grant me your permission. I am blessed and grateful to have met you. I shall come to see you whenever I wish to be purified.'

When Rama had spoken these wonderful words, the sage, who was rich in austerities and who saw through eyes of righteousness, was filled with happiness. He said, 'Your words are truly wondrous, Rama, and they are eloquent. You are the joy of the Raghus and the purifier of all that is in the worlds. Anyone who sees you even for a moment, Rama, is cleansed and worthy of living in heaven, worshipped by the gods. Any creature on earth that looks upon you with a negative eye shall die and go to hell, to be punished there by Yama. Go in peace and calmly, there are no dangers on your path. Rule your kingdom righteously, for you are the refuge of the world.' Rama honoured the great sage and the others who were rich in austerities. He mounted gold-decorated Pushpaka, free from anxiety. The hosts of sages all around blessed Rama as if he were Indra worshipped by the immortals. Seated in Pushpaka, Rama seemed like the moon near a rain-filled monsoon cloud.

And so, worshipped everywhere, Rama reached Ayodhya around noon. He dismounted from Pushpaka and released the beautiful chariot which could go where it willed. He entered the central part of the city and said to the guard who stood at the gate, 'Go to Lakshmana and Bharata, those men who carry their valour lightly. Tell them of my arrival and ask them to come to me without delay.'

## Sarga 74: Rama Consults His Brothers about a Sacrifice

The doorkeeper, commanded thus by Rama of unsullied deeds, summoned the two princes into the king's presence. Rama saw that his beloved Lakshmana and Bharata had arrived and he embraced them, saying, 'I have completed the tasks of the twice-born appropriately. Now I wish to do more of what is enjoined by dharma. The two of you are as my own self and so I want you to organize the great rajasuya sacrifice that I wish for. It will make dharma eternal. Mitra, who put an end to his enemies, attained the status of Varuna by performing this auspicious rajasuya with all the oblations. And Soma, who performed the rajasuya appropriately, attained fame in all the worlds and established himself. Think about how we might achieve the greatest benefit and let me know.'

Bharata, who was skilled with words, joined his palms and said, 'On you, good man with mighty arms, rests all righteousness, even the entire earth itself, as do fame and limitless power. The kings of the earth look upon you as the lord of the world, in the same way as the immortals regard Prajapati. The people regard you as a father, your majesty, for you are the end of all beings on earth. Why would you perform this sacrifice which would lead to the destruction of all the royal lineages in the world? All the men on earth who are attached to their manliness will be destroyed by anger. You are a tiger among men, you are distinguished by your virtues. The earth is already in your control. It does not deserve to be destroyed.' Bharata's words were filled with sweetness and when he heard them, valorous Rama was filled with immeasurable happiness.

He said sweetly to the man who increased Kaikeyi's joy, 'I am pleased, I am satisfied with what you have said just now. You, too, are a tiger among men, and your words are powerful and filled with righteousness. They will protect the earth. You know dharma. I had planned to perform the great rajasuya sacrifice, but I have changed my mind after listening to your excellent speech. A king's dharma is to protect his people through sacrifices. And so I shall listen to your advice which is both good and appropriate.'

## Sarga 75: Lakshmana Suggests the Ashvamedha

After wise Bharata had spoken to Rama, Lakshmana also spoke auspicious words to him. 'There is the ashvamedha, the bull among all sacrifices, and it is difficult to perform. It purifies one of all misdeeds and it will purify you as well. In the past, we have heard that Indra, whose mind was vast, performed this horse sacrifice and was cleansed of the sin of killing a brahmin. Long ago, apparently, in the war between the gods and the asuras, there was a mighty daitya named Vritra, highly regarded in all the worlds. He was a hundred yojanas long and his height was three times that. He looked on the three worlds with affection at all times. He knew dharma, he knew about actions, he stood firm in wisdom. He ruled the entire earth righteously and with concentration. The earth produced all that the heart might desire – flowers and juicy fruits and roots – during his reign. It produced grain without being ploughed and so, the kingdom of great-souled Vritra was abundant and prosperous and wondrous. "I shall perform the best of austerities," he thought. "For austerities are the greatest glory and the greatest happiness."

'He entrusted his people to his eldest son Parameshvara and embarked on the practise of the most terrifying austerities dedicated to all the gods. As Vritra performed his austerities, Indra grew agitated. He went to Vishnu and said, "Mighty-armed one, Vritra has brought the worlds under his control by performing austerities. That righteous one is so strong that I am not able to subdue him. Lord of the gods, if he continues to do this, the worlds will be under his control for as long as they exist. You look upon him with great favour, mighty one, but Vritra would not live for a single moment if you become angry. He shall have dominion over the worlds as long as he is favoured by you, Vishnu. Be gracious to the worlds, glorious one, and they will be peaceful and free of sickness. The sky dwellers are all looking to you, Vishnu. You must help them to kill Vritra as you have always helped good people. Vritra cannot be endured! We have no refuge. Shelter us!"'

## Sarga 76: The Killing of Vritra

Rama, the killer of enemies, heard Lakshmana's words and said, 'Tell us the entire story of how Vritra was killed.'

Lakshmana, who increased his mother Sumitra's joy, began to tell the divine story of Vritra.

'Listening to thousand-eyed Indra and all the other sky dwellers, Vishnu said to them, "I had a friendship with great-souled Vritra in the past. And because of that, I will not kill the great asura. But I certainly want to do what will make you all happy. So I will tell you how Vritra can be killed. I will divide my essence into three parts and with it, there can be no doubt that thousand-eyed Indra will be able to kill Vritra. One part will enter Indra, a second part will enter his thunderbolt, a third will enter the surface of the earth. And then, Indra will be able to kill Vritra."

'"If you say so, it shall certainly happen, slayer of daityas!" said the gods to the lord of gods. "May all be well with you. We will leave as we are eager for the death of Vritra, the asura. You have shared your own effulgence with Indra with great generosity."

'Led by thousand-eyed Indra, the gods went to the forest where Vritra was and they saw him, the best among the asuras, practising austerities. He was blazing with splendour, as if he would drink up the three worlds or burn the sky. The gods were very agitated. "How shall we kill him? How shall we be victorious?" Even as they were panicking, thousand-eyed Indra grabbed his thunderbolt and, with both arms, he flung it at Vritra's head.

'The thunderbolt blazed, flaming like the doomsday fire and the worlds trembled when it struck Vritra's head. Wise and glorious Indra was concerned that the killing of Vritra was inappropriate and so he ran away and wandered through the worlds. But though he fled, Indra was pursued by the sin of killing a brahmin and his limbs were covered with wounds which caused him great pain.

'Indra disappeared after he had killed the enemy and so the gods, now with Agni at their head, worshipped Vishnu, the lord of the three worlds, many times. "God, you are the supreme refuge, you are the father of the worlds, lord. You have appeared as Vishnu to protect all creatures. Vritra was killed by you, but the sin of brahminicide has gone to Indra. Tell us, how can he be liberated from that suffering?"

'Vishnu said, "Let him make a sacrifice to me and I will purify him, the wielder of the thunderbolt. Let him worship me with the horse sacrifice which is filled with merit and once again, he will be Indra among the gods, free of fear." Having instructed the gods with these words which were like nectar, Vishnu went on his way as the gods continued to praise him.'

## Sarga 77: The Sin of Brahminicide

After narrating the main part of the story of Vritra's killing, Lakshmana, the best of men, went on to tell the remaining part. 'When heroic Indra had killed Vritra who had terrified the gods, he was set upon by Brahminicide, for the sin of killing a brahmin had become a woman. He reached the end of the worlds weakly and lost consciousness. He stayed there for a while, lying on the ground like a great serpent. The whole world was disconsolate when Indra disappeared. The earth was as if eclipsed and even the forests dried up. The gods grew agitated as the world was being destroyed and then, they remembered the sacrifice that Vishnu had told them about earlier. All the gods, with their teachers and the great sages, went together to where Indra lay, stupefied with fear.

'Seeing thousand-eyed Indra so confused by Brahminicide, they approached him and began the performance of the ashvamedha sacrifice. That great ashvamedha performed by Indra cleansed him of the sin of killing a brahmin, best of men. When the sacrifice was complete, Brahminicide approached the gods and said, "Where shall I stay?" The gods were in a good mood. They said, "Divide yourself into four parts, you dangerous woman!" In their presence, Brahminicide chose the places where she would reside, places that were difficult to live in. "I declare truly that one part of me will live in the abundant rivers, a second part of me will live in trees. With my third part, I shall live for three nights inside young women who are full of pride and I will be the destroyer of their pride. With my fourth part, I shall take shelter with brahmin-killers who have never spoken falsely before."

'The gods replied, "It shall be as you say, naked woman! It shall all be so. Now do as you please!"

'The gods were terribly pleased and they all praised thousand-eyed Indra who was now free of fatigue and of sin. Indra praised and honoured the wonderful sacrifice and the entire world was relieved when Indra was re-established. This is the effect of the ashvamedha sacrifice. Undertake it, your majesty!'

## Sarga 78: The Story of Ila

Eloquent Rama, the effulgent one, smiled when he heard what Lakshmana had to say. 'Best of men, you have told us the story of Vritra's killing and the fruits of the ashvamedha sacrifice,' he said. 'We have heard that in the past, the son of Prajapati Kardama, Ila by name, righteous and glorious, was the ruler of Bahlika. That illustrious king had brought the whole earth under his control and he nurtured his kingdom as if it were a child.

'He was worshipped constantly by the gods, the generous daityas, the great asuras, by the nagas, rakshasas, gandharvas and the great-souled yakshas, because they were afraid of him. All the three worlds feared the anger of that great man. The king of Bahlika was wise and illustrious and he stood firm in righteousness and valour. In the pleasant month of Chaitra, he went to a lovely forest to hunt along with his retainers and soldiers and vehicles. The great-souled king killed hundreds and thousands of animals in the forest but he was not satisfied with that massacre. He killed all kinds of animals until he came to the place where Kartikeya, the great commander of the gods' armies, was born. Accompanied by his invincible attendants, Shiva, god of gods, was enjoying himself there with Parvati, daughter of the mountain. Shiva, whose flag carries the bull, had taken on the form of a woman to please the goddess who stood near a mountain waterfall. All the living beings in that region of the forest that were male somehow became female. At that very time, King Ila, son of Kardama, who had killed thousands of animals, approached the area. He saw that all the animals and birds and snakes had become female and that he and his companions had also become female. He was overcome by a great sadness when he saw what had happened to him. When he realized that it was because of Shiva, Uma's lord, he grew agitated. With his soldiers and retainers and vehicles, the king sought refuge with the god of the blue throat and the matted locks.

Illustrious Shiva, giver of boons, laughed and said to Prajapati's son, "Stand up, stand up, royal sage, man of great vows, mighty son of Kardama. Choose a boon for your dead masculinity, dear fellow!"

'The king was struck with sorrow and he refused Shiva, rejecting the form of a female. He asked the best of the gods for another boon. Sadly, his heart filled with sincerity, the king bowed to the goddess Parvati. "Beautiful goddess, giver of boons to the entire world, the sight of you is never in vain. I bow to you, show me your grace." Parvati, who was standing beside Shiva and had his respect, recognized that the royal sage's plea was heartfelt and she said these auspicious words to him, "Half your boon will be given to you by Shiva and half of it by me. Ask me for the boon of being either a man or a woman." The king was delighted when he heard this wondrous offer from the goddess. He said, "Goddess, if you are pleased with me, then let me be the most beautiful woman in the world for a month and a man again in the next month." The goddess with the lovely face understood what the king wanted and so she said, "It shall be as you say! When you are a man, you will forget that you were a woman and when you are a woman, you will forget that you were a man!"

'And so, the king, the son of Kardama, was a man for one month and for the next month, he was the most lovely woman in all the three worlds.'

## Sarga 79: Ila and Budha

Lakshmana and Bharata were amazed when they heard Ila's story from Rama. They joined their palms and asked Rama for details about the condition of that great-souled king. 'Why did the king choose to become a woman, which is difficult? And what did he do when he became a man?' Hearing their curious questions, Rama told them more about what happened to the king.

'The first month that he became a woman, Ila was surrounded by women who used to be his male companions. As the most beautiful woman in the world with eyes like lotus petals, he went on foot to a forest of trees and bushes and creepers. The others abandoned their mounts and vehicles and wandered around, enjoying the mountainous region. In that forest, which was not far from the mountain, was a beautiful lake filled with different kinds of birds. There, Ila saw Budha, the son of Soma, blazing with his own marvellous beauty, like the moon himself. He was performing severe austerities in the middle of the lake and so he was difficult to reach. But he was young and glorious and could go wherever he pleased. Ila and her companions, who were previously men, were surprised to see him lying submerged.

'Budha saw Ila and was struck by the arrows of love. He was disturbed and started moving in the water. Gazing at that most beautiful woman in the world, he wondered, "Who is this woman, more beautiful even than the goddesses? I have never seen a woman as lovely as this before – not among the gods, the nagas, the asuras nor the apsaras. She would be a match for me, if she does not belong to someone else." Having decided that, he came out of the water on to the shore. When he got to his hermitage, there were four lovely women there. He called out to them and greeted them. He asked them, "Who is that woman, the most beautiful in all the world? Why has she come here? Quickly, tell me the truth!"

'They heard his gentle question and his soft words and the women replied in sweet voices: "This lovely-hipped lady is our mistress for all time. She has no husband and has come to this forest with us on a whim." He heard the women's confusing words and went into a trance to find out the truth of the matter. He discovered all that had happened to the king and then, that bull among sages, said to the women, "Gentle ladies, sort-of-men live on the slopes of this mountain. You should live here, too. Let room be made. All of you will be constantly nourished by roots and fruits and plants. And as women, you will obtain the sort-of-men as husbands." When the many women who had been turned into sort-of-women heard the words of Soma's son, they worshipped the mountain in various ways.'

## Sarga 80: King Ila Becomes a Woman

When they had heard about how the sort-of-women came to be, Lakshmana and Bharata said to Rama, lord of the people, 'That is amazing!' And having related this much, illustrious and righteous Rama went on to tell them more about that son of Prajapati. 'When he saw that the sort-of-women had vanished, the best of sages smiled and said to the woman who was rich in beauty, "I am the beloved son of Soma, lovely one. You have a beautiful face. Give yourself to me and look upon me with affection."

'The lovely woman, who had been abandoned by her friends in that deserted place, listened to his request and replied, "Dear man, I am under your control and at your pleasure. Son of Soma, do with me as you please!"

'He was filled with joy at her words and took his pleasure with her. As the lustful Budha enjoyed lovely-faced Ila, the second month of spring passed as if it were only a moment. When the month was over, Ila, who had a face like the full moon, rose from the bed as the illustrious son of Prajapati. He saw Budha practising austerities in the water with his arms held above his head. He said, "Sir, I came to this inaccessible mountain with my retainers. But I can't see them or my army. Where could they have gone?" The sage heard what the king who had lost his memory said and replied with fine words in a reassuring voice, "Your servants were killed in a mighty hailstorm. You were frightened by that hurricane and you came and fell asleep in my hermitage. Calm down, my dear man. Do not be frightened or anxious. You can stay here as long as you like, eating roots and fruits."

'The king was comforted by his words but upset about the death of his companions. He said, "I have lost my servants but I cannot abandon my kingdom. I cannot stay here even for a moment. Give me leave to depart, brahmin. My eldest son, Shashabindu, is righteous and illustrious. I will bestow the kingdom on him. I left my followers and my happy wives behind; I cannot stay here. What you said cannot be acceptable to me!"

'Then the sage Budha said the most wondrous thing to the king. Reassuring him he said, "Stay here. Enjoy yourself. Do not be agitated by your actions, mighty son of Kardama. Stay here for a year, and then I will act for your benefit." The king made up his mind to stay when he heard the words of Budha, who was a brahmin of unsullied deeds. After a month, he became a beautiful woman and enjoyed sexual pleasures. And then a month later, he became a man and worried about his duties as a king. After nine months, Ila with the lovely hips, gave birth to Budha's child, a son who was named Pururavas. Ila handed her son, who was strong and like his father in splendour, to Budha as soon as he was born. And thus it was that Budha comforted the king who had become a woman and enjoyed telling him stories of righteousness.'

## Sarga 81: The Power of the Ashvamedha

When Rama had spoken thus about that wondrous birth, illustrious Lakshmana and Bharata said, 'What did Budha do with his beloved after she had lived with him for a year? You must tell us about that as well, best of men.'

Hearing those repeated questions and those sweet sentences from the two of them, Rama went further with the story of the Prajapati's son. 'When heroic Ila had become a man again, Budha, the wise, summoned the magnanimous and illustrious sage Samvarta as well as the sage Chyavana who was the son of Bhrigu, and Arishtanemi, Pramodana, Modakara and the sage Durvasas. Eloquent Budha, seer of truth, focused his mind and spoke firmly to those like-minded ones who had gathered there. "This mighty king is Ila, the son of Kardama. You all know what has happened with him. Act for his benefit."

'As they were talking among themselves, mighty, effulgent Kardama came to the hermitage with the great twice-born sages Pulastya, Kratu, Ashtakara and the greatly effulgent Omkara. The sages were delighted to see each other and because they wanted the best for the king of Bahlika, they conferred among themselves. For the sake of his son and with his best interest in mind, Kardama said, "Twice-born men! Listen to my words which are for the good of the king! I see no other remedy for this problem than Shiva, who carries the bull on his banner. There is no sacrifice more dear to him than the ashvamedha. We should perform this difficult sacrifice for the sake of the king!"

'When they heard what Kardama had to say, the best among the twice-born decided to perform the ritual as an offering to Shiva.

'Samvarta had a disciple, Marutta by name, who was a royal sage and a conqueror of enemy cities. He performed the great sacrifice to appease Shiva in the vicinity of Budha's hermitage. When the sacrifice was completed, Shiva was exceedingly happy. He came to Ila and said to the brahmins, "I am pleased by this ashvamedha that has been performed by the best among the brahmins. What can I do to please the king of Bahlika?" Those twice-born men with concentrated minds gratified Shiva so that Ila could have his masculinity back. Shiva was pleased. He restored Ila's maleness and vanished.

After the sacrifice was over and Shiva had disappeared, all the brahmins, those who could see the future, left the way they had come.

'Ila left Bahlika and settled in the middle region in the place famously known as Pratishthana. While Ila, Prajapati's mighty son, ruled in Pratishthana, Shashabindu, conqueror of enemy cities, became king of Bahlika. And when Ila died and attained the best of Brahma's realms, his son, Pururavas, became the king of Pratishthana.

'Such is the power of the ashvamedha! Ila, who had become a woman, regained his maleness and overcame other difficulties as well.'

## Sarga 82: Preparations for the Sacrifice

Rama, of limitless splendour, finished telling that wonderful story to his brothers. Then, he spoke words filled with righteousness to Lakshmana. 'Invite Vasishtha and Vamadeva, Jabali and Kashyapa and all the best brahmins who can conduct the ashvamedha. After I have consulted them about how to perform this auspicious sacrifice, I will release myself into a meditative state.' Lakshmana quickly summoned all the brahmins to an audience with Rama. They saw Rama, invincible in war and like unto a god, and they bowed at his feet and worshipped him. Rama joined his palms before the best of brahmins, and spoke to them in words filled with dharma about the ashvamedha. When the leading brahmins heard about the sacrifice, they were very pleased.

Rama understood their intentions and said to Lakshmana, 'Send for Sugriva, with the great soul and the mighty arms. Bring the powerful monkeys that live outdoors. Let them enjoy the pleasures of this great event. And also strong, courageous Vibhishana, surrounded by his rakshasas who can go where they please. Bring him to the ashvamedha. And those kings that want to please me, let them come with their retainers to this grand sacrificial arena. From one corner of the land to the other, invite all the righteous brahmins and the great sages, rich in austerities, along with their wives.

'Order the construction of a huge sacrificial hall on the banks of the river Gomati in the Naimisha forest, for that is the most sacred of places. Go ahead, mighty one, with hundreds of thousands of mules laden with rice and mustard seeds and lentils. Wise Bharata, too, should go ahead, with millions of gold coins. Let him organize merchants who have things for sale, actors and dancers, those who know the Vedas, the young and the old, brahmins who have concentrated minds, servants and skilled craftsmen and experts and my mothers and the princes and those that live in the palace, a golden statue of my wife and acolytes who have been initiated into the sacrifice – let Bharata go ahead with all this.'

## Sarga 83: Rama's Great Sacrifice

All that was needed was sent ahead with Bharata and a horse, entirely black and with all the auspicious marks, was set free. Rama instructed Lakshmana and the sacrificial priests to watch over the horse and he went with his army to the Naimisha forest. Rama saw the magnificent sacrificial hall and was very pleased. He said, 'This is splendid!' While Rama lived in Naimisha, the kings came there with their people and he welcomed them all. He distributed food and clothes among them and to their attendants and their servants who had come there. Bharata and Shatrughna looked after all the kings while the great-souled monkeys who had come with Sugriva busied themselves serving the brahmins food. Rakshasas wearing garlands, who had come with Vibhishana, stood by the sages of great austerities as servants.

The well-appointed horse sacrifice carried on and Lakshmana kept an eye on the horse as it wandered free. During that sacrifice, the only words heard were 'give me' as the needs of the petitioning priests were met by servants. Monkeys and rakshasas distributed things as everyone watched. No one was dirty or poor or miserable – Rama's sacrifice was filled with happy prosperous people. Great-souled sages, who had lived long lives, could not remember another sacrifice that had been marked by such an abundance of charity. It seemed as if endless quantities of gold and silver and gems and clothes were given away. Sages rich in austerities said that they had never seen anything like this, not even in the past, not from Indra, nor Varuna nor Yama nor Soma. Monkeys and rakshasas stood everywhere, giving away clothes and food by the handful, as much as people wanted. Loaded with all the virtues, the sacrifice of Rama, lion among men, went on in this way for a whole year, lacking nothing.

## Sarga 84: Valmiki Brings Rama's Sons to the Sacrifice

As the sacrifice continued, the sage Valmiki came there with his students. He saw the opulence of the sacrifice which rivalled anything performed by the gods and set up camp near the settlements of the great sages. He built a few pleasant huts there and then he said to Kusha and Lava, 'Go and sing the Ramayana in its entirety. Sing with emotion and sincerity. Sing among the sages and the brahmins, sing on the road and on the highways. Sing in the camps of the kings. Sing at Rama's door, at the site of the rituals. Sing especially in front of the priests performing the sacrifice. Sustain yourself with the sweet fruits that grow on the mountains and your voices will remain melodious. You shall not grow tired if you eat those fruits. If Rama asks you to sing among the sages, do so, keeping in mind all the finer points of the art. Observe all the rules of music and song that I have taught you. Sing only twenty cantos a day, and sing them sweetly. Do not hanker after wealth and gifts. What use are such things to those who live in forest settlements and eat only roots and fruit? If the king should ask you whose sons you are, tell him only that you are Valmiki's students. Tune your instruments as I have taught you. Sing with all your heart, sing sweetly and without concern for anything else. Start at the very beginning. Be sure not to show any disrespect to the king, for this righteous ruler is the father of all creatures. In the morning, collect your thoughts, calm your minds and after you have tuned your instruments, sing the poem as it deserves to be sung.'

Thus spoke the sage, giving his students careful instructions.

The two boys held the sage's wonderful instructions in their hearts, like the ashvins when they were taught by Bhrigu. And they went to sleep happily, eager to begin their task.

## Sarga 85: Rama Listens to Valmiki's Poem

The twins woke in the morning and after they had bathed and performed the morning worship, they began to sing as the sage had instructed them to do. Rama listened to the poem composed by the great teacher. It was melodiously set to music and was quite unique, the first of its kind. As he heard more and more of the wonderful poem which was bound by the rules of metre and which was set to music, he became extremely curious. In the pauses between the rituals, Rama would make the boys sing in front of the sages, kings and respected scholars. He made them sing before those who knew the legends of the past and in the presence of venerable old brahmins. The sages and powerful kings were all delighted with the poem and they gazed at the young boys as if drinking them in with their eyes. 'These boys look so much like Rama, they could well be mirror images of him,' they said to each other. 'But for their matted hair and their simple clothes, we cannot tell which is Rama and which are the singers!' The boys from the hermitage continued to sing so sweetly that the audience went into raptures. Their music was so lovely that it seemed divine rather than human and the listeners simply could not get enough of it. The boys began their song with the first canto, with the arrival of Narada, and then they went on to sing twenty cantos a day on a regular basis. When Rama heard the first twenty cantos, he said to his brother Bharata, 'Give eighteen thousand gold pieces to these boys immediately!' But Kusha and Lava would not accept the shining gold. 'What can we do with this?' they asked with surprise. 'We live in the forest and we eat only roots and fruit. What do we need this gold for?' Rama and the others were amazed at their response.

Eager to hear the rest of the poem, Rama asked the boys who shone with splendour, 'What is this poem about? Who composed it? Where does that great sage live?'

'It was composed by the blessed sage Valmiki who has come to attend your sacrifice. The poem tells the story of your life in great detail in five hundred cantos. If you like, you and your brothers can hear the entire poem in the intervals between the rituals.'

'Excellent,' said Rama.

The boys took his permission and returned to the sage's hut. And Rama went back to the sacrificial enclosure with the kings and the sages.

## Sarga 86: Rama Summons Sita

Rama listened to that lovely poem for many days in the company of kings, sages and monkeys. He learned from the poem that Kusha and Lava were the sons of Sita. In the midst of the assembly, Rama said, 'Go to the sage with this message. Tell him, "If Sita is really innocent and virtuous, let her come here with your permission and clear her name!" I would like to hear what the sage has to say on the matter and I am also curious about whether Sita would be inclined to prove her innocence. Find out all this and come back quickly! Let Sita prove her innocence tomorrow morning in front of this entire assembly. I can establish the sincerity of my intentions at the same time.'

The messengers went at once to the sage and told him what Rama had said. Valmiki immediately understood what Rama wanted to do and said, 'Bless you! Sita will do as Rama says because for a woman, her husband is like a god!'

The messengers returned and Rama was delighted with the news. 'Blessed sages, you and your disciples and the kings and their retinues shall watch as Sita proves herself!' he said to the assembly. 'Anyone else who is interested can also come along!'

The sages praised Rama when they heard his words and the kings said, 'No one other than you would be so magnanimous!' Now that he had decided what was to be done the next day, Rama, the slayer of his enemies, dismissed the gathering.

## Sarga 87: Valmiki Confronts Rama

When the night had passed, the king went to the sacrificial enclosure and sent for the effulgent sages – Vasishtha, Vamadeva, Jabali and Kashyapa; Vishvamitra, whose asceticism was of long years, and Durvasas whose asceticism was great; Agastya, Shakti, Bhargava, Vamana; Markandeya whose life was long, and Maudgalya whose austerities were wondrous; the Bhargava Chyavana and dharma-knowing Shatananda, effulgent Bharadvaja and Suprabha, the son of Agni. All the heroic rakshasas and mighty monkeys gathered out of curiosity. Thousands of kshatriyas, vaishyas and shudras also assembled, eager to see Sita take her oath of purity.

When Valmiki heard that everyone had arrived and that the crowd was as still as a mountain, he hurried there with Sita. Sita walked behind the sage with her head bowed. Her palms were joined, her mind was fixed on Rama and her eyes were filled with tears. A roar of approval went up from the people who grieved deeply in their hearts when they saw Sita following Valmiki as Shri follows Brahma. Some shouted Rama's praises, others praised Sita and still others praised them both. Valmiki made his way through the throng with Sita and went up to Rama. 'This is the virtuous and righteous woman you abandoned in the forest near my hermitage even though she is innocent,' he said. 'You renounced her because you feared people's gossip. She has now come to prove her innocence. You should let her do so. Her two sons, these wonderful bards, are your sons, Rama. I swear this is the truth. I am the tenth son of Prachetas, Rama, and I have never told a lie. These are your sons! I have practised austerities for thousands of years. May I lose all the merit I have gained if Sita is not innocent! I determined that Sita was innocent with my five senses and my mind and I gave her shelter near a forest waterfall. This blameless woman never behaved inappropriately and she thinks of her husband as a god. You were so scared of a little gossip! Now, she will prove herself in front of you!'

## Sarga 88: Sita Enters the Earth

Rama looked at Sita who was as lovely as a goddess. He joined his palms and said to Valmiki, 'It shall be as you say, for you know dharma. But your words have been proof enough for me. Sita has already declared her innocence before the gods. And I abandoned her, even though I knew she was innocent, because I feared a scandal. You must forgive me for that. I also know that these two boys are my sons. When Sita proves herself before the world, I shall be able to love her again!'

Realizing that Rama wanted Sita to prove herself, all the gods arrived, led by Brahma. The adityas, Indra, Shiva, the vishvadevas and the troops of maruts, the ashvins, the sages, gandharvas and hosts of apsaras came too. Just then, Vayu released a gentle breeze, redolent with divine perfumes. As it wafted through the assembly, it made everyone calm and happy. The people who had come from other countries marvelled at this, thinking that such a wondrous thing could only have happened long ago, in the Krita Yuga.

Everyone watched as Sita, wearing an ochre robe, joined her palms. Her head was bowed and she kept her eyes on the ground. 'If I have never thought about any man other than Rama, let the goddess Madhavi create a chasm for me!' As soon as she had finished speaking, a truly wondrous event occurred. A splendid celestial throne appeared from within the earth. It was borne on the heads of immeasurably strong nagas who had taken on celestial bodies and were adorned with jewels. Then, the goddess of the earth lifted Sita in her arms and with all due honour, she placed her on the throne. Heavenly beings showered Sita with blossoms as they watched her descending into the earth.

'Well done!' cried the gods with delight as they stood in the air. 'Such a thing is worthy only of someone like you, Sita!'

The kings and the sages at the site of the sacrifice expressed their amazement, and all the moving and unmoving creatures of the earth and sky, the large-bodied danavas and the pannaga kings of the underworld were deeply moved. Some shouted for joy, others slipped into meditative trances, some gazed at Rama and others at Sita in a state of utter bewilderment. They were awed by Sita's entry into the earth, and for a whole hour it seemed as if the entire universe was spellbound.

## Sarga 89: Rama's Sorrow

When the sacrifice was over, Rama was terribly depressed that Sita was no longer with him. The entire world seemed empty to him. He was overcome by his grief and he knew no peace of mind. He rewarded the brahmins suitably and sent them away, along with the kings, the rakshasas and the monkeys. When they had all left, he went back to Ayodhya carrying Sita in his heart. He did not marry again and for every sacrifice after that, he placed a golden statue of Sita by his side. For ten thousand years, Rama performed the horse sacrifice and then the vajapeya for ten times longer, with much gold and wealth, as well as the agnishtoma, the atiratra and the govasa, giving more and more. A long time went by as mighty Rama actively pursued dharma and ruled his kingdom wisely and well. The bears, the monkeys and the rakshasas lived under his control and every day, the vassal kings did what would please Rama. The rain god sent the rains on time and the people in the cities and in the countryside were happy and prosperous. Under Rama's rule, no one died an untimely death, no calamities occurred and no one acted unrighteously. After many years, Rama's illustrious mother died, surrounded by her sons and her grandsons. Soon after, Sumitra and Kaikeyi followed her. They were all reunited with Dasharatha in heaven, where, together, they enjoyed the fruits of dharma. Rama distributed gifts to the brahmins and the ascetics at appropriate times to ensure the welfare of his mothers equally. He also performed many difficult sacrifices which entailed the donation of wealth for the benefit of his paternal ancestors.

## Sarga 90: Rama Settles Bharata's Sons

After some time had passed, Yuddhajit, the king of the Kekayas, sent his own teacher, effulgent Gargya, the son of Angiras, to the great-souled Rama. As a sign of his affection he also sent ten thousand magnificent horses, blankets, jewels, bright cloths and many beautiful ornaments.

When Rama heard that the great sage Gargya had arrived with gifts from Ashvapati, Yuddhajit's uncle, he came to meet him from two miles away with his brothers. He honoured Gargya, accepted the gifts from him and offered his own gifts in return. Rama then asked about the well-being of his uncle and of the sage. After the sage was seated, Rama said, 'Blessed one, what message has my uncle sent with you, who are so eloquent and like Brihaspati himself?'

The sage heard Rama and began to describe the purpose of his wondrous visit. 'Mighty one, bull among men, this is what your affectionate uncle wants you to hear. The land of the gandharvas is rich in roots and fruit. It straddles both sides of the river Sindhu and is very beautiful. It is protected by hundreds of thousands of warlike gandharvas, armed with weapons, who are the sons of Shailusha. Defeat them and live in that beautiful gandharva city, which has no future other than you. Take pleasure in this. Heed my words for they are to your advantage.'

Rama was pleased to hear this message from his uncle which had been delivered by the great sage. He said, 'Very good,' and looked over at Bharata. Joyfully, he grasped the sage's hand and said, 'Great sage, these two boys shall conquer that city. They are Taksha and Pushkala, the sons of Bharata, and under my uncle's protection, they shall stand firm in dharma. Led by Bharata, these young men will go there with their armies and kill the sons of the gandharvas. And then they will occupy both cities. Righteous Bharata will return to me after he has entered the two cities and installed his sons there.'

Rama finished speaking to the great sage and then he instructed Bharata to set forth with his army after crowning his two sons. Bharata departed with his two sons under an auspicious star, placing Gargya at the head of his army, which seemed as if it had been sent by Indra, invincible even to the gods. Rama followed it for some distance. Flesh-eating creatures and bloodthirsty rakshasas went ahead of Bharata and thousands of terrifying ghouls, eager to eat the flesh of the gandharvas, came along, as did thousands of lions and tigers and boar and high-flying birds. After a month and a half on the road, the army reached Kekaya, which was filled with happy and healthy people.

## Sarga 91: Bharata Secures His Sons' Kingdoms

Yuddhajit, king of the Kekayas, was thrilled when he heard that Bharata, the commander of the troops, had arrived along with Gargya. With a huge company of people, he set off immediately to fight the godlike gandharvas. Bharata and Yuddhajit, both men of great valour, reached the city of the gandharvas with their armies and their foot soldiers. The heroic gandharvas gathered when they heard that Bharata had arrived, yelling in all directions and eager to fight. A hair-raising, violent war commenced that lasted for seven terrible days with neither side the winner.

Angrily, Bharata, Rama's younger brother, unleashed a frightful weapon against the gandharvas. It was called Samvarta and it belonged to Yama. Bound in death's noose by the Samvarta, three million gandharvas were rent apart and killed by that great-souled one. Those who lived in the heavenly realms could not remember a battle so fierce, when, in the blink of an eye, so many were slaughtered. Bharata, son of Kaikeyi, killed the heroic warriors and occupied those two wonderful cities, so rich in wealth, placing Taksha in Takshashila and Pushkala in Pushkalavati.

Bharata spent five years in the pleasant lands of the gandharvas. The two cities were filled with wealth and jewels and riches, adorned with groves of trees and seemed to compete with each other, striving for supremacy in virtues. They were studded with gardens and lakes and well-appointed markets and they were made all the more attractive by large homes and splendid mansions and magnificent temples to the gods. Rama's younger brother lived there for five years and then he returned to Ayodhya. As Indra would greet Brahma, resplendent Bharata greeted great-souled Rama, who was like dharma made manifest. He related all that had happened with the massacre of the gandharvas and Rama listened happily to the story of the occupation of that region.

## Sarga 92: Rama Settles Lakshmana's Sons

Rama listened along with his brothers and experienced great joy. Then he said to his brothers, 'Lakshmana, your two sons, Angada and Chandraketu, are fit to rule, for they are skilled in dharma and firm in their resolve. I will crown both these virtuous men. Find them suitable regions as kingdoms, pleasant and free from hindrances, dear one, regions where they will not be harassed by other kings, where the hermitages of sages will not be destroyed, where they can be free of transgression.' When Rama had spoken thus, Bharata replied, 'There is a region called Karapatha which is pleasant and secure. Angada, who has a great soul, can be settled in that city and for Chandraketu, there shall be another beautiful and secure place.'

Rama accepted Bharata's words and since that region was already protected by him and under his control, he settled Angada in a pleasant city called Angadiya. Chandraketu, who was built like a wrestler, was settled in the Malla region and his city, which was known as Chandrakanta, was as beautiful as a heavenly city. Rama, Bharata and Lakshmana, all of them invincible warriors, were well pleased and anointed the young men.

After being crowned, the two princes were firmly established – Angada in the west and Chandraketu in the north – along with their soldiers and retinues. Lakshmana followed Angada and the rear of Chandraketu's army was brought up by Bharata. Lakshmana stayed in Angadiya for a year and when his invincible son was secure in his position, he returned to Ayodhya. Bharata, too, stayed away for a little more than a year and then came back to Ayodhya to sit at Rama's feet. Lakshmana and Bharata, utterly righteous, served at Rama's feet and because of their affection for him, they did not realize how much time had gone by.

Ten thousand years passed in this way as they performed their duty of taking care of the people. Completely satisfied, standing in righteousness, steady in concentration, they lived surrounded by prosperity. The three brothers were like three sacrificial fires that blazed when fed with oblations.

## Sarga 93: Time Approaches Rama

Years later, as Rama was pursuing the path of dharma, Time arrived at his door in the form of an ascetic. 'Tell Rama I have come to see him on an urgent matter,' he said to resolute Lakshmana. 'I am the messenger of an effulgent and splendid sage and I have important business with Rama.'

Lakshmana went quickly to Rama and said that an ascetic had come to see him. Rama commanded that he be admitted at once and Lakshmana led in the ascetic who blazed like fire. Rama shone with his own splendour and the ascetic greeted him sweetly, saying, 'May you prosper, Rama!' Rama honoured him with arghya water and made the customary enquiries. He led the ascetic to a resplendent throne and seated him. 'Welcome, splendid one! Give me the message from the sage who has sent you!' said Rama.

'I can only tell you what he said where no one else can either see or hear us,' said the ascetic. 'If you care for the message that the sage has sent, then whoever sees or hears us must be put to death, Rama!'

'Send away the doorkeeper and stand there in his place,' said Rama to Lakshmana. 'I shall have to kill anyone who sees or hears our private conversation!'

Then, Rama turned to the ascetic and said, 'Tell me, what is the message? Deep in my heart, I already know what it is, but tell me anyway.'

## Sarga 94: Rama Is Called Back to the Gods

'Listen, mighty Rama, and I will tell you why I am here,' began the ascetic. 'Brahma, the grandfather of the gods, has sent me. I am Time, the destroyer of all. Blessed Brahma, the ruler of the worlds, has asked that you come back and protect your own realm! Long ago, you shrank the worlds and then, lying on the waters, you produced me. You had already created the great serpent, Ananta, upon whose coils you lay and through maya, you created two mighty creatures, Madhu and Kaitabha. This earth with its mountains was made from a pile of their bones. You produced me from a lotus, bright as the sun, that arose from your navel, and gave me the task of creating all beings. When you gave me this responsibility, I worshipped you as the lord of the world and said, "Protect all creatures, for you have given me that power!"

'You must look after all beings because of your indestructible and eternal nature as Vishnu. You helped your brother Indra, Aditi's son, to increase his wealth. And then, when all creatures were being tormented, you became mortal in order to kill Ravana. You decided that you would live in the world of men for eleven thousand years. You were born on earth of your own free will. Now your human life has ended and you must come back to me. But if you still want to protect your subjects, you are free to do so. May all go well with you. This is what Brahma said: "If you do return to the realm of the gods, they will be relieved of their anxiety because you, Vishnu, are there to protect them."'

Rama smiled and said to Time, the destroyer of all things, 'I am glad you came here with this message from Brahma. May all go well with you! I shall return to where I came from. You arrived even as I was thinking about you. There is nothing left for me to consider. But I still have a few duties to discharge towards those who depend on me. When I have completed them, I shall do as Brahma says.'

## Sarga 95: Durvasas Visits Rama

While the two of them were talking, the blessed sage Durvasas arrived at the door, eager to see Rama. 'I want to see Rama at once, before my purpose in coming here is defeated,' he said to Lakshmana.

Lakshmana honoured him and said, 'What do you need? Tell me, what have you come for? Rama is very busy right now. Can you wait for a while?'

Durvasas flew into a rage and looked at Lakshmana as if he would consume him with the fire from his eyes. 'Go at once and tell Rama that I am here. Or, I shall curse you, Rama, the city and the entire kingdom as well as Bharata and all your children! I cannot control my anger!'

Lakshmana considered the matter and said to himself, 'It is better that one man, I myself, die, than all creatures be destroyed!' He made up his mind quickly and went in to see Rama. Rama dismissed Time and came out with Lakshmana.

He honoured the sage who shone with splendour and, with his palms joined, he said, 'What can I do for you?'

'Listen, lover of dharma,' said the sage. 'Today I have completed one hundred years of practising austerities and I am very hungry. Satisfy my desire to eat!'

Rama ordered a delicious meal for the sage and Durvasas ate his fill of the food that was as fine and sweet as nectar. He thanked Rama and praised him and went back to his hermitage. Rama was very happy until he remembered Time's words. He recalled their frightful implications and burning with grief, he hung his head and was utterly silent.

'This cannot be true,' he thought to himself.

## Sarga 96: Lakshmana's Death

Lakshmana noticed that Rama was depressed and dull like an eclipsed moon. 'Do not grieve for me, Rama,' he said gently. 'Do as Time said, for it has been ordained. Kill me without hesitation and fulfil your promise. The man who breaks his word goes to hell! If you love me and want to make me happy, then kill me without any second thoughts or misgivings! You must nourish dharma, Rama!'

Rama's senses were in a whirl when he heard what Lakshmana said. He sent for his ministers and the family priest and told them what had happened. They were silent when they heard the story and then, Vasishtha said, 'Mighty one, I knew long ago that this calamity, this separation from Lakshmana, was going to happen! Time is all-powerful. You must abandon Lakshmana and keep your word. Dharma is destroyed when a man breaks his promise. And when dharma is destroyed, you can be sure that the three worlds, with all their moving and unmoving creatures, with the gods and the sages, will also perish. You are responsible for protecting the three worlds. If you kill Lakshmana today, you will have established the universe firmly.'

'I must renounce you, Lakshmana, or else dharma will be violated,' said Rama when he heard Vasishtha's words which were filled with purpose and meaning. 'It will be all the same to good men whether I kill you or abandon you or am separated from you!' Lakshmana's eyes filled with tears and he left hurriedly, but he did not go to his own home. He went straight to the banks of the Sarayu where he stopped the activities of his senses and ceased to exhale. When his breathing stopped, the gods, apsaras and groups of sages rained flowers from the sky. Unseen by others, Indra lifted Lakshmana's body and took him to heaven. Thus, Lakshmana reverted to his original state as one quarter of Vishnu and the gods and sages rejoiced and celebrated and honoured him.

## Sarga 97: Rama Prepares to Join the Gods

Rama was filled with grief when Lakshmana left. He called together his ministers and the family priest and said to them, 'Today, I want to anoint righteous Bharata king of Ayodhya. He can rule the kingdom and I shall retire to the forest. Collect the materials for the coronation as quickly as you can. I want to go the way Lakshmana has gone.' The citizens were terribly upset when they heard this and they threw themselves on the ground at Rama's feet as if they were dead. Bharata fainted when he heard Rama's words and then, immediately rejected the kingdom. 'I swear on truth and on my place in heaven that I do not want the kingdom. What use is it to me without you, Rama? Divide the kingdom between Kusha and Lava and consecrate them kings. Send messengers to Shatrughna at once and tell him about your imminent departure for heaven!'

Vasishtha saw how upset the people were. He said, 'Rama, my child, look how the citizens have thrown themselves on the ground. You must find out what they want and fulfil their wishes,' he said.

Rama raised the people up and asked, 'What do you want me to do?' and they replied, 'We shall go wherever you go! That would give us the greatest happiness and would also fulfil our highest duty. We want to follow you!'

Rama saw that the people were truly devoted to him and he agreed to their plans. That very day, Rama anointed Kusha and Lava kings of Kosala. He gave them three thousand chariots each, ten thousand horses and elephants and huge quantities of money and jewels. Once he had established them in their own separate cities, he sent messengers to Shatrughna.

## Sarga 98: Rama Says Farewell

Prodded by Rama's command, the messengers went swiftly to Madhura, not stopping along the way. After three days and three nights, they reached Madhura, and there they told Shatrughna all that had happened: Rama's renunciation of Lakshmana, Rama's promise, the coronation of his two sons and the people's decision to follow him, about the beautiful city called Kushavati which wise Rama built on the slopes of the Vindhya mountains for Kusha, and about the beautiful city of Sharavati for Lava, and how the people, determined to follow Rama and Bharata, had abandoned Ayodhya. When they had related all this to the great-souled Shatrughna, the messengers said, 'Make haste, your majesty!' and then they were silent.

Shatrughna listened to the terrible news about the destruction of his lineage and summoned his people as well as Kanchana, the family priest. He told them all that had happened and also told them of his decision to join his brothers in their departure. The king anointed both his sons, giving Madhura to Subahu and Vaidisha to Shatrughati. He divided the army of Madhura and he made his sons kings by establishing them in wealth and grain. He left Vaidisha and Shatrughati and went in a single chariot as swiftly as he could to Ayodhya. There, he saw great-souled Rama blazing like a fire, dressed in robes of fine silk and surrounded by sages of indestructible righteousness. He greeted Rama with his palms joined. Shatrughna, knower of dharma, controlled his senses and spoke words which were righteous in their intent. 'I have anointed both my sons and settled them with wealth. I am here to follow you. Know that this is my decision. Do not say or do anything otherwise. I would prefer not to disobey your commands.'

Rama saw that his resolve was firm and so he said to Shatrughna, 'Let it be so!'

When this conversation had ended, the monkeys who could change their forms at will and the bears and the troops of rakshasas arrived in great numbers. The sons of the gods, the sons of the sages and the sons of the gandharvas all came too, knowing that Rama's end was at hand. All the creatures gathered there greeted Rama and said, 'We have come here, illustrious king, so that we can go with you. Rama, bull among men, if you leave without us, you will have destroyed us as certainly as if you had struck us with Yama's staff.'

Rama spoke gently to Vibhishana and to the monkeys and bears. 'Vibhishana, you are the mighty lord of the rakshasas. You have to rule as long as there are citizens in Lanka. Protect your people with honour and do not question me further!'

Rama then said to Hanuman, 'You had decided to live on earth. Do not break that promise. As long as my story lives in the world, so long shall you live, best of monkeys. Keep your promise and fulfil my wish!'

Addressing the rest of the monkeys and bears, Rama said, 'You can come with me as you had wished.'

## Sarga 99: Rama's Departure from Ayodhya

Early the next morning Rama, with the broad chest and the lotus eyes, called for the priest and said, 'Let the sacred fires be lit. Make sure they are carried ahead of us on the highway, along with the white canopy.' Vasishtha ensured that all the rites and rituals for setting out on a great journey were performed correctly. Rama went forth wearing dazzling white clothes, carrying a bunch of kusha grass in his hand and uttering mantras to invoke Brahma. He left his home and walked down the road, shining like the sun. He did not speak to anyone or look at anything.

Shri walked on his left holding a lotus, the earth walked on his right and his own majesty walked in front of him. His great bow and arrows took human form and followed him. The Vedas appeared in the form of brahmins and Savitra, the protector of all, and the sacred syllables were also there. The great sages and brahmins followed Rama because the doors of heaven had been opened wide. All the women and children, the young and the old, the servants and retainers from the inner apartments came, too. Bharata and Shatrughna went along with their retinue and attendants. The sacred fires were carried in front and the brahmins walked behind them with their wives and children. The ministers and their families also came and the happy and prosperous citizens of Ayodhya followed their king, enthralled by his many virtues.

With immense delight, the people bathed and chattered and enjoyed themselves. No one was unhappy or wretched or miserable and it was a miracle that everyone was so happy. Even the people of the countryside, who had only come there to watch, decided to follow Rama to heaven. The monkeys, bears and rakshasas, the townspeople and the country folk walked behind Rama with calm and collected minds.

## Sarga 100: Rama Enters Vishnu

About half a mile from Ayodhya, Rama reached the river. He gazed upon the pure waters of the Sarayu as Brahma, the grandfather of the worlds, surrounded by the gods and the great-souled sages in their shining celestial vehicles, arrived at the place from where Rama was preparing to ascend to heaven. A rain of flowers fell and a pleasant breeze blew. The apsaras and gandharvas gathered in crowds and Rama stepped into the Sarayu.

Then Brahma spoke from the skies. 'Come Vishnu! May all be well with you! It is our great good fortune that you have arrived, Rama! Enter your own effulgent body along with your godlike brothers. Return to your essential nature as Vishnu. Or, enter the eternal ether. You are the last resort of the world, though there are some that would not recognize you, large-eyed one, without Maya, who has always been your companion. You are beyond thought, wondrous, indestructible and the totality of everything. Enter your own body, if that is what you wish!'

Wise Rama thought for a while after he heard Brahma's words and then, along with his brothers, he entered his own body which was Vishnu's effulgence. When the divine one had become Vishnu, all the gods with Indra and Agni at their head, the troops of maruts and the sadhyas worshipped him. The hosts of celestial sages, the gandharvas and the apsaras, the great birds, the serpents, the yakshas, daityas, danavas and rakshasas were thrilled. Filled with immeasurable happiness, they shouted 'Good! Good!' as all those who lived in the heavens were purified. Effulgent Vishnu then said to Brahma, 'We must provide for all these people who have followed me out of love. They are devoted to me and are willing to give up their lives for my sake.' 'They can all go to the realm known as Santanika,' said Brahma, teacher of the worlds. 'Any creature that gave up his life thinking of you and is devoted to Rama can live there. It is a wonderful place, second only to my own realm.'

The monkeys were reunited with the gods from whom they were born and the bears returned to the nagas and yakshas that had created them. The crowd moved to Gopratara on the banks of the Sarayu, their eyes filled with tears of joy. Humans who entered the waters happily were freed from their earthly bodies and climbed into celestial chariots. Even those that were in animal form, along with all the moving and unmoving creatures, assumed glorious divine bodies when they touched the waters of the Sarayu. With the bears and monkeys who had been born of the gods, they lived happily in the heavens. Brahma was pleased and he returned to the sky with the other gods.

This story, along with the Uttara, is honoured by Brahma. It is known as the Ramayana and was composed by Valmiki.

Vishnu, who pervades the three worlds, both the moving and unmoving beings, returned to heaven as before, and there the gods, gandharvas, the siddhas and the great sages would listen to this poem, the Ramayana, with great pleasure.

This story grants long life and good fortune, it destroys sins. The Ramayana is equal to the Vedas and is recited by the wise when we remember the ancestors. Those without sons shall gain sons, those without wealth shall gain wealth. Half a verse of this poem is sufficient to get rid of all sins. Even the man who sins daily will be purified if he reads a single verse. Anyone who recites this should be given clothes and cows and gold for if he is satisfied, all the gods are pleased. The man who recites the Ramayana, which grants long life, shall have sons and grandsons in this world and glory after death in the next. He who recites the Ramayana with concentration in the morning, at noon and at night shall never have problems.

The lovely city of Ayodhya will be deserted for a long time. It shall be revived when a king named Rishabha takes it.

This story, which grants long life, along with the Bhavishya and the Uttara, has been composed by the son of Prachetas and is sanctioned by Brahma.

# ESSAYS

# THE UTTARA KANDA AS A MAHAPURANA

Just as the Harivamsha provides a crucial epilogue to the Mahabharata, we could argue that the Uttara Kanda of Valmiki's Ramayana performs the same function. Each of these epilogues impinges retrospectively on the story that we have just received, forcing us to consider it anew.

The Harivamsha leaves us in no doubt about Krishna's essentially divine nature even as it creates a mortal lineage (vamsha) for him. It stitches together multiple (and possibly entirely disparate) Krishna narratives – the child in the villages around Mathura, the enchanting lover in Vrindavana and finally, the politicized prince of Dwarka, cousin to the Pandavas – and presents us with a seamless, composite Krishna, the avatara of Vishnu. The Harivamsha highlights the miraculous aspects of Krishna's life – the wondrous circumstances that surround him as well as the wondrous circumstances that he generates, whether it is lifting the mountain Govardhana, dancing with a hundred gopis at the same time or slicing off Shishupala's head with his discus in the Kaurava assembly. After the Harivamsha, we are bound to see all of Krishna's actions in the Mahabharata (and before), however troubling their consequences, as those of a god acting in the world of men to save dharma. And because these are the acts of a god, imbued with divine purpose, the ends justify the means. It matters little how many times Krishna violates the rules of war or how many times his actions are unethical, for their moral ambiguity is subsumed under Krishna's ultimate and righteous purpose, the restoration of dharma.

The stories of Krishna's life, the Mahabharata in particular, now become the most fundamental story that humans like to tell, that is, the story of good versus evil. Or – perhaps more accurately, in the case of Hindu stories – the confrontation between dharma and adharma. Classical Hinduism makes Vishnu appear on earth nine times to uphold dharma and save humankind. The Mahabharata's Harivamsha fits into that series of avatara narratives, as does the Uttara Kanda of Valmiki's Ramayana, which rounds off the idea of Vishnu-as-Rama acting in the human world to eliminate the adharma represented by Ravana.[18]

The ideas, tenor and vocabulary – indeed, the very theology of the Uttara Kanda – places the composition of this seventh book of what we call the Valmiki Ramayana in a time when the avatara theory was firmly established and possibly central to Hinduism. It is likely that this was a few hundred years after the middle books of the Valmiki Ramayana were compiled, perhaps around 300 CE. This was also the period when the earliest layers of the earliest Mahapuranas were put together. As sectarian Hinduism grew, changed and flourished during the first millennium CE, the relative significance of particular deities also fluctuated – and it is reasonable to argue that the Puranas represent the evolving and revolving importance of these deities. Since it is likely that the Harivamsha and the Uttara Kanda were contemporaneous with the early Puranas, it should come as no surprise that they resemble them in form and content and, most of all, in attitude. In their specific case, both the Harivamsha and the Uttara Kanda establish the supremacy of Vishnu in the pantheon and of his avataras in mythology.

---

[18] There is a most peculiar similarity between the Harivamsha and the Uttara Kanda, placing the divine Krishna and Rama in the service of brahmins. In the Uttara Kanda, a brahmin arrives at Rama's door, wailing that his young son has died for no reason. He says that this could only have happened if there was adharma somewhere in Rama's kingdom. Rama discovers that a shudra is practising austerities and he kills him. At once, the brahmin's son is restored to life. In the Harivamsha, a brahmin accuses Arjuna of not being able to protect his sons who keep getting taken away by malevolent forces. Arjuna, deeply humiliated, appeals to Krishna for help. After crossing the seven seas and a mountain of darkness, Krishna finds the brahmin's four sons and returns them to him.

Among other things, the classical Puranas remind us that the conflict between the gods and the anti-gods (that is, those who oppose the gods, be they rakshasas, asuras, daityas, danavas, or even humans) is constant and cyclical. Power shifts between the rulers of heaven and earth and the underworld. As the anti-gods take control of the three worlds, and they often do, the gods prepare to defeat them by any means necessary. When avataras enter the picture, defeating the anti-gods is no longer simply about regaining power – it becomes about restoring dharma, the hierarchical rules of action and behaviour by which everyone in the three worlds knows what they should do. But the Puranas also establish the fundamental pluralism of Hinduism – the same stories are told again and again from different perspectives. The gods rise and fall according to who is telling the story and, if you like, in the end, everything is really an illusion.

The Uttara Kanda of Valmiki's Ramayana spends its early chapters relating the history of Ravana's family to Rama. It is Agastya who tells these stories and we, along with Rama, are led to the understanding that generations of Ravana's family had been rapacious and aggressive. In this narrative, Vishnu has continuously fought the rakshasas led by Ravana's forebears, always coming to the rescue of gods and humans when rakshasas threaten to gain control of the three worlds. By creating this multi-generational, multi-yuga and essentially cyclical narrative, the Uttara Kanda elevates the story of the Ramayana to the cosmic level, to the eternal struggle for power between the gods and their opponents. Rama, Vishnu's current avatara, is merely doing what Vishnu has always done. With this new perspective, we lose the poignant particularity of Rama's story as it was before: in the books of the Valmiki Ramayana that precede the Uttara Kanda, we have a story of jealousy and betrayal, of love and loss, of lust and power that centres around very particular individuals, with Rama, Sita, Lakshmana and Ravana at its core. Until we encounter the Uttara Kanda, Rama and Sita's love story is unique to them, Lakshmana's devotion to his brother is his singular quality, Ravana's ill-advised abduction of Sita is because of his personal character and temperament. Once the Rama–Ravana conflict becomes just one more in a series of battles between the gods and demons of various kinds (rakshasas, daityas, danavas, asuras), we are forced to see the story as part of a cosmic cycle, a cycle most often depicted in the Puranas.

The Uttara Kanda story of Ravana's ancestors, in true Puranic style, starts far away from him in place and time. There was once a brahmin sage named Pulastya, a son of Prajapati, who was practising fierce austerities near the hermitage of Trinabindu, a royal sage. Trinabindu's daughter becomes accidentally pregnant by Pulastya and when her son is born, he is named Vishravas. Vishravas marries the daughter of the sage Bharadvaja and their son is named Vaishravana. Vaishravana grows up virtuous and noble and his penances attract the attention of Brahma, who offers him a boon. Vaishravana says that he would like to be one of the guardians of the four quarters. Brahma agrees and makes him the lord of wealth and gives him the magical flying chariot Pushpaka. Vaishravana's father sends him to live in the beautiful city of Lanka and soon, 'Lanka became prosperous and was filled with thousands of happy and contented rakshasas because of his rule'.[19]

Rama experiences the same confusion that we do when he hears about Vaishravana and Lanka.

> Rama shook his head and for a moment, he gazed at Agastya, whose body shone like the three fires on a sacrificial altar. He said, smiling, 'Blessed one, I was surprised to learn that Lanka already belonged to the flesh-eating rakshasas. We had heard that the rakshasas were born from the bloodline of Pulastya. Now you are suggesting a different origin for them. Were they more powerful even than Ravana, Kumbhakarna, Prahasta and Vikata? And Ravana's sons? Who was their ancestor, brahmin? What was his name and how strong was he? For what crime were they driven out so long ago by Vishnu? Relate all this to me in detail, flawless one. Dispel my curiosity as the sun dispels darkness.'[20]

Hearing Rama's elegant words, Agastya was surprised and he said to him,

> Prajapati Brahma, born from a lotus, created water and then created living beings to protect the waters. Living beings were tormented by hunger and thirst and they presented themselves humbly before Brahma and said, 'What shall we do?' Brahma smiled and said, 'Protect

[19] Sarga 3.

[20] Sarga 4.

> these waters!' Some of the hungry ones said, 'We shall protect', and others among them said, 'We shall worship!' Brahma, the Creator, said to them, 'Those that said that they would protect shall become rakshasas and those that said they would worship shall become yakshas!'[21]

Four generations after the rakshasas have been created by Brahma, the rakshasas Mali, Sumali and Malyavan are born, the sons of Sukesha.[22]

> They were as steady as the three worlds, as firm as the three fires on a sacrificial altar, as formidable as the sacred chants, as terrible as disease. Sukesha's sons blazed like the three fires and they grew quickly, like a disease that has been ignored. When they learned that their father had obtained his boons through great austerities, the brothers went to Mount Meru, determined to perform penances. The rakshasas accepted harsh rules, best of kings, and began their penance which terrified all living beings. They heated up the three worlds, the gods, the asuras and humans, by these practices and by truthfulness, self-control and good actions.
>
> Eternal Brahma, the four-faced one, arrived in a flying chariot and said to the rakshasas, 'I have come to offer you boons!' Realizing that Brahma, surrounded by Indra and the hosts of gods, was going to give them boons, the rakshasas shook like trees. They joined their palms

---

21 Sarga 4. As Wendy Doniger points out in a personal communication, this is an old story that appears in the Brahmanas.

22 Doniger also quotes a marvellous story from the Matsya Purana (*The Origins of Evil in Hindu Mythology*, University of California Press, 1976, pp.129–30) where the rakshasa Sukeshin (Sukesha) has been instructed by sages to practise his own dharma, that is, the dharma of a rakshasa, which also includes the worship of Shiva. Sukesha does this and spreads the word among his people, thus becoming the 'good' rakshasa, which leads to a series of problems and an eventual confrontation with the sun. Shiva has to intervene to restore the rakshasas and their city. With Ravana also being a devotee of Shiva, the idea that rakshasas worship Shiva makes them automatically oppositional to Vishnu and his avataras and followers. Just before Ravana challenges Kartavirya Arjuna to fight, there is an elaborate description of him and his ministers establishing a lingam on the banks of the Narmada and worshipping it with flowers. See Sarga 31.

in respect and said, 'If you are pleased with our austerities and wish to give us boons, then make us unbeatable, killers of our enemies and long-lived. Let us be superior to others and attached to one another.'

'It shall be so,' said Lord Brahma to Sukesha's sons. After that, Brahma, who loved brahmins, returned to his realm.

Then, Rama, when they received those boons which had made them fearless, the night-stalking rakshasas began to obstruct the gods and the asuras. The gods and the sages and the charanas were troubled but they could find no one anywhere who would protect them and they suffered like men in hell.[23]

Soon enough, the gods and sages find themselves under siege and appeal to Shiva to help them. Shiva sends them to ask Vishnu for help, because, 'He is the Lord, he will kill them.' It is interesting that Shiva appears in the story of the rakshasas as much as he does, mainly as a giver of boons, for he has made no other appearances in the Valmiki Ramayana up to now. Of course, he always sends the agitated and fearful gods to Vishnu, who then steps in to defeat the arrogant rakshasas who have been empowered by boons from both Shiva and Brahma. When the gods do approach Vishnu, they remind him of the other demons he has killed, Madhu and Kaitabha, and the text assumes that we (and Rama) already know of these killings. Further, the Uttara Kanda often refers to Vishnu as Janardana and Narayana, which adds to the Purana-like atmosphere of the final book of Valmiki's Ramayana.[24] When Malyavan hears that it is Vishnu who is coming to subdue them, he says to his brothers, 'Vishnu has promised the frightened gods that he will destroy us. What do you think would be appropriate? He has killed Hiranyakashipu and other enemies of the gods. It is not easy to defeat Vishnu who wants to kill us.'

A terrible battle ensues between the rakshasas on one side and Vishnu on the other. When he has finally defeated them, Agastya says to Rama,

---

[23] Sarga 5.

[24] There is an extreme instance of this in Sarga 6 where Vishnu is called Madhava (Krishna).

'And so it was, Rama, that the rakshasas were defeated several times in battle by lotus-eyed Vishnu and they lost many of their leaders. They left Lanka and went to live in the underworld with their wives, unable to face Vishnu in battle and tormented by fear. Those who were descended from Salakantaka and famous for their valour, joined the rakshasa Sumali. The rakshasas that you killed were all descendants of Pulastya. Mali, Sumali and Malyavan were all more fortunate and stronger than Ravana. No one other than Vishnu – the lord of the gods, Narayana, holder of the conch, the discus and the mace – could have killed those rakshasas. You are that four-armed god, the eternal Narayana, the invincible and imperishable lord, born to kill the rakshasas.'[25]

Again, as in the Puranas, the visual iconography of Vishnu as the one who holds the discus and the conch begins to appear more and more frequently in the Uttara Kanda, as do the epithets Narayana and Janardana.

As if it were not enough that Rama-as-Vishnu is bound to fight Ravana in this essentially Puranic universe, there is another story in the Uttara Kanda that brings Rama's mortal ancestors into the picture. Ravana, as he covers the earth demanding that kings confront him in battle, reaches Ayodhya, where he challenges King Aranyana. Aranyana's army is routed and eventually, the king himself falls from his chariot.

The rakshasa laughed at the Ikshvaku monarch and said, 'This is what you get for taking me on in combat! There is no one in the three worlds that can match me in a duel. Perhaps you did not hear of my strength because you were engaged in drunken pleasures.' The king, his voice fading, said, 'What can I do now? The march of time is inexorable. I was not defeated by you, rakshasa. You praise yourself. I have been felled by time, of which, good sir, you were only an instrument. What can I do now that my life is ebbing away? Because of what has happened to the Ikshvakus today, let me tell you something, rakshasa. If I have given gifts, if I have performed sacrifices, if I have done good deeds, if I have done penance, if I have ruled my people well, then let my words

[25] Sarga 8.

> come true. In this very family of the great-souled Ikshvakus, there shall be born a king of great energy who will take your life.' When that curse was uttered, flowers rained from the sky and drums sounded like the rumbling of thunder from the clouds. Then the king went to heaven and after he had departed, the rakshasa also went on his way.[26]

Aranyana's pronouncement joins a series of curses that Ravana will carry to his death.

After Vishnu has fought generations of rakshasas, we come to the moment at which Ravana and his siblings are born. Sumali comes up from the underworld, where the rakshasas have been driven (again, a Puranic idea that those who oppose the gods dwell in the underworld and are pushed back there after a defeat). He brings his daughter Kaikasi with him and encourages her to seek marriage with the son of Pulastya, the sage Vishravas.

> At that time, Rama, the brahmin son of Pulastya was performing the agnihotra sacrifice, blazing like the fourth fire. Concerned for her father's honour and unaware of the dark hour, the girl went and stood before him, looking down at her feet. When he saw that girl with the lovely hips, whose face was like the full moon, that magnanimous one, blazing like a fire, said, 'Whose daughter are you, my dear, and why have you come here? What is your purpose? Tell me truly, my pretty one.' The girl joined her palms and said, 'You should be able to guess why I am here with your powers. Know that I have come here on the orders of my father. My name is Kaikasi. You can know the rest.'
>
> The sage entered a state of contemplation and spoke. 'I can see what is in your heart, my dear. You have come to me at this dark hour, so listen, for you must know what kind of sons you will bear. They shall be dreadful – dreadful in appearance and friends with dreadful people. My lady with the lovely hips, you shall give birth to rakshasas of cruel deeds!' She bowed to him when she heard those words and she said,

[26] Sarga 19. This story carries narrative elements and tropes that are common in the Puranas, for example, the 'happy death' where the person knows that he is being liberated from life not by his killer, but by time. There is also the prediction that the killer's own death will occur in a particular way.

> 'Sons such as these cannot be born from a brahmin!' The sage replied, 'The last son that is born to you will be righteous, in conformity with my lineage.'
>
> In time, the girl gave birth to a dreadful creature who had the repulsive form of a rakshasa. He had ten heads and huge teeth, he was dark as collyrium, he had coppery lips and twenty arms, huge mouths and flaming hair. Jackals spewed flames from their mouths as he was born and carnivorous beasts circled him in the inauspicious direction. Indra rained blood and the clouds rumbled menacingly. The sun dimmed and huge meteors fell. His father, who was like Grandfather Brahma, named him. 'Since this one has ten heads, he shall be called Dashagriva!' Mighty Kumbhakarna was born next, the likes of whose enormous strength had never been known before. Then, the girl named Shurpanakha, with the hideous face, was born. Kaikasi's last son was the righteous Vibhishana.[27]

The Bala Kanda of Valmiki's Ramayana, the first book (also likely to have been composed in the Puranic period), makes doubly sure that Rama enters his story as no ordinary mortal. As the gods and other celestial beings had gathered to beseech Vishnu to save them from Ravana's ancestors, so too, they gather to beg Vishnu to save them from Ravana himself. Initially, they approach Brahma and say to him,

> 'Lord, the rakshasa Ravana obstructs us all because of the favours that he has received from you. He is strong and brave and none of us can subdue him. Long ago, when you were pleased with him, you gave him a boon and now we have to suffer this constant oppression ... We live in constant fear of that rakshasa who has a terrifying face. You must think of a way to kill Ravana!'
>
> Brahma thought for a while and then he said, 'There is a way to kill this dissolute creature. "May I be invulnerable to gods, gandharvas, yakshas and danavas!" were the words Ravana spoke and I replied that it would be so. He was contemptuous of humans in general and so he

[27] Sarga 9.

> did not ask for protection from them. Therefore, he can be killed only by a human being.' ... At that very moment, the effulgent Vishnu arrived at the gathering ... The gods praised him with hymns and songs and then they said to him, 'O Vishnu, we plead with you for the welfare of the three worlds! ... Become a human being and destroy Ravana, the enemy of the three worlds, for he cannot be killed by gods or divine beings in battle!' ...
>
> Praised by all the gods, Vishnu humbly asked them a question, although he already knew the answer. 'How can this king of the rakshasas be killed? Tell me and I will use that very method to kill this creature who torments the rishis!'
>
> The gods cried out together, 'Be born as the son of a mortal woman and kill him in battle! ... In the old days, Ravana scorned humans and so he did not include them in his boon of invulnerability. O enemy-burner, Ravana can only be killed by a human.' Vishnu considered the words of the gods and decided to choose King Dasharatha as his father.[28]

The other gods are persuaded to help make Vishnu's enterprise a success.

> When Vishnu had become the offspring of the great-souled Dasharatha, Brahma addressed the other gods. 'Heroic Vishnu, the ocean of truth, desires what is best for us all. You should create mighty beings who can change their shape at will in order to help him ...
>
> 'Beget sons upon the apsaras and gandharvis, upon the daughters of the yakshas and the pannagas, the rakshas and the vidyadharas, upon kinnaris and vanaris. Let them have the form of monkeys and let them be equal to yourselves in valour!'
>
> ...
>
> The gods followed Brahma's instructions and created sons in the form of monkeys. The great-souled rishis, the siddhas and the uragas also ensured that mighty sons were born to creatures that lived in the forest ...

---

28 Sattar, *Valmiki's Ramayana*, chap. 4.

> These heroic warriors, who could change form at will, were created in the thousands for the purpose of killing Ravana and they were unmatched in strength, courage and valour.[29]

Once again, the involvement of all the gods serves to underline the cosmic nature of the conflict between Rama and Ravana. When we view the Bala Kanda and Uttara Kanda as Puranic, we are able to understand why there is such a marked difference between these and the middle books of the Valmiki Ramayana, not just in style and language, but also in intent and purpose. It is in these first and last books that Rama's divinity is unequivocally declared, something of which the middle books are less sure. Once again, the elevation to divinity and the reconfiguring of the conflict as a cosmic one does much to depersonalize Rama's troubles and his triumphs. But, in doing so, the elevation introduces another layer of interpretation and participation for us – we now have to contend with what it means for a god to come to earth. How would s/he act if s/he were faced with what it means to be human? What does it mean to be good? To do good? How does a god answer these questions in her/his actions, speech and thought? The fact that there are more Rama stories where he is a god must lead us to consider that Hindu culture finds the story of the divine (however flawed or problematic) on earth more compelling than the one about a human who tries to be perfect.

---

[29] Sattar, *Valmiki's Ramayana*, chap. 4.

# THE STORY OF RAVANA

The Uttara Kanda could almost be thought of as Ravana's book because it is his story and the story of his ancestors that dominates the narrative. Of course, all the stories that are told about Ravana in the Uttara Kanda serve the kanda's larger agenda, which is to make sure that there are no questions left unanswered about how and why things happened the way they did. Other essays in this volume make the point that the Uttara Kanda is the book of overdetermination, where multiple and infallible reasons are provided for events and actions. Ravana, too, is wrapped in a tapestry of curses that ensure he will die. But the curses he carries with him also explain why he did not touch Sita while she was in captivity.

Because Ravana has to remain the antagonist, his attitude towards Sita and the fact that she remains unharmed in Lanka can have nothing to do with his inherent nobility. Rather, Sita's safety is guaranteed by the curses that several women before her have already placed on Ravana.

## Ravana's Women

In the Valmiki Ramayana, although Ravana torments Sita and threatens her and cajoles her and tries to persuade her that he is a better consort than her exiled husband, he never touches her after he has abducted her.

After the harrowing ride through the air in Pushpaka held fast in Ravana's arms, Sita remains inviolate for all the time that she is in captivity. There is a poignant moment when, after Ravana has tried to seduce her with accounts of his wealth and power, Sita places a single blade of grass between herself and her abductor, as if daring him to cross that line. The innocuous blade is imbued with a power that exists only in her imagination. As Sita tells Hanuman, there had been a moment in the forest when she, wet from her bath in the river, was attacked by a crow who pecked her on her breast. Rama saw her fear and picked a blade of kusha grass. He breathed a mantra over it and sent it after the crow who sought refuge from it in all the three worlds but eventually, came back to Rama for protection. Because Rama could not recall the mantra, he sent the blade of grass into the crow's eye, blinding it. Sita sends this story back to Rama as a message with Hanuman, reminding him that if he could bear such anger towards a mere crow, how much more would he bear towards Ravana. But Sita does not know – as none of us do at that point in the story – that Ravana keeps away from her for reasons far more deadly than her faith in her husband and a blade of grass.

The Uttara Kanda takes great pleasure in telling stories about the number of women that Ravana violated, each one of them adding to the reasons for his leaving Sita unmolested because each encounter left him with karmic residue, if not an outright curse. Once again, the text is answering the question that needs to be asked: if Ravana was, indeed, so very villainous, if he was a rapacious rakshasa (as he should be, given the nature of all rakshasas), why did he not take advantage of Sita's vulnerability when she was captive in Lanka? Why did he not force himself upon her? Yet again, these are questions for the Valmiki Ramayana more than they are for any other tellings of Rama's story. With bhakti producing its own series of narrative overdeterminations, Rama's apotheosis also elevates Sita to the status of a goddess and then, her own power is enough to keep Ravana at arm's length.

When the Uttara Kanda opens, we, along with Rama, begin to hear about Ravana's forefathers as soon as the sages arrive at his court. Rama is surprised that the sages single out Indrajit for special praise and asks why that is the case. In reply, Agastya begins the story of Ravana's great-grandfather, Pulastya, who was a brahmin, a son of Prajapati. Pulastya declares that any woman who comes within his line of sight in the grove where he is meditating will become pregnant. Trinabindu's daughter does not know this and so becomes unwittingly pregnant and then, is married off to Pulastya.

She produces a marvellous son called Vishravas who becomes a sage. The rakshasa Sumali urges his daughter to approach Vishravas and offer herself to him because, like all daughters, she has become a burden to her father.

> 'Being the father of a daughter is the greatest of all worries for those who seek respect, for you never know who will accept your daughter in marriage. An unmarried daughter causes uncertainty in three families – her father's, her mother's and the family into which she will be married. Go, then, my daughter, to Vishravas, the best of sages, born in the line of Prajapati, descendant of Pulastya. Choose him for yourself. Undoubtedly, my daughter, you will have sons like him. He is the lord of wealth and equal to the sun in brightness.'
>
> At that time, Rama, the brahmin son of Pulastya was performing the agnihotra, blazing like the fourth fire. Concerned for her father's honour and unaware of the dark hour, the girl went and stood before him, looking down at her feet. When he saw that girl with the lovely hips, whose face was like the full moon, that magnanimous one, blazing like a fire, said, 'Whose daughter are you, my dear, and why have you come here? What is your purpose? Tell me truly, my pretty one.' The girl joined her palms and said, 'You should be able to guess why I am here with your powers. Know that I have come here on the orders of my father. My name is Kaikasi. You can know the rest.'
>
> The sage entered a state of contemplation and spoke. 'I can see what is in your heart, my dear. You have come to me at this dark hour, so listen, for you must know what kind of sons you will bear. They shall be dreadful – dreadful in appearance and friends with dreadful people. My lady with the lovely hips, you shall give birth to rakshasas of cruel deeds!' She bowed to him when she heard those words and she said, 'Sons such as these cannot be born from a brahmin!' The sage replied, 'The last son that is born to you will be righteous, in conformity with my lineage.'
>
> In time, the girl gave birth to a dreadful creature who had the repulsive form of a rakshasa. He had ten heads and huge teeth, he was dark as collyrium, he had coppery lips and twenty arms, huge mouths and flaming hair. Jackals spewed flames from their mouths as he was

> born and carnivorous beasts circled him in the inauspicious direction. Indra rained blood and the clouds rumbled menacingly. The sun dimmed and huge meteors fell. His father, who was like Grandfather Brahma, named him. 'Since this one has ten heads, he shall be called Dashagriva!'[30]

In the Uttara Kanda, Ravana grows up tempestuous and volatile. Through the focused and unwavering practise of austerities, he makes himself practically invincible and then, sets about to become the most powerful and feared creature in the three worlds. His quest for world domination is carried out by defeating kings and capturing and/or having sex with women. Vishravas's brahmin nature is inherited entirely by Vibhishana, leaving Ravana to live out the rakshasa temperament he gets from his mother's side of the family. Apart from a propensity to war and arrogance, this temperament (or, arguably, this dharma) is most conspicuously displayed in his interactions with women, well before he abducts Sita.

> As he returned home well pleased, wicked Ravana captured the daughters of the gods, sages and gandharvas along the way. In his vehicle, the rakshasa imprisoned women and virgin girls whom he found attractive, after killing their families. Ravana took the young women of the pannagas, yakshas, humans and rakshasas, of the danavas and the daityas. They had long hair and comely limbs, their faces were like full moons, their breasts heavy. All those young women were stricken with grief. They trembled and were overcome with sorrow. They shed tears which were like fire, born as they were from the fires of grief and fear. Pushpaka blazed on all sides with the fire of their sighs and appeared like a fire altar holding the sacrificial fires within it. Some of those virtuous, sorrow-laden women wondered if they would be eaten, others if they would be killed. They remembered their mothers and fathers and brothers and sons and their sisters and, overwhelmed with sorrow, they wailed together:

---

30 Sarga 9.

'What must my son be doing without me? And what of my mother and brother, who are drowning in an ocean of sorrow?'

'How will I live without my godlike husband! Ah, death, I beg you, take me to Yama's realm!'

'What bad deeds did I commit before, in another body? I am a fallen woman, sunk into this ocean of grief!'

'At the moment, I see no end to this sorrow. Damn this world of men, there is nothing lower than this!'

'Our families are destroyed in front of Ravana's strength, weak like stars before the rising sun.'

'This mighty rakshasa who invents new methods of destruction! He behaves so badly but does not realize it.'

'He is as powerful as he is wicked. But taking the wives of others in this way is not appropriate.'

'This perverted fellow delights in the wives of others, he is sure to be killed because of a woman's actions.'

Ravana's lustre dimmed and his energy was depleted when he was cursed by the women who were devoted to their husbands and who were firm in their goodness. Even as they lamented, Ravana, the king of the rakshasas, entered the city of Lanka and was honoured by the night-stalking rakshasas.[31]

The episode with the abducted women points us back to two other incidents in the Uttara Kanda with individual women which have already occurred and which seal Ravana's fate. After conquering many kings, Ravana decides to take on his own half-brother Kubera, the virtuous lord of wealth and

[31] Sarga 24. This passage seems to speak directly to Valmiki's Sundara Kanda, where, as Hanuman searches for Sita in Ravana's private apartments, he sees innumerable beautiful women. 'With Ravana peacefully asleep, it seemed as if the golden lamps watched over those splendid women with fixed, unblinking eyes. There were women from the families of royal sages, daityas, gandharvas and rakshasas and they had all come to Ravana out of love. None had been carried away against her will, they had all been won over by Ravana's personality. None had ever loved another or been the wife of another, none except Sita, the daughter of Janaka.' Sattar, *Valmiki's Ramayana*, chap. 46.

guardian of one of the four quarters of the earth. He defeats him and his army of yakshas soundly and then, he takes from him Pushpaka, the magical flying chariot, as part of the spoils of victory. Now, Ravana wanders the earth even more freely than before and reaches the Himalayas. Agastya says to Rama:

> 'And so, your majesty, mighty Ravana roamed the earth. When he arrived at the forests of the Himalayas, he wandered around. He saw a young woman who was wearing an antelope skin and had matted locks. She was practising austerities fit for the sages and she was shining like a goddess. He looked at that beautiful woman of great vows and he was overcome with desire. Laughing, he asked her, "What are you doing, my pretty lady, contradicting your youth in this manner? Your actions are in contrast to your beauty. Whose daughter are you, pretty one? You are flawless, who is your husband? I ask you and so tell me quickly, what is the purpose of these austerities?"
>
> 'Addressed by the ignoble rakshasa, that girl, rich in austerities, welcomed him appropriately and said, "My father is named Kushadhvaja and he is righteous, a brahmin sage. He is the son of Brihaspati and equal to him in wisdom. He is constantly engaged in the study of the Vedas and since I was born to him through them, I am called Vedavati. The gods, gandharvas, yakshas, rakshasas and pannagas have all been to my father to ask for me in marriage. But my father did not give me to any of them, lord of the rakshasas. I will tell you the reason for that. Listen, strong-armed one. My father wanted only Vishnu, best of the gods, lord of the three worlds, as a son-in-law. And so he would not give me to anyone else. A wicked daitya named Shambhu, who was arrogant because of his strength, heard about this and wanted me. He grew angry and one night, while my father slept, he killed him. My illustrious mother pathetically embraced my father's body and entered the fire with him. I have placed Vishnu in my heart since then so that I can carry out my father's wishes in that regard. I want to fulfil the wishes of my dear father and so I have embarked on this vow and have undertaken these austerities. I have told you everything, bull among rakshasas. I want to take shelter in Vishnu as my husband. Go now. I

also know who you are, son of Pulastya. I know everything that happens in the three worlds because of my austerities."

'Struck by the arrows of the god of love, Ravana climbed down from his chariot and spoke to that girl of great vows. "Lady, you have lovely hips, but you are arrogant, indeed, to have made up your mind thus. Such austerities that create merit are for the elderly, doe-eyed girl. You are rich in all the virtues, it is not right for you to behave like this. You are the most beautiful woman in the three worlds. Your youth is slipping away, my timid one! Who is this Vishnu that you speak of? He cannot compare with me in valour or austerities or pleasures or strength, pretty lady. I want you."

'"Stop this, stop this!" said the girl to the night-ranging rakshasa. The rakshasa grabbed her harshly by the hair. Vedavati was enraged. She cut off her hair with her hand and created a fire in order to kill herself. She said, "Ignoble creature! I do not wish to live because of the way you have insulted me. Watch me, rakshasa, as I enter this fire! I shall be born again for your destruction because you have humiliated me, a woman without protection and in danger. A woman cannot kill a man, even if he is wicked. And if I curse you, I will use up the power I have gained from my austerities. If I have done anything good, given gifts, sacrificed to the fire, I shall be the daughter of a righteous man, but I shall not be born of a female womb." She entered the blazing fire and a rain of flowers fell from the heavens.

'You, Rama, were able to kill the enemy because of her anger,' said Agastya. 'You have taken refuge in the form of a heroic man. In the same way, this illustrious woman has appeared among men again. She has emerged from a field that is being ploughed, blazing like the fire on a sacrificial altar. Her name is Vedavati in the Krita Yuga. In the Treta Yuga, born for the destruction of that rakshasa, men have called her Sita because she was born from a furrow.'[32]

In this episode, we see a reversal of the sage–apsara trope that is so common in Hindu mythology. Here, it is the woman who is celibate and practising the

[32] Sarga 17.

austerities that will increase her power and it is the male who is the seducer, or, as in this case, the potential violator. Vedavati has appropriated all the external signs that we usually associate with male ascetics, the antelope skin and the matted hair. And it is also clear that her ascetic practice is most unusual for a woman. Ravana seems to be attracted as much by her determination and her unlikely demeanour as he is by her ravishing looks. He is also intrigued by the juxtaposition of opposites: a young and beautiful woman wilfully denying her youth and beauty as she imitates the behaviour of a renunciant. Vedavati explains herself to Ravana and tells him that she is, in fact, waiting for another husband to claim her. Ravana is not deterred by her words or by her actions or the idea of a husband in the wings. He mocks her even as he demands that she surrender to him. When she resists him, he grabs her by the hair. She cuts off her hair with her hand and as she leaps into the fire to escape Ravana, she curses him. Or rather, she vows to be reborn for his destruction but not from a human womb. Agastya explains to Rama (and to us) that Vedavati returns in the Treta Yuga as Sita, born from a furrow that King Janaka ploughed.

Vedavati's story, in many ways, replicates Sita's. To begin with, like Sita, Vedavati suggests that she, too, has a non-human birth (she was born to her father 'through' the Vedas, hence her name). Vedavati jumps into the fire to preserve her chastity; and at the end of the war, it is Sita who enters the fire to prove hers. The woman ascetic and the male aggressor is a feature of both episodes, Sita being a forest dweller when Ravana abducts her and very much the solitary renunciant when she is in captivity. But there is another element of replication in these parallel narratives, one that elevates both stories and their actors to a cosmic level. The husband that Vedavati is waiting for in the Krita Yuga is Vishnu while in the Treta Yuga, Sita's husband is Rama (who is Vishnu in the Uttara Kanda). In both these cases, it is Ravana who tries to violate her.[33]

This is the first of the stories of overdetermination that explain Ravana's defeat. But it is Ravana's practically incestuous rape of the apsara Rambha

---

33 The fact that Ravana takes Vedavati away, as it were, from Vishnu is also part of the cycle of Uttara Kanda stories that places the conflict between Rama and Ravana on a cosmic level, a conflict that has causes and effects over individual lifetimes and yugas. See the essay on the Uttara Kanda as a Mahapurana in this volume for more on this.

which more explicitly addresses why he did not assault Sita. Ravana comes to Kailasha again, the lower reaches of which are guarded by his brother Kubera and his yakshas. He settles there to rest, enraptured by the serene beauty of the region.

> At that very moment, Rambha arrived there. She was the best of all the apsaras. Her face was like the full moon and she was adorned with celestial flowers. Decorated with special designs of fresh flowers from all six seasons, she was veiled in a cloth as blue-black as a rain cloud. Her face was like the moon, her brows like beautiful bows, her thighs like an elephant's trunk, her hands like blooming lotuses. Ravana saw her as she passed through the army camp. The rakshasa king, overwhelmed by the arrows of love, rose and grabbed her by the hand as she walked shyly by. He smiled and said, 'Where are you going, my lovely? What have you planned for yourself? Whose lucky time has come, that he gets to enjoy you? Who are you going to satisfy tonight, who shall drink the nectar of your lips fragrant with lotus and lily? Who shall touch these breasts of yours, my pretty one, like golden urns and so tightly pressed together? Your hips are lovely, wide as a golden circle themselves and encircled by a golden belt. Who shall mount into these heavens tonight? There is no one more virile than me – not Indra, not Vishnu and not the ashvins. It is not good, pretty one, that you try to go past me! Rest here, on this beautiful rock, wide-hipped lady. I alone am the lord of the three worlds, there is no one that compares with me. Ten-headed Ravana, lord of the three worlds, pleads with you like this, with his palms joined. Accept me!'
>
> Rambha trembled and clasped her hands together. She replied, 'I beg you, do not speak to me in this way. You are my elder! You should protect me from others if I am sexually assaulted, for by rights, I am your daughter-in-law. What I am saying is the truth!' As she stood there with her head bowed low, Ravana said to her, 'You are my daughter-in-law only if you are my son's wife.'
>
> 'It is true,' Rambha replied to Ravana. 'Bull among rakshasas, I am legally the wife of your son. The son of Vaishravana, your brother, is dearer to him than his own life. He is known in the three worlds as

Nalakubara. He is like a brahmin in his righteousness, but he is like a kshatriya in valour. He is like the fire when he is angry but like the earth in his patience. I have made an appointment with the son of Vaishravana Kubera, the guardian of the quarters. I have adorned myself in this way with him in mind. He is attached to no one but me and likewise, I am to him. For this truth alone, king, you should release me, scorcher of enemies! Righteous Nalakubara is eagerly waiting for me. Do not come in the way of your son. Let me go! Bull among rakshasas, walk the path trodden by good men. You are worthy of my respect, and I am worthy of your protection!'

Overcome with lust, the mighty rakshasa mocked Rambha's righteous words. Inflamed by passion and desire, he violated her. When he let her go, Rambha's flower decorations were torn and she was agitated, like a river in which an elephant has played. Trembling, shamed and terrified, she went to Nalakubara. She fell at his feet with her palms joined. Great Nalakubara saw the state that she was in and he said to her, 'What is this, my lovely? Why have you fallen at my feet?' Sighing and trembling, she told him everything exactly as it had happened. 'Lord, ten-headed Ravana is on his tour of the three worlds. He has camped here along with his army. He saw me passing by as I was coming to you. He grabbed me and asked me whom I belonged to, scorcher of enemies. I told him everything exactly as it was but because he was overcome with passion, he did not hear anything I had said. My lord, I pleaded with him saying I am your daughter-in-law. But he put that aside and he raped me violently. You must forgive me for this transgression, destroyer of pride. A woman's strength does not match up to a man's!'

Vaishravana's son was enraged when he heard that. He put himself into a trance and meditated on what she had told him. In a moment, he saw what had happened. His eyes red with anger, he took some water in his hand. He sprinkled it around, according to custom, and then he unleashed a terrible curse upon the king of the rakshasas.

'My dear, because he took you violently against your will, he can never approach another young woman against her will. His head will split into seven pieces if he ever sexually violates another woman!'

> When this terrible curse, which was like a blazing fire, was uttered, celestial drums sounded and flowers rained from the sky. All the gods, with Prajapati Brahma at their head, rejoiced, recognizing the destiny of the worlds and the death of the rakshasa. Ravana lost interest in having sex with women who did not desire him when he heard that hair-raising curse.[34]

How much more overt, more brimming with desire, more steeped in power, more violent is this episode with Rambha compared to Ravana's harassment of Vedavati. It is for these reasons that the curse that follows his rape of Rambha is as severe as it is. And just in case we missed the point, the curse (that Ravana's head would explode if he touched another woman against her will) is celebrated from the heavens with a rain of celestial flowers and the story ends with Ravana's renunciation of 'sex with women who did not desire him'. The incestuous overlay of Rambha being Ravana's daughter-in-law is an overstatement in terms of how transgressive this act already is.

However, despite the state of emotional agitation and physical distress in which Rambha meets her husband, Nalakubara feels the need to go into a meditative trance before he can believe her and unleash his wrath upon his uncle Ravana. It is also hard to ignore the fact that it is not Rambha who curses her rapist, it is her husband who does that. In that one moment, the story goes from being primarily about the rightful punishment for Ravana's habitual sexual aggression, the violation of Rambha and her reaction to it, to being, in fact, the story of Rambha's husband and his honour.

Taking into account the larger context in which this story is told, we can see that once again, it is actually Rama who is being persuaded by the brahmins around him – Agastya, in particular – that a married woman's chastity is the fulcrum upon which a man's honour is balanced.

## Ravana's Other Curses

The curses from the women ensure that Ravana stays away from Sita but they do not make his death inevitable. There is another series of curses that

34 Sarga 26.

ensure not only that Ravana is killed, but that he is killed by Rama and his monkey allies.

As Ravana pursues his conquest of the kings on earth, he reaches Ayodhya.

> Ravana, king of the rakshasas, approached Ayodhya which was well protected by Aranyana the way Amaravati is by Indra. He went to the king and said, 'Give me battle or declare, "I have been defeated." This is my command.' Enraged, Aranyana said to the king of the rakshasas, 'I'll give you single combat, you rakshasa king!' Since Aranyana had already heard about Ravana, he had prepared an enormous army. The king's army came forth, eager to kill the rakshasa. With many thousands of elephants and horses and chariot-warriors and foot soldiers, the army covered the earth in a moment. But when the king's army encountered Ravana's army, it was consumed like offerings in a sacrificial fire.
>
> The king watched his great army dissolve, like rivers rushing into an ocean. In anger, he twanged his bow, which was like Indra's, and he came close to Ravana. He released eight hundred arrows on to the head of the king of the rakshasas. But the arrows that struck bothered him not a whit and were like a shower of rain upon a mountain. Then, in anger, the king of the rakshasas struck the king on his head with his palm and the king toppled from his chariot. Stunned and trembling, he fell from his chariot like a great sala tree in the forest struck by lightning.
>
> The rakshasa laughed at the Ikshvaku monarch and said, 'This is what you get for taking me on in combat! There is no one in the three worlds that can match me in a duel. Perhaps you did not hear of my strength because you were engaged in drunken pleasures.' The king, his voice fading, said, 'What can I do now? The march of time is inexorable. I was not defeated by you, rakshasa. You praise yourself. I have been felled by time, of which, good sir, you were only an instrument. What can I do now that my life is ebbing away? Because of what has happened to the Ikshvakus today, let me tell you something, rakshasa. If I have given gifts, if I have performed sacrifices, if I have done good deeds, if

> I have done penance, if I have ruled my people well, then let my words come true. In this very family of the great-souled Ikshvakus, there shall be born a king of great energy who will take your life.' When that curse was uttered, flowers rained from the sky and drums sounded like the rumbling of thunder from the clouds.[35]

Of course, that descendant is Rama. But what of the ragtag army of monkeys and bears that Rama brings with him to Lanka? How could those root-and-fruit-eating forest dwellers have defeated the mighty rakshasas? The Uttara Kanda makes sure we know how that could have happened.

One day, Ravana was wandering at will in his magical Pushpaka when all of a sudden, it could go no further.

> When the chariot stopped, surrounded by his ministers, the rakshasa wondered, 'How can this chariot, which moves according to the wishes of its owner, have stopped? Why is it not going any further? Why has it stopped against my will? What could be on this mountain that has stopped it?'
>
> Maricha, who was wise and knowledgeable, said to Ravana, 'There must be a reason why Pushpaka is not going forward.' Then, mighty Nandi, Shiva's retainer, approached them confidently from the side and said to the king of the rakshasas, 'Turn back, Ravana! Shiva is frolicking on this mountain! Birds and serpents, yakshas, daityas, danavas or rakshasas – no living beings can access this place!' Enraged, his eyes coppery with anger, Ravana dismounted from Pushpaka and stood at the base of the mountain. 'Who is this Shiva?' he said. He saw Nandi standing by the god's side, holding a shining spear and looking like a second Shiva. The rakshasa noticed that he had the face of a monkey and he mocked him and laughed like a thundering rain cloud. Blessed Nandi, who was not separate from Shiva's body, grew angry. He said, 'Wicked rakshasa! You saw my monkey form and you had contempt for me. You laughed at me, in your folly. Because of that, monkeys will be born for the destruction of your clan. They shall have my form, my

[35] Sarga 19.

energy and my valour. I could kill you right now, but I will not, for you are already slain by your own deeds!'[36]

The bizarre end that Nandi's curse forces on to Ravana's own life and the destruction of his people takes away our pleasure in a narrative of such wonders and magic that monkeys with stones and tree trunks could have triumphed over rakshasa weaponry and fighting skills. The curse also points back to what we already know from the Bala Kanda (another later addition to what we call the Valmiki Ramayana) – that when Vishnu was persuaded to come to earth as Rama in order to destroy Ravana, the gods who appealed to him for help themselves created splendid sons on monkeys and bears. In yet another moment of anxiety, the Uttara Kanda doubles the ante for majestic Ravana's defeat by assuring us that it was not simply possible, but that it was inevitable.

Through these stories, we are reminded that fundamentally, it is Ravana's rakshasa nature that is the cause of his ultimate defeat since it is his arrogance that leads Nandi to curse him. This inherent rakshasa nature is also the reason for his collecting a series of curses from and related to women. Vedavati curses him because he cannot contain his sexual desire and assaults her. Nalakubara's curse is because of Ravana's rape of Rambha. It is this same rakshasa nature that propels him to abduct Sita.

As discussed at greater length in the essay on the Uttara Kanda as a Mahapurana, Ravana's behaviour in the Uttara Kanda is placed in a long series of aggressions and transgressions by the rakshasas of Lanka, his forebears. By creating this context, the Uttara Kanda attempts to draw a picture of the essential nature of the rakshasas – they are greedy, warlike, driven by a lust for power and, in the case of Ravana in particular, simply by lust. They use the boons they receive from the gods for self-aggrandizement

---

[36] Sarga 16. We are more used to thinking of Shiva's Nandi as a bull. In fact, all representations of Nandi are in that form. It is odd that the Uttara Kanda chooses to make a monkey of him. We can assume that it was only to create a curse whereby monkeys would be responsible for the destruction of Ravana's people, if not for the death of Ravana himself. Coming from Shiva's attendant, Nandi's curse also strikes a blow at the idea of Ravana as a privileged devotee of Shiva, a position that is articulated in many para-Ramayana stories about Ravana.

and not to establish the rule of dharma in the three worlds. It has often been noted by both readers and scholars that the rakshasas of the Ramayana are not like other rakshasas, the ones that we meet in the Mahabharata, for example, or those in other Puranas. Yes, there are misshapen and terrifying rakshasis that guard Sita in Lanka and Shurpanakha and Kumbhakarna are monstrous. But Ravana himself is charismatic and powerful, ruling over a kingdom that is prosperous and orderly. Vibhishana studies the Vedas and is attracted to a dharma of truth and justice, as it were. Indrajit is a warrior of elegance and grace and not a brutish fighter like other rakshasas. Hanuman's first impression of the rakshasas of Lanka mirrors our surprise.

When Hanuman reaches Lanka in the Sundara Kanda, this is what he sees.

> Hanuman could sense the pride the rakshasas had in their strength and heroism ... Hanuman saw rakshasas who were among the most intelligent of all beings, others who were devout and pious and those who were eloquent and learned. He was delighted to see that some of them were handsome and virtuous and followed the rules of good conduct. But he also saw rakshasas who were ugly and deformed and seemed to have wicked ways.[37]

The sight of Ravana leaves him even more wonderstruck. After Hanuman has set Lanka on fire, he is captured and taken before the king.

> Ravana blazed with his own splendour and with the brilliance of his golden crown which was studded with pearls. His jewels were dazzling and he wore the finest silks. His body was anointed with rare red sandal paste. He sat upon a crystal throne inlaid with diamonds. As Hanuman gazed at him in wonder, the rakshasa king reminded him of a rain cloud on the peaks of Mount Meru. Though the rakshasas had beaten Hanuman badly, he could not help but be impressed by their king. He was stunned by his glory and effulgence.
>
> 'How magnificent he is!' thought Hanuman. 'What beauty, what courage, what grace! He has all the signs of a great king! Had he not

---

[37] Sattar, *Valmiki's Ramayana*, chap. 46.

been so unrighteous, he may well have been the protector of the world, of the heavens, even of Indra himself!'[38]

Clearly, the rakshasas of Lanka are a far cry from the ones that we are more familiar with from other texts and stories – who live in the forest, who are gigantic, often hairy, who gain their powers at night and are hostile and dangerous to other creatures. In a sense, Hanuman puts his finger on it when he says that if Ravana had not been so unrighteous, he would have been admirable and heroic.

The Uttara Kanda sets out to emphasize this more general unrighteousness, for otherwise we might have some sympathy for the mighty monarch who was destroyed because of a single impulsive transgressive act – stealing the wife of another man. The Uttara Kanda sets itself the task of a crucial narrative correction, which is that Ravana and his forebears were quintessentially rakshasic. The more rakshasa-like Ravana becomes, the more appropriate he is as an opponent for Rama-as-Vishnu and the more important it becomes that he be killed.

[38] Sattar, *Valmiki's Ramayana*, chap. 51.

# THE BANISHMENT OF SITA

The banishment of the pregnant Sita into the forest is surely one of the most poignant moments in the Ramayana. In the Valmiki text, it occurs in the middle of the Uttara Kanda at a seemingly tranquil time when, after his coronation, Rama has been absorbed in stories about the exploits of Ravana and other beings that he has encountered in the course of his previous adventures. The stories are being told to him by various sages, chief among them being Agastya. Often, the stories are triggered by a question, by Rama's curiosity about why things were the way they were or how someone had been defeated. After a number of these tales have been told, Rama dismisses the monkeys and bears who had followed him to Ayodhya. In the same way that he had honoured the kings who had attended his coronation with gifts, Rama is generous in his presents to his allies as well. There are tearful farewells, but the forest dwellers return to their own lands. At that very moment, there is a voice from the sky. Pushpaka, the wondrous flying vehicle, has returned, pleading to be in Rama's service now that it has been released by Kubera. Rama honours the vehicle and sends it away promising to call it when needed. Rama then listens with pleasure to his brother Bharata's report that during his month as ruler of Ayodhya, his kingdom has prospered, his people are healthy and happy and they wish for his long and successful reign.

Rama retires to his pleasure gardens with Sita where they eat and drink and are entertained with music and dance. Between these pleasures, both Rama and Sita attend to their duties, religious and secular. Sita takes care of her mothers-in-law and Rama attends to matters of state. Very soon, Sita is pregnant and Rama is delighted, promising to fulfil her every wish. She asks that she be allowed to visit the sages in the forest, to spend a night with them and eat only roots and fruits, reliving the simple joys of their time away from the city.

Rama goes to his court where his advisers and others in his royal retinue are waiting for him. They, too, tell him amusing stories and Rama says to one of them,

> 'What do they talk about in the city, Bhadra? The city dwellers and those that live in the country, what do they say? About me? About Sita? And Bharata and Lakshmana? What about Shatrughna and my mother Kaikeyi? For kings are criticized when they are new rulers.'
>
> Bhadra joined his palms and said, 'The citizens speak highly of you, king. Dear sir, bull among men, both the people of the city and those of the country talk a lot about your victory over ten-headed Ravana.'
>
> Rama said to Bhadra, 'Tell me everything as it is, without omitting anything. Tell me the good and the bad things that are being said by the citizens. There are those who want to hear only the good and not the bad. Speak to me with confidence, without fear or anxiety. Tell me exactly what the city dwellers and the country folk are saying.'[39]

It is possible that Rama has been emboldened to ask for the truth because he has only recently heard glowing reports from his brother about the state of the kingdom and his people's contentment. Whether or not that is the case, Rama is clearly not prepared for what he hears next.

> Bhadra joined his palms and with a steady mind, he said to radiant Rama, 'Listen, king, to what the citizens are saying, the good and the bad, on the streets and in the markets, in the forests and in gardens. "Rama did a difficult thing when he built the bridge over the ocean, such a thing had never been done before, not even by the gods and the danavas. He destroyed invincible Ravana along with his army and his

[39] Sarga 42.

chariots. And he brought the monkeys and bears under his control, along with the rakshasas. He killed Ravana in battle and he brought Sita back. He turned his back on anger and led her into his own house. How could he take Sita back into his heart? How could he enjoy pleasures with her when she had been snatched from him by Ravana and had even sat on his lap? Ravana had taken her to Lanka and kept her in the ashoka grove – she was at the mercy of the rakshasas. How can Rama not be repulsed? We shall have to treat our wives in the same way – for whatever a king does, his subjects must do the same." This, and various other things, are what the citizens are saying, king, in the city and everywhere in the country.'

Rama grew agitated when he heard this. He said to his friends, 'What is this? Tell me!'

They hung their heads and bowed to him and replied, 'It is sad, but it is true!'

...

Rama, scorcher of his enemies, dismissed them all when he heard what they had said. After he had sent his friends away, he began to worry about what he should do.[40]

Rama sends for his brothers at once and they arrive to find him downcast and depressed. He tells them about the people's gossip and says that he is heartbroken. He knows that Sita is innocent because the gods, Agni and Vayu, had returned her to him after the trial by fire in Lanka. But he cannot ignore the feelings of his people. And so, he says to his brothers,

'Those who are infamous in this world descend to the realms of ghosts and stay there as long as their infamy is discussed. The gods do not like people of ill repute, they admire those who are famous. All great-souled people are motivated by compliments. Bulls among men, I would give up my life and you from fear of a scandal. How can I do less in the case of Janaka's daughter? It is because of this that you see me drowning in an ocean of sorrow. I have never experienced a sorrow greater than this.

[40] Sargas 42 and 43.

> 'Tomorrow morning, Lakshmana, let Sumantra have the chariot ready. Climb into it with Sita and leave her on the borders of the kingdom. The hermitage of the great-souled sage Valmiki, which is like heaven, lies on the far shore of the Ganga. Leave her in that desolate place, joy of the Raghus, and come back quickly. Do as I say, Lakshmana! Do not speak to me ever again about the matter of Sita. I will be greatly displeased if you try to obstruct me. I swear by my arms and by my life that I will not abide anyone speaking against my wishes. If you have any respect for me and are obedient to my commands, do as I say and take Sita away from here at once. Sita has already told me that she wishes to visit the sages' dwellings on the banks of the Ganga. Her wishes will now be fulfilled!'
>
> Having said this, Rama, the soul of dharma, his eyes filled with tears, departed, surrounded by his brothers.[41]

Clearly, Rama is distraught at what he has to do. And yet, the cruelty of his words and his actions, his determination to do what is right as a king are at odds with his emotions.[42]

Why is Rama so sensitive to this gossip, so much so that he banishes the wife that he loves to the forest, not even sure if he will ever see her again. How did things come to this pass, since after the final battle in the Yuddha Kanda, Sita is proven innocent through the trial by fire? The gods, sages, siddhas and charanas all applaud her chastity from the heavens. Her earthly witnesses, apart from her husband and brother-in-law, are rakshasas, the monkeys and bears, many of whom join Rama's triumphal return to Ayodhya. The Yuddha Kanda (and, arguably, the entire story) ends happily with Rama restored to his rightful place as king, his beloved wife, his devoted brother and his valiant allies by his side. Most importantly for this ending of the story, Sita's chastity has been proven, she has been vindicated and Rama has taken her back.

The Uttara Kanda unstitches this happy end, leaving a tangle of loose ends that it will tie up in its own way with entirely different implications for how we consider all that has gone before.

---

41 Sarga 44.

42 For a longer explanation of why Rama might have done this, see Arshia Sattar, *Lost Loves: Exploring Rama's Anguish* (New Delhi: HarperCollins India, 2019).

Temporally, the Uttara Kanda locates itself in the time right after Rama's coronation and stays with him until he ascends to heaven. As such, we find that the Uttara Kanda plays the part of the audience of the text, asking the questions, raising the doubts that sceptical readers and listeners might have about the events that took place in the earlier part of the story. This time, the question is simple, if devastating: what did Sita do when she was a prisoner in Lanka? Surely, she must have succumbed to Ravana's power, if not his charisma. Perhaps she surrendered to him just in order to survive. Worse, Sita is now pregnant.

In order to mitigate the subtext of sexual desire and choice that these real questions contain, the overt complaint that Rama's citizens make is expressed rather more aspirationally. Citizens need to follow the example of their king, they need to behave as well as he does. Now that the king has taken back a wife who has been in the house of another man, the citizens will have to do the same – and they do not have Rama's exalted capacity to do the best thing at all times, to always stand firm in dharma. Nevertheless, however the citizens' concerns are framed, the first stones against Sita have been cast. And the worm of doubt wriggles into the tradition that tells this story. Or perhaps it is the other way around – that the later tradition betrays an anxiety about what happened in Lanka and writes an addendum to the story in which its doubts are placed in the mouths of devoted citizens.

By the time the Uttara Kanda is composed and appended to the older books of the Valmiki Ramayana, bhakti has become the central emotion of Hinduism. Rama has become a god, an avatara of Vishnu, who acts in the world of men to restore (rather than merely preserve) dharma. Once Rama is god, his wife can be no less than a goddess, his companions no less than amshas, parts, or the offspring of other divinities. Bhakti tellings of the Ramayana do not have to ask and answer the same questions as Valmiki's Uttara Kanda poses and then answers. For example, the sixteenth-century *Ramcharitmanas* of Tulsidas, which invites the listener to drown in the loving ocean of Rama's deeds, avoids the problem of Sita's chastity. Since she is a goddess, she disappears the moment Ravana arrives in the forest to abduct her. She is replaced by a chhaya Sita, a shadow Sita, who is neither defiled by Ravana's touch nor subject to any of the pressures that a lesser Sita might have been. In the eighth book of the *Ramcharitmanas,* in the Lavakusha

Kanda, Lord Rama is told that a washerman in the city had criticized Sita. Rama knows that he now has to ask Sita to leave. Addressing her as the goddess, Rama asks her to ascend to heaven, leaving her shadow form behind to undergo the trials and tribulations that are to come. Kamban's twelfth-century Tamil *Iramavataram*, also imbued with bhakti and, therefore, concerned with the desecration of a god's wife, relates the moment of Sita's abduction such that Ravana never touches her. He gouges the earth upon which she stands and carries it away. There is none of the physical violence perpetrated on Sita's body that we experience in Valmiki's text. Kamban goes even further in his protective stance towards the god and his wife and ends his tale of Rama at the moment of his coronation. In his story, Sita is spared the humiliation of her banishment and the second trial to establish her conjugal fidelity after her sons are born.

Like so many other later renditions of Rama's story, both the Tamil and the Hindi versions have historical authors who can manipulate the story as they need to preserve a married woman's chastity, whereas it is the tradition itself that has to emend the more ambiguous story that it receives from Valmiki. Sarga 44 in the Uttara Kanda (quoted in part above) can be read in two ways. One, in which Rama's outburst about never being questioned or spoken to about Sita again could be seen as his extreme grief – that he never wants to be reminded about what he has had to do to his beloved wife, that the very thought of her abandoned in the forest would make it impossible for him to function. On the other hand, this could well be the voice of a later anxiety about married women and their behaviour. This voice says that if there is even the slightest suspicion around their relations with other men, women must be punished, even if the woman is the wife of the king or, as it is in this case, the wife of a god acting as a man on earth.

To soften the blow of the man-god's brutal actions, the sargas that follow Lakshmana leaving Sita in the forest tell an interesting story. Lakshmana, profoundly upset by what has just happened, says to Sumantra, the royal charioteer who is also a wise family counsellor,

> 'Look at wise Rama's sorrow, born of Sita's torment! What greater sorrow could Rama possibly have than rejecting his wife, Janaka's daughter, whose conduct has been pure? I think it is destiny that has

caused Rama's separation from Sita, for it is only destiny that cannot be avoided. Angry Rama abides by destiny in order to kill the gods, gandharvas, asuras and rakshasas. In the past, he lived in the desolate forests of the Dandaka for nine years and then another five because of my father's words. At that time, too, he suffered immense grief because of his separation from Sita. But now, I think he has committed a very cruel act after listening to citizens' idle talk. Which person who takes refuge in dharma, charioteer, would act in such a dishonourable way towards Sita based on the low and vulgar talk of common people?'[43]

Although Lakshmana is upset and critical of Rama, he tries to mitigate that criticism by suggesting that Rama could not act against fate.[44] But Sumantra takes the argument for the constraints upon Rama's free will even further when he tells Lakshmana about the sage Durvasas's prediction from a long time ago. Sumantra says that King Dasharatha had asked the sage,

'Blessed one, how long will my dynasty last, how long will Rama live and how long will my other sons live? And what will be the lifespan of Rama's sons? Speak as you will, blessed one, about the destiny of my family.'

Effulgent Durvasas related everything to Dasharatha in chronological order. He declared, 'Rama will be the ruler of Ayodhya for a long, long time. And his brothers will be happy and prosperous. But it is also certain that this righteous man will, for some reason, forsake Maithili for a long period. For ten thousand years and then another one thousand, Rama will rule and then he will depart for Brahma's realm. Rama, conqueror of enemy cities, will establish his dynasty firmly by

---

43 Sarga 49.

44 It is interesting that this same Lakshmana, in the Ayodhya Kanda, rails against Rama taking refuge in the idea of destiny when he agrees to go into the forest to honour his father's decree. Lakshmana berates Rama, saying, 'How can a man like you, who stands so strong and proud in the dharma of a kshatriya, sing praises of this thing called destiny? Fate is the refuge of the weak and the impotent ... No capable man would ever be oppressed by the workings of destiny. And a real man would never allow fate to frustrate his aims.' Sattar, *Valmiki's Ramayana*, chap. 16.

> performing many horse sacrifices.' Having narrated everything about his dynasty to the king, the wise, effulgent sage fell silent. When both the sages had finished speaking, Dasharatha honoured the great-souled ones and returned to his own incomparable city.
>
> I heard all that the sage had declared so long ago and I kept it in my heart. Things cannot be any other way. And so, Lakshmana, you should not grieve on account of Sita or of Rama. Be resolute, best of men![45]

Being the book of overdetermination, in which many explanations are proffered for the same event or deed, the Uttara Kanda again resorts to the lowest common denominator in a constellation of multiple causes: the prediction.

The prediction differs from the boon and the curse in that the latter have something to do with the deeds of the people they affect. For example, Ravana gets his extra powers and invincible weapons because he has worshipped Shiva and Brahma. Dasharatha is cursed to die in the absence of his beloved son by the parents of a young boy whom he accidentally kills. A prediction has no cause, it merely is. And by virtue of simply being so, it is even more infallible than a boon or a curse, both of which can be modified.

Returning to the larger text for a moment, the anxiety about married women is brought to our attention in the Bala Kanda as well, in the story of Ahalya. Like the Uttara Kanda, the Bala Kanda, too, is written later and lays great emphasis on Rama's divinity. In one of the episodes that serve to highlight Rama's divine nature, Vishvamitra tells Rama what had happened at an abandoned hermitage that they pass on their way home after killing the yakshi Tataka. Gautama had lived there with his beautiful wife Ahalya. But Indra, the king of the gods, desired her and one day, when Gautama was away, Indra took his form and seduced Ahalya.

> 'Slim-waisted lady, the passionate man does not wait for the right season. I want to make love to you now!' Ahalya recognized Indra in his disguise but she was curious about the king of the gods and agreed to sleep with him. When her desire had been satisfied, she said to the

[45] Sarga 50.

> best of the gods, 'I am completely fulfilled, Indra! Now go from here quickly and protect yourself and me from my husband!'[46]

Gautama returns as Indra is leaving and curses both him and Ahalya. In this version of the story, Indra loses his testicles[47] and Ahalya is made formless.

> Then Gautama cursed his wife. 'You shall live on air, without food, and you shall sleep on ashes. You shall be invisible to all creatures as you do penance in this hermitage! You shall be purified only when Rama, the invincible son of Dasharatha, comes to this forest. Wicked woman, when you offer hospitality to Rama, you shall be freed of your lust and passion. You shall regain your earlier form in my presence!'[48]

Vishvamitra urges Rama and Lakshmana to enter the hermitage and 'do the right thing by liberating Ahalya'.

> Even though Ahalya was invisible to the gods and the asuras and the people of the world, Rama and Lakshmana were able to see the fortunate woman who shone with the power of her austerities. Her celestial beauty was the result of a special effort by the creator. She appeared like a flame veiled in smoke, like the light of the full moon covered by a delicate mist, like the sun's rays reflected by water, so beautiful that she was almost an illusion.
>
> Gautama's curse had made her invisible to all beings until the moment she saw Rama. The princes touched her feet, and recalling Gautama's words Ahalya welcomed them. With a serene mind, she honoured them with the arghya ritual. Flowers rained from the sky and the sound of celestial drums was heard as the gandharvas and apsaras

46 Sattar, *Valmiki's Ramayana*, chap. 9.

47 Indra complains to the gods about his lost testicles and in sympathy, they replace them with those of a ram.

48 Sattar, *Valmiki's Ramayana*, chap. 9.

> gathered. The gods honoured Ahalya who had been reunited with her husband because of her austerities.[49]

Ahalya is punished for her transgression and then restored not only to her beautiful body but also to her role as a good and virtuous wife.

We have to ask ourselves why certain stories appear at particular places in the Ramayana as well as in other texts. It is clear that the Ramayana is self-conscious, it knows itself. It is even more self-conscious in the books that have been added later, books that have been written to point the central story in particular directions and towards particular interpretations.

The Ahalya story in the Bala Kanda sets the tone for what is to come in the Uttara Kanda, when the queen herself must be punished, not for what she has done but for what other people *think* she might have done. In the Bala Kanda, Rama is a fourteen-year-old boy when he is taken by Vishvamitra to kill Tataka. He is told the story of Ahalya and made aware of how seriously such a transgression can and should be taken. Surely, this plays on his mind when, in his later life, he is confronted with the veiled accusations about his wife's conduct. Whether or not we believe that there is a narrative continuity for the character and person of Rama (in that what he was exposed to as a young boy will have an effect on him when he is a grown man and a king), we can see that the first and the last books of the Valmiki Ramayana are overtly concerned with the chastity of married women. The incidents reflect and refract each other in several ways. Sita's second exile into the forest, where she must live as an ascetic in Valmiki's hermitage, recalls the austerities that Ahalya must practise in order to regain her human form. These austerities make it possible for Ahalya to be restored to her husband in Rama's presence.[50] After her ascetic life, Sita's

49 Sattar, *Valmiki's Ramayana*, chap. 9.

50 As an indication of the importance of the Ahalya story, the Uttara Kanda has its own version in Sarga 30. Here, it would appear to be Indra's story, explaining why he was defeated by Meghanada, Ravana's son, who, after this stunning victory over the king of the gods, was known as Indrajit – conqueror of Indra. When Indra is pathetic after having been defeated, Brahma explains to him how this could have happened. He reminds Indra that he had done something wrong in the past and says, 'Long ago, lord of the immortals … I formed a blameless woman with beauty

exoneration, too, is in Rama's presence and in public, at the great sacrifice he is conducting.[51]

Sita's exoneration and glorious apotheosis in the Uttara Kanda, however, is also something that we might regard with mixed feelings, given the overall position that the Uttara Kanda takes in terms of the story that has gone before. If, as we suspect, the Uttara Kanda is adjusting the way we think about women in the text and in society, then in the Valmiki Ramayana, no matter how many times and in how many ways Sita is proven innocent, she cannot

---

and virtue. I gave her the name Ahalya, by which she was known. After I had created that woman, lord of the gods, I began to think about whom she should belong to. But you, Indra, destroyer of cities, you fixed your mind on that woman and thought of her as your wife because you were superior to her! I entrusted her to the great-souled Gautama and after many years of looking after her, he gave her back. Now that I was sure of the great sage's patience and knew that his austerities were complete, I gave her to him as a wife. The righteous sage enjoyed her but the gods were disappointed that I had given her to Gautama. You were angry and in the mood for love. You went to the sage's hermitage and saw the woman, shining like a flame. Filled with lust and anger, you violated her, Indra. Gautama saw you in his hermitage and enraged, he cursed you. That led to a change in your circumstances, lord of the gods.

'"You shall fall into your enemies' hands in battle, King Vasava, because you fearlessly violated my wife!" said Gautama. "Idiot! This passion that you have unleashed will stay among all men, have no doubt about that! Whoever commits this same transgression shall bear one half of its consequences. The other half will fall on you. Your position will never be secure, destroyer of cities, because of your unrighteous deed. Whoever becomes the king of the gods shall be unsteady in his position – this is the curse I declare and cast upon you!" Gautama, a man of great austerities, then berated his wife, "Disappear from the vicinity of my hermitage, you badly behaved woman! You were rich in youth and beauty and that made you restless. You will no longer be the only beautiful woman in the world. This beauty, which was so hard to obtain, shall now belong to all beings. All of this will come to pass because of your blunder."'

[51] In fact, this happens twice. In captivity, too, Sita has lived like an ascetic. Her first exoneration is also in Rama's presence and in public, when she appears on the battlefield after the war and has her trial by fire. Perhaps this is a more important episode because it is here, in the Valmiki Ramayana, that the gods tell Rama who he really is. Rama's divinity and Sita's chastity are established in the selfsame moment.

stay with her husband, the maryadapurushottama, the ideal man (and god), once a whiff of scandal had touched her.

While the Uttara Kanda asks narratively important (if naive) questions about who and what and how and where and when, the answers it provides tend to shut down the story in terms of our engagement with the characters and the choices they make. Typically, the answers tend to resort to either the infallibility of Rama's divinity or one of several inevitabilities generated through boons, curses and predictions. These eliminate the possibility that characters in the Valmiki Ramayana, be they human or divine, make choices at all. As readers and listeners, we are no longer able to think about the crucial dilemmas that they face and how and why they decide to act in the way that they do. On the other hand, if we see Rama's actions through the later lens that bhakti offers us, we can think more deeply about what it means for a god to act in the world of men. Such a lens could significantly deepen and broaden our idea of divinity itself. It also keeps open the thrilling possibility of encountering the divine in our lives.

For all that the Uttara Kanda has papered over the cracks in terms of why Rama had to ask Sita to leave, there is one crack that remains open, its paper peeling. Whether or not it is an apotheosis, we can still see Sita's departure as her choice. In the Yuddha Kanda, at the trial by fire, her first test of chastity, Sita says, 'If my heart has never strayed from Rama, let the god of fire, eternal witness to all that happens in the world, protect me!'[52] In the Uttara Kanda, at her second trial during Rama's great sacrifice, Rama says,

> 'When Sita proves her innocence before the world, I shall be able to love her again!' ... Everyone watched as Sita, wearing an ochre robe, joined her palms. Her head was bowed and she kept her eyes on the ground. 'If I have never thought about any man other than Rama, let the goddess Madhavi create a chasm for me!'[53]

In the Uttara Kanda, Sita asks to be taken away.

---

[52] Sattar, *Valmiki's Ramayana*, chap. 67.

[53] Sarga 88.

Despite everything that the Uttara Kanda does to persuade us that this story about a woman accused of infidelity has been sealed in approved ways, the peeling crack allows us to see Sita for ourselves: not as a woman who was manipulated by an increasingly patriarchal structure, but as a woman who opted out of a system that had robbed her of her dignity. And this is what enables us to enter the universe of the Ramayana and make it our own.

# THE KILLING OF SHAMBUKA

One day, when all seems well in Ayodhya, a brahmin comes to Rama, wailing, his dead son cradled in his arms. He accuses Rama of not doing enough to be a good king, else his child would not have died.[54] Narada supports the brahmin's argument by telling Rama that he must find the cause of this disruption in the natural order – that a child should die for no reason – and eliminate it as soon as possible. He also describes the state of dharma in each of the yugas, declaring that in their time, the Dwapara Yuga, a shudra cannot and must not take on the performance of austerities. As king, Rama is beholden to address this transgression. Rama travels through his kingdom in the magical Pushpaka and finds Shambuka, a shudra, performing austerities, violating the dharmic and cosmic order that Narada has described. Rama acts simply and effectively: he kills the shudra. The brahmin's son comes back to life and dharma is restored in the Ikshvaku kingdom. Rama then visits the hermitage of Agastya, is praised for his righteous killing, and comes back home.

---

54 Of course, this accusation reminds us of the opening scene in Sophocles' *Oedipus Rex* when a plague falls upon the city of Thebes. The people are convinced that there is something unclean in the city and Creon, the king's brother-in-law, has to persuade them that he will leave no stone unturned to discover the horror that is causing them to suffer the loss of their children and loved ones. It turns out that the horror is the king himself, in his incestuous relationship with his mother. Rama is also the transgressor here, although his transgression is not personal.

This astounding episode is narrated smack in the middle of the Uttara Kanda, in Sargas 64 to 67. What comes immediately before it is a perfectly bland chapter where Shatrughna begs to be allowed to return to Ayodhya from the kingdom that he has been ruling for the last twelve years because he wants to be close to Rama. After spending five nights with him, Rama persuades Shatrughna that he should go back to his kingdom. Shatrughna does so and then, on the morning of his departure, his brothers watch him drive away into the distance. Nothing prepares us for the physical, emotional or social violence of the chapter that follows. We are literally slapped awake from the stupor into which we had been lulled as we listened to the almost routine expansion of the Ikshvaku lands and their division among Rama's younger brothers to ensure that they are not each other's rivals.

It is the utter mundaneness of the episode, the unadorned clarity of its purpose, that is so shocking. Rama sets out, gladness flooding his heart, he sees Shambuka and has the utmost respect for what he has undertaken, Shambuka reveals that he is a shudra and even before he has finished speaking, Rama has cut off his head with his gleaming sword. Unlike in the other instances in the Uttara Kanda where Rama must act as king, for example, the moment when he has to banish a pregnant Sita into the forest, Rama shows no confusion, no sadness, no hesitation when he has to kill Shambuka. It is the absence of Rama's inner thoughts and feelings here, his blind obedience to Narada's scheme, that make this incident so very brutal.

But there is another brutality that underlies this story, that makes it necessary for Rama to kill Shambuka. And that is the brutality of caste. Ayodhya's pre-eminence as a city is predicated on the fact that within it, all the four castes live and act within the strict hierarchy that has been prescribed for them.

In the Bala Kanda, as Ayodhya is being described as an ideal city, the caste system is depicted thus:

> Ayodhya was ruled by the great king Dasharatha who was learned in the Vedas ...
>
> Always associated with the truth, King Dasharatha supported the three upper castes and ruled his city the way Indra ruled Amaravati.

> ... Even though Ayodhya had thousands of brahmins, people did not neglect the performance of household sacrifices and rituals. Brahmins were committed to the performance of public rituals and were allowed to accept gifts. They were learned and had conquered their senses because of their exalted characters.
>
> ... The kshatriyas placed the brahmins first and the vaishyas followed the kshatriyas. And the shudras, according to their duty, served the other three castes.[55]

In the hierarchy of castes that is securely in place in Ayodhya, it is clear that the brahmins in the city play a large public ritual role. This public role is confirmed and ratified by their presence at the royal court, first with Vasishtha, Jabali and others in Dasharatha's time and then continued and further enhanced by Agastya and his cohort in the time of Rama's reign. At the court, the brahmins are not merely ritual priests, they are also powerful advisers who cover both the temporal and the religious realms that the king must guard. The Uttara Kanda opens with the arrival of Agastya and eight other sages, each of them mighty in reputation and powerful in their supra-human capacities. The sages surround Rama and begin to tell him stories, replicating, as it were, the public performance of a royal sacrifice where the patron king and all the others present hear the stories of the king's ancestors and his lineage. The difference in the opening chapters of the Uttara Kanda (where the greatest of all sacrifices with its cataclysmic consequences is yet to be performed) is that the stories Rama hears are not the tales of his own proud and illustrious family, but tales of Ravana's forefathers and their sustained tyranny over the three worlds. In these stories, it is typically Vishnu who defeats the rakshasas.[56] The message of these stories is ultimately quite clear: that unrighteousness gets the upper hand every now and then and has to be destroyed. Now, it is Rama-as-Vishnu's duty to be the instrument of this destruction so that the three

[55] Sattar, *Valmiki's Ramayana*, chap. 3.

[56] In a sense, Rama-as-Vishnu is listening to his own story, his actions and deeds from another time. This also replicates the situation at his own sacrifice when his sons tell him the story of his own life, his life as Rama in the world of men.

worlds can be safe and so that dharma – a dharma designed and dictated by the powerful brahmin sages who are telling him these stories – can stand firm.[57]

Through these stories and by the middle of the Uttara Kanda, along with Rama, we are led to the idea that unrighteous behaviour is not restricted to rakshasas and other oppositional beings alone. Such dangerous behaviours and disruptive acts can be found closer to home, among Rama's subjects and citizens, even among members of his family. The Ikshvaku kings had long been upholders of dharma, rooting out the practices and the people that made its edifice unstable and vulnerable to collapse. One can imagine that the dharma these warrior princes upheld with such valour and dedication over generations was located within the parameters of the kshatriya code, one that protected the weak and moderated the strong. What the Uttara Kanda seeks to establish is that the Ikshvakus must now protect a dharma dominated by brahmin practices and ideologies, a dharma that must at all costs maintain their fundamental superiority in all the three worlds. The killing of Shambuka is but a single moment in this larger schema. It is not simply that Shambuka is practising austerities apparently reserved for the upper castes, it is that he wants to attain heaven in his human body, that he wants to achieve great fame and that he wants to be like a god. His so-called violations in this world of men will ensure his place in heaven, among the gods, thereby carrying this subversion of human hierarchy into the next world as well.

Returning for a moment to the idea of kshatriya dharma, we have seen Rama reject that dharma for himself in the middle books of the Valmiki Ramayana, albeit at times of high emotion. His first rejection of kshatriya

---

[57] Sreekanta Nair's modern Malayalam play, *Kanchana Sita*, reveals a Rama held in thrall by brahmins after his return from exile. Even his beloved brother Bharata is appalled by the extent to which, when making decisions for his personal and his public life, Rama subdues his own instincts and intuitions in order to appease the powerful priestly class that has surrounded him. Brahmin control over kings has also been noticed by the Bangla writer Buddhadeva Bose in his *Mahabharater Katha* (The Tale of the Mahabharata) where he suggests that the first half of the Mahabharata is a kshatriya work centred around Arjuna, while the second half of the epic has a brahmin orientation and revolves around Yudhishthira. I thank Arunava Sinha for discussing this with me.

dharma is when he tells Lakshmana and his mother about his exile. Lakshmana is incensed and suggests that together they imprison their father, Dasharatha, who has clearly become senile as demonstrated by this ridiculous decree on the eve of Rama's coronation. Rama responds by saying to Lakshmana,

> 'Dharma is the most important thing in the world, truth is established because of it. And obeying a father's command is the highest dharma of all, as is conforming to the wishes of a mother and a brahmin. I cannot disobey my father simply because Kaikeyi, our mother, asked him to command me thus. Give up your ignoble ideas inspired by the duties of a kshatriya! Follow my example. Take refuge in dharma and not in violence.'[58]

Is there a dharma that is higher and more noble than that of the kshatriya code of behaviour (which already includes obedience to brahmins)? Rama seems to suggest as much in this admonition to his brother.

Later, when Bharata comes to Nandigrama with his royal retinue to persuade Rama to take back the kingdom, Rama gives him a discourse on kingship in the presence of Dasharatha's brahmin advisers. Jabali, the materialist, provokes Rama by suggesting that there are no family ties, that there is no need to obey the wishes of his father, that he should simply come back to Ayodhya and become king. Rama is moved to a passionate rebuttal and at the end of it, he says,

> 'It is clear to me that every man must hold to the truth, that it is his dharma. It is for this reason alone that ascetics command so much respect. I renounce the dharma of a kshatriya because it is fundamentally unrighteous even though it has some good things about it. It attracts the base, the cruel, the greedy and those inclined to be wicked.'[59]

---

[58] Sattar, *Valmiki's Ramayana*, chap. 16.

[59] Sattar, *Valmiki's Ramayana*, chap. 26.

As Rama seeks a dharma that he can truthfully abide by – rather than one that is dictated to him by caste – Sita also suggests to him that dharma can be a choice. During their days in the Dandaka forest, she expresses concern that as he continues to carry his weapons, the mark of his kshatriya-ness, he will draw violence to himself.

> 'Now that you are here with your brother and both of you are armed, you shall see many forest creatures. Inevitably, you will be tempted to use your arrows. Like dry fuel bursts into flame when it is near a fire, so too, a kshatriya's passions are ignited when he has a bow at hand …
>
> 'May it never happen that you attack the rakshasas of the forest without reason, simply because you carry a weapon. I cannot bear the thought of innocents being killed, O hero! A kshatriya should use his bow in the forest only to protect the oppressed. What a difference there is between the life of weapons and that of the forest, between the vows of a kshatriya and those of an ascetic! We must learn to respect the code of behaviour of the world we now inhabit. Here, the mind is perverted by extreme proximity to weapons. You can return to the code of the kshatriyas when we go back to Ayodhya!'[60]

Since Rama has already questioned an inherited dharma and seems to be seeking a personal truth that can let him act ethically in the world, it is all the more disturbing that the Rama we are presented with in the Uttara Kanda upholds a brahminized dharma that is dictated to him by the cabal that surrounds him. Narada's role in the Shambuka story cannot pass unremarked: he explains that brahmins were superior but now, since kshatriyas rule like brahmins, the hierarchy has been mitigated (though not erased). He says to Rama,

> 'In the Krita Yuga, Rama, only brahmins became ascetics. Your majesty, non-brahmins never became ascetics under any circumstances. In that yuga, the shining brahmins were dominant, they were immortal and they could see the future. Then came the Treta Yuga, where the men of

---

[60] Sattar, *Valmiki's Ramayana*, chap. 28.

> glory were kshatriyas, and they ruled as the brahmins had done before. The great-souled men of this age were not superior in their heroism and practise of austerities to those in the previous yuga. Brahmins had been superior to the kshatriyas, but in this yuga, both were equal in power. Because there was no perceptible difference between the brahmins and the kshatriyas, the system of the four castes was established everywhere. Adharma stood on one foot on the surface of the earth and the twice-born became apathetic because of their attachment to adharma. Lifespans diminished. Only those who were dedicated to truth and righteousness performed auspicious activities.
>
> 'In the Treta Yuga, both brahmins and kshatriyas performed austerities and all the other people served them – this was the highest dharma for vaishyas and shudras. Shudras, especially, had to worship everyone. Then, the second foot of adharma descends and so that becomes known as the Dwapara Yuga. In this Dwapara Yuga, decay will prevail and, bull among men, adharma and lawlessness will increase. In the Dwapara Yuga, vaishyas will take to ascetic practices. But, bull among men, shudras cannot access this, the dharma of fierce asceticism. In the future, in the Kali Yuga, best of kings, men without caste shall take on great austerities and those born of shudra wombs will also perform penances. But it is the greatest unrighteousness, Rama, for a shudra to appropriate this in the Dwapara Yuga.'[61]

In these essays, we have assumed that the Uttara Kanda of Valmiki is a later composition than the middle books. As such, it can embody and encourage an entirely different world view and endorse a completely different politics with regard to caste. In the middle books, there are enough instances of brahmins being elevated and being accorded more than the usual respect. However, there are no clear instances of dharma as articulated by them being the dharma which Rama must uphold and disseminate. In the middle books, the very idea of dharma that Rama acts upon can be questioned. In fact, it is questioned within the text itself by Vali when Rama shoots him in the back

[61] Sarga 65.

while he is fighting another opponent.[62] One could argue that the dharma that Rama seeks to impose on others is the dharma of Ayodhya, already misplaced in its applications outside that particular city.[63] Taking Sita's words in the Dandaka forest into account, the dharma of Ayodhya would have been a kshatriya dharma upheld by the Ikshvaku kings and not the brahmin dharma that Rama is being persuaded to endorse in the Uttara Kanda.

In a variant edition of the Uttara Kanda, the killing of Shambuka has more details. Once the shudra is beheaded, the gods, led by Indra and Agni, appear, shouting 'It is good! It is good!' and a shower of perfumed blossoms falls from the sky. The gods are pleased and they thank Rama for doing something that will benefit them and offer him a boon. They say to Rama, 'Because of your actions, this shudra will not attain heaven.' Rama asks that the brahmin's son be brought back to life since his untimely death had been due to Rama's carelessness. The gods reassure him that the boy is already alive and well and persuade him to visit Agastya's hermitage. There, Rama is congratulated again for his decisive intervention and is offered a magnificent divine ornament fashioned by Vishvakarma, perhaps as a reward for eliminating the danger posed to the gods by Shambuka's ascetic practice. Rama says that he cannot receive gifts because he is a kshatriya. He maintains that it is his dharma to give gifts and that of a brahmin to receive them. Agastya then tells him this story.

> 'Long ago, Rama, in the Krita Yuga, when all beings lived in Brahma, all living beings were without a king, though the king of the gods was Indra of a thousand sacrifices. Living beings came to Brahma in order to have a king. They said, "You have established Indra as the king of the gods. We ask you for a king of the world, a man best among men,

---

[62] Vali says, 'Why did you do this to me, a harmless monkey who lives in the forest and eats roots and fruits, who had no quarrel with you but was concentrating on fighting with someone else? You are a prince, handsome and distinguished. You carry all the outward signs of dharma. How could someone like you, born a noble kshatriya, who has all his ethical doubts resolved by the wise, how could you do something so cruel, hidden under the trappings of dharma?' Sattar, *Valmiki's Ramayana*, chap. 38.

[63] For more on this, see Arshia Sattar, 'Three Cities and the Search for Dharma', in *Lost Loves: Exploring Rama's Anguish* (New Delhi: HarperCollins India, 2019).

> by worshipping whom we shall be free of all wrongdoing. We cannot live without a king. This is our decision." Brahma, best of the gods, summoned the guardians of the four quarters along with Indra. "Give me a part of your effulgence," he said to them and all the guardians gave him a part of their effulgence. Then, Brahma sneezed and engendered King Kshupa and bestowed on him all the effulgence that the guardians of the four quarters had shared. He gave Kshupa as a king to the living beings. With Indra's effulgence, he ruled the earth, with Varuna's he nurtured the bodies of living beings, with Kubera's he gave them wealth and with Yama's he was able to rule over all living beings. You have a part of Indra's effulgence, Rama! You should accept this, for my sake, dear one!'[64]

Once again, Rama is being persuaded to act like a brahmin and he willingly does so, even though the logic of why he can accept gifts in the story is not entirely clear. If, as a king, he can accept gifts, he is already eroding one of the pillars upon which his code of behaviour as a warrior stands. The royal obligation that Rama acts upon when he kills Shambuka is an obligation driven by a strict caste hierarchy and an equally strict code of who can do what and when. While Narada acknowledges that brahmins and kshatriyas can share power and experience a cosmic era of relative equality, together they must ensure that the other lower castes remain constrained, particularly in respect of their access to religious merit – and therefore, to the heavens – through their actions. Further, when Rama kills Shambuka, he violates another caveat of the kshatriya code, one that Sita warns him against in the forest in relation to the rakshasas. She says,

> 'There are three major weaknesses that arise from desire. One is telling lies. The other two are much worse: one is lusting after another man's wife and the other is cruelty without a justified cause for hostility ... the third weakness which men succumb to because of their passions, the

---

[64] Translated by Arshia Sattar from the *Srivalmikiramayanam Satika* (Bombay: Nirnayasagar Press, 1930).

inflicting of violence and cruelty upon other beings without reason or enmity, that weakness appears to be present in you now.'[65]

Like Vali, Sita points out that a kshatriya, especially an exemplar like Rama, is not expected to kill on behalf of the enmity and hostility of others. Narada and the other brahmins have convinced Rama that he can betray the tenets of the code of behaviour that he grew up with because there is, apparently, a more important dharma at stake.

[65] Sattar, *Valmiki's Ramayana*, chap. 28.

# THE DEATH OF LAKSHMANA

As the other essays in this book have noted, the Uttara Kanda specializes in overdeterminism, that is, it gives us many reasons for why something happens the way it does. At its most obvious, this narrative device seals the fate, as it were, of free will. Characters act not out of choice but out of necessity, sometimes from a necessity that they don't even know about. In the universe of overdeterminism which always pulls back to the big picture, Rama banishes Sita from his kingdom not from the desire to be above reproach himself, but because it has been ordained. This is what Sumantra tells Lakshmana after he has abandoned Sita near Valmiki's hermitage. We do not know if Rama knew that his wife's second exile was bound to happen, because we hear the 'secret' for the first time when Lakshmana hears it. But like Lakshmana, we are being persuaded to forgive Rama his cruelty to his wife – it is not his act that has banished her, it is in her destiny. And in his.

Given the corrective tenor of the Uttara Kanda, we can suggest that the purpose of placing actions outside the realm of individual judgement and choice is to exonerate Rama's deeds. Typically, in the Hindu world, it is deeds in the past or karma that is the narrative (and metaphysical) instrument that prevents us from seeing actions and events as contingent. But in the Uttara Kanda, it is also the new dharma, which Rama must first establish and then uphold, that makes these problematic actions necessary. The new dharma is that of the brahmins, specifically, the powerful brahmins, led by Agastya, who surround Rama when he becomes king.

The kshatriya dharma that Rama follows in the middle books of the Ramayana allows one to rail against fate, as Lakshmana does when Rama announces the news of his banishment. Kshatriya dharma can also be rejected, as Rama declares on more than one occasion. Further, Sita questions the propriety of the warrior's code when they are living in the forest as ascetics. Vali criticizes the dharma by which Rama kills him and also the dharma that permits Rama to kill him in the way that he does – with no personal enmity, from behind, from a hiding place and when he was engaged with another opponent.

But the dharma that the brahmins present Rama with cannot be questioned. Or, rather, it is a dharma that Rama chooses not to question. In that sense, he surrenders his kingship to a code and a world view that lies outside the dharma into which he was born and in which he was trained. This new dharma demands that he kill Shambuka, persuades him to send his wife away and allows him to see his brother's death as something that had been predicted and was, therefore, inevitable. Also startling in the Uttara Kanda is the fact that while people are described as dharma-knowing, standing firm in dharma, righteous, etc., there are no discussions of dharma at all. In the middle books of the Valmiki Ramayana, there are several occasions to discuss dharma. Further, Rama thinks about dharma often, exploring its dimensions for his own actions as well as trying to understand it through the actions of others. In the Uttara Kanda, there is only Narada's disturbing speech in the Shambuka episode. There, too, it is a declaration of what dharma is rather than a discussion or a debate. We are told every now and then about the perfection of ramarajya – material prosperity, happy and contented citizens, the absence of disease and discomfort – but the only dharma that seems to prevail there is one of obedience to a hierarchy of power.

While Rama's actions in the Uttara Kanda are doubly justified – first, by his divinity and second, by the duties of a king who is being advised by brahmins – one could argue that the people who love him most – Sita and Lakshmana – are disturbed by the man that Rama has become. Sita's astounding choice at her second public trial, where she asks the earth to swallow her if she has been true, shows that she is willing to leave the husband who seems to be no longer true to his own will and desires.[66] More than once, Rama says that he has always believed in Sita's innocence, that these public trials are for the sake of other people and their doubts. Yet, he chooses not to defend her and he acts against her from what appear to be motivations not his own. Rama has chosen his public dharma as a king, suggested to him by his brahmin advisers, over his more instinctual individual dharma as a husband.

Years after Sita's departure from this world, Lakshmana chooses to leave Rama by doing what he knows will bring the curse of death upon him. By this act, perhaps he, too, is judging Rama, realizing that he has lost his brother even as he has gained a monarch. We must also remember the many times that Lakshmana has had to act on Rama's behalf in very unpleasant circumstances. It is Lakshmana who has to mutilate Shurpanakha, to light the fire (at Sita's request) for her public trial at the end of the war, to take Sita into the forest under false pretences when Rama banishes her.

Rama's reign has continued uneventfully, and soon it is time for him to ascend to heaven, to become what he really is, that is, a part of Vishnu. Time, disguised as an ascetic, comes to the palace and asks to be admitted into Rama's presence. Lakshmana takes him in and Time says to Rama that he can only deliver the message he has in private. Time says, 'If you care for the message that the sage has sent you, then whoever sees or hears us must be put to death, Rama!' Rama, trusting no one more than he does Lakshmana, asks him to guard the door himself. Unexpectedly, the sage Durvasas, who cannot be crossed, arrives to see Rama.

> While the two of them were talking, the blessed sage Durvasas arrived at the door, eager to see Rama. 'I want to see Rama at once, before my purpose in coming here is defeated,' he said to Lakshmana.
>
> Lakshmana honoured him and said, 'What do you need? Tell me, what have you come for? Rama is very busy right now. Can you wait for a while?'
>
> Durvasas flew into a rage and looked at Lakshmana as if he would consume him with the fire from his eyes. 'Go at once and tell Rama that

66 For more on this, see Arshia Sattar, *Lost Loves: Exploring Rama's Anguish* (New Delhi: HarperCollins India, 2019).

I am here. Or, I shall curse you, Rama, the city and the entire kingdom as well as Bharata and all your children! I cannot control my anger!'

Lakshmana considered the matter and said to himself, 'It is better that one man, I, myself, die, than all creatures be destroyed!' He made up his mind quickly and went in to see Rama. Rama dismissed Time and came out with Lakshmana.

He honoured the sage who shone with splendour and, with his palms joined, he said, 'What can I do for you?'

'Listen, lover of dharma,' said the sage. 'Today I have completed one hundred years of practising austerities and I am very hungry. Satisfy my desire to eat!'

Rama ordered a delicious meal for the sage and Durvasas ate his fill of the food that was as fine and sweet as nectar. He thanked Rama and praised him and went back to his hermitage. Rama was very happy until he remembered Time's words. He recalled their frightful implications and burning with grief, he hung his head and was utterly silent.

'This cannot be true,' he thought to himself.

...

Lakshmana noticed that Rama was depressed and dull like an eclipsed moon. 'Do not grieve for me, Rama,' he said gently. 'Do as Time said, for it has been ordained. Kill me without hesitation and fulfil your promise. The man who breaks his word goes to hell! If you love me and want to make me happy, then kill me without any second thoughts or misgivings! You must nourish dharma, Rama!'

Rama's senses were in a whirl when he heard what Lakshmana said. He sent for his ministers and the family priest and told them what had happened. They were silent when they heard the story and then, Vasishtha said, 'Mighty one, I knew long ago that this calamity, this separation from Lakshmana, was going to happen! Time is all-powerful. You must abandon Lakshmana and keep your word. Dharma is destroyed when a man breaks his promise. And when dharma is destroyed, you can be sure that the three worlds, with all their moving and unmoving creatures, with the gods and the sages, will also perish. You are responsible for protecting the three worlds. If you kill Lakshmana today, you will have established the universe firmly.'

> 'I must renounce you, Lakshmana, or else dharma will be violated,' said Rama when he heard Vasishtha's words which were filled with purpose and meaning. 'It will be all the same to good men whether I kill you or abandon you or am separated from you!' Lakshmana's eyes filled with tears and he left hurriedly, but he did not go to his own home. He went straight to the banks of the Sarayu, where he stopped the activities of his senses and ceased to exhale.[67]

Once again, Rama has been persuaded by the brahmins in his court to abandon those whom he loves best because of a dharma that they can see and that they proceed to define for the king. It is ironic that Rama says, 'It will be the same to good men whether I kill you or abandon you or am separated from you!' These possible judgements of himself (and the fear of infamy) are the same as the ones he takes into consideration when he decides to send Sita into the forest after their return to Ayodhya – 'good men', whoever they are (and we can take an educated guess at that) will not care about the reasons why Rama needed to be separated from his loved ones. For them, it is simply enough that the expulsion of first Sita and then Lakshmana from Rama's life is in accordance with the dictates of dharma.

Rama hears Time's brutal condition for maintaining the privacy of their meeting and as he has done so many times before, he appoints Lakshmana to take care of the momentous task by asking him to guard the door. Lakshmana agrees, knowing that even a trivial interruption of their meeting could cost him his life. And when he is confronted by Durvasas, he decides that it is better for him, alone, to die than to have the worlds destroyed because of the sage's anger. When Rama is distraught at what has happened, Lakshmana urges his brother 'to kill him' (though that is not in fact necessary) so that dharma will be firmly established. It is only when he leaves for the river that we have some sense of Lakshmana's own devastation, his sadness at leaving his brother, his family and his life in the world. Maybe, he senses that Rama is soon to leave the world and he cannot bear to live without him. Or, perhaps his tears are for the man his brother has become.

---

[67] Sargas 95 and 96.

Lakshmana, the proud kshatriya, who, so often in the past, reminded Rama of his own duties as a warrior and a prince, accedes to the new dharma that his brother, now king, must establish and uphold. In the Ayodhya Kanda, when Dasharatha's fraught decree exiles Rama to the forest and Rama decides to honour his father, Lakshmana bursts out in anger.

> 'You seem perturbed about the violation of dharma and the doubts that may arise in the minds of others. This is most unlike you, Rama. Such confusion does not become you.
>
> 'How can a man like you, who stands so strong and proud in the dharma of the kshatriya, sing praises of this thing called destiny. Fate is the refuge of the weak and the impotent ... I feel only contempt for a dharma that makes even someone as resolute as you vacillate like this! It is your attachment to dharma that confuses you!
>
> 'I cannot accept that all this happened because of fate. An explanation like that is for cowards, not for the brave! No capable man would ever be oppressed by the workings of destiny. And a real man would never allow fate to frustrate his aims. I will show you which is stronger, fate or manliness. The people will see that fate, which reversed your consecration, has been defeated by my courage.
>
> 'My courage will turn back this fate which comes rushing headlong at us, like a rogue elephant that has broken his bonds and ignores its goad ... I am stronger than any fate and anyone who opposes me shall suffer the consequences!'[68]

Here, as when Rama is with Sita (both at the trial by fire and her banishment into the forest), and in the last instance when he refuses to defend Lakshmana against Time's curse, Rama bows to a dharma that Lakshmana does not comprehend. Each time, Lakshmana surrenders to his older brother's understanding of the situation. But it is only when Rama chooses to honour Dasharatha's besotted promise to his young wife that Lakshmana challenges Rama. He cites kshatriya dharma, which, to him, seeks justice even if that justice comes through violence. Lakshmana is also reacting to what Rama

[68] Sattar, *Valmiki's Ramayana*, chap. 16.

said before his outburst, which is, 'Dharma is the most important thing in the world, truth is established because of it. And obeying a father's command is the highest dharma of all, as is conforming to the wishes of a mother and a brahmin. I cannot disobey my father simply because Kaikeyi, our mother, asked him to command me thus. Give up your ignoble ideas inspired by the duties of a kshatriya. Follow my example. Take refuge in dharma and not in violence.'[69]

It is through the person of Lakshmana and his increasing distress that we see how Rama, a prince born to live in and uphold the code of a warrior, is led away from the creed of a kshatriya towards a way of life that empowers brahmins as a class and favours the values that they cherish. In the Uttara Kanda, Rama's actions are justified by the advice that the brahmins give him and by fate, or earlier predictions. There is a marked difference between Lakshmana's impassioned arguments against dharma and fate in the Ayodhya Kanda and his acceptance of the end of his time on earth in the Uttara Kanda. The Uttara Kanda might want us to believe that, like his brother, Lakshmana, too, has given up the fight for his birthright to live and act as a warrior.

But we can also choose to consider seriously the fact that Lakshmana literally walks into a curse that he knows will result in his death. Surely, this is an act of free will within what has become an excruciatingly determined universe. Consoling Rama and encouraging him to fulfil the conditions of the curse, Lakshmana produces an extraordinary set of arguments that range from the fact that his death has been ordained, to filial love and the nurturing of dharma. None of them sound like the Lakshmana that the reader has gotten to know in the story, certainly not the Lakshmana who has argued against fate as well as against dharma and has clearly shown his discomfort at having to do things which made him uneasy. Asking for his own death is perhaps the only completely independent act that Lakshmana has ever done and it is significant that when he does choose to act from his own volition, there is no return. What makes his independence even more poignant is the fact that his exit from the world of men is quiet and solitary. Though the gods rain flowers and Indra comes and carries his body away to heaven, Lakshmana takes his last breath alone, free at last of the expectations

---

[69] Sattar, *Valmiki's Ramayana*, chap. 16.

that others have of him and equally free of his own deeply felt obligations. It is also his first and only breach with the dharma he lived by, as a man, as a brother and as a warrior. Yet, it shows us that the hermetically sealed universe of cause and effect that the Uttara Kanda attempts to create can be punctured, depending on how we choose to read the final book in the Valmiki Ramayana.

# 'RAMA'S LAST ACT'[70]

In the eighth century CE, Bhavabhuti reminded us about the importance of Valmiki's Uttara Kanda by writing his magnificent play, *Uttararamacharita* (The Last Act of Rama), the very title of which evokes Valmiki's Uttara Kanda. The exquisite structure of Bhavabhuti's masterpiece is predicated on his intimacy with Valmiki's Uttara Kanda and what I would like to believe is his discomfort with its content. Like us, he cannot accept a Rama so in the thrall of his brahmin advisers that he sends his wife away with no compunctions or regrets, a man who can while away his time listening to stories about the greatness of his own deeds and the worthiness of his opponents. Bhavabhuti's Rama is a broken man, a man who has lost his wife and has to create a golden statue of her in order to fulfil her ceremonial role. His Sita is equally a tragic heroine who loves her husband despite all that has happened, not a woman ready to renounce her husband at a huge public sacrifice. Using all that was available to him in terms of his understanding of the original text, his extraordinary talent as well as the genre in which he was writing, Bhavabhuti provides an alternative ending to Valmiki's poem as he rewrites the last kanda as a nataka. He telescopes all the critical events that occur after Rama regains the throne of Ayodhya – Sita's banishment, the

[70] I borrow this title from Sheldon Pollock's translation of Bhavabhuti's *Uttararamacharita* (New York: Clay Sanskrit Library, New York University Press, 2007).

killing of Shambuka, Rama's great sacrifice, his reunion with his sons – but turns the end of the poem around so that his work conforms to the genre constraints of the nataka and allows Sita and Rama to be reunited. In doing so, he also provides a critique of Valmiki, showing that another end to the story is not only possible, but that it might even be necessary. Bhavabhuti seems to think it is desirable as well.

The Rama of Valmiki's Uttara Kanda is a king: respectful to his brahmin advisers, attentive to the needs of his people, generous to his allies, aware of how he must rule his kingdom and dominate the lands around Kosala. For the most part, the private Rama has disappeared and we see primarily the king in public, learning more about the world that he has re-entered and about the significance of his actions, both past and present. That Bhavabhuti knows Valmiki's text well is clearly established when he quotes Valmiki's famous outpouring of grief in the shloka metre and when he refers to characters and incidents from Valmiki's Uttara Kanda. But he uses these same elements to craft a challenge to the denouement of Valmiki's story. He does this largely by unveiling the private Rama who has been hidden by the demands of statecraft and the aura of divinity that shroud him in Valmiki's text. Bhavabhuti shows us a Rama wracked by guilt, distraught at the loss of his beloved and tormented by what he had to do to her, a man going through the motions of being king and detached from the idea that he is god. Neither his kingship nor his divinity can restore to him what he has lost, since they are, in fact, the cause of it. For the queen cannot be tainted and a goddess must remain pure.

Bhavabhuti's play opens with Rama and a heavily pregnant Sita attending an exhibition of paintings that depict their lives. As Sita tires and falls asleep, Bhadra comes to Rama and tells him about the townspeople's gossip and the aspersions that are being cast on Sita's character and conduct. Sita is banished and Rama is heartbroken at what he has had to do. Twelve years later, on his way to kill Shambuka, Rama finds himself in the sylvan groves where he and Sita had spent their happiest times. In a surreal sequence, Sita speaks to Rama. But she is invisible and so he can only sense the comfort of her presence; he can neither see her nor hear her. However, he is able to say to her all that he wants to and Sita is reassured of his love and continuing devotion to her, something that Valmiki's Sita had to live without while she lived in the forest with her sons.

Upping the emotional ante of the tragedy, Bhavabhuti brings Janaka, a grieving Kaushalya and even Shanta, Rama's sister, into the action. Janaka and Kaushalya encounter a young boy, Lava, Rama's son, but they do not recognize him. Having introduced these characters who are completely absent from Valmiki's Uttara Kanda, Bhavabhuti flips back into that very text by keeping Lava a student of Valmiki's who is learning the Ramayana without yet knowing that he is Rama's son. Meanwhile, the horse for Rama's ashvamedha sacrifice wanders on to the scene and Lava stops it, which brings him face to face with his cousin Chandraketu, Lakshmana's son. The wandering horse that is stopped by the unknown young boys in the forest is not in Valmiki's text, but Bhavabhuti continues with this incident regardless. In his play, Kusha arrives to help Lava mount the challenge that stopping the horse entails. The boys call upon the magical jrimbhaka weapons which have been promised to them at birth and this, rather than the recitation of the Ramayana (as in Valmiki's text), is what makes Rama realize that they are his sons.[71] The magical weapons also do not feature in the Valmiki Ramayana and so there, it is the story, specifically the mention of Sita's banishment, that becomes the epiphanic moment through which Rama knows his sons. Meanwhile, as Bhavabhuti's drama continues, the boys accept Rama as a 'father in dharma' and a series of double entendre statements between them and Rama lift the play to emotional heights that Valmiki's restrained text simply cannot attain. Once again, Bhavabhuti has reached into the human heart of the epic poem and laid bare the anguish of being separated from those whom one loves most.

The main play contains Sita's banishment. In Act Two, we know that Sita is somehow in another world but we don't know how and when she got there. Apparently, Rama and Lakshmana and her family in the play are not aware that she has left the human world – they only know that Rama banished her when she was pregnant. In Valmiki's Uttara Kanda, both Sita's banishment

---

[71] Here, Bhavabhuti exploits the 'abhijnanam', the token by which people are recognized for who they are, a trope that we are more familiar with from Kalidasa's *Abhijnanashakuntalam*, where it is the king's signet ring that establishes the truth of Shakuntala's person and her son's claim to the throne.

and her departure into her mother's (the earth's) arms take place at the conclusion of Rama's great sacrifice. In the *Uttararamacharita,* the conclusion of the sacrifice has yet to occur, as we surmise from the wandering horse.

A dizzying series of reflections and refractions and slippages in time and space between Bhavabhuti's play and Valmiki's original poem segue to the point where, in the *Uttararamacharita,* we are brought to the brink of a play within a play in which Sita appears, having just given birth to her twin sons. But even as the play is being performed, Rama and Lakshmana, who are in the audience, respond as if the real Sita were before them. For the first time, they see and become aware of how Sita must have suffered in her abandonment. Sita says that she is without a protector and in a moment of abject despair, she begs her mother, the earth, to take her away. The mighty weapons materialize to bless the boys and the earth promises Sita that her sons will be cared for by Valmiki. As Sita vanishes, the play within the play ends. Rama falls into a faint, distraught by the fact that he will never see his wife again. But Lakshmana calls out, 'Help, Valmiki! Is this the moral of your poem?'[72] A voice off stage announces a miracle. The real Sita appears and revives Rama and then asks for her sons. Valmiki appears with Lava and Kusha and introduces them to their grandparents. Rama, unable to believe his eyes, says, 'Though all this is really happening to me I still cannot believe it. Then again, such is the nature of good fortune.' Valmiki's astonishing response is, 'Dear Rama, is there some further good turn I can do for you?'[73]

Surely, this is Bhavabhuti at his most audacious: he brings Valmiki into his (Bhavabhuti's) play to fix the flawed (in Bhavabhuti's opinion) ending to the story that Valmiki has written long ago.[74]

Bhavabhuti's play has always been admired for its virtuosity in terms of form and content. But perhaps something more can be said about the

---

[72] Pollock (tr.), Bhavabhuti, *Rama's Last Act*, p. 381.

[73] Pollock (tr.), Bhavabhuti, *Rama's Last Act*, p. 389. Although this is a line that appears conventionally at the end of many natakas, it seems to carry an extra weight here because it is Valmiki who speaks to Rama, the man whose story he has already written with a different ending.

[74] I owe much of my understanding of the symbiotic relationship between the *Uttararamacharita* and Valmiki's Uttara Kanda to Girish Karnad's brilliant foreword to Pollock's *Rama's Last Act*. Pollock (tr.), Bhavabhuti, *Rama's Last Act*, pp. 19–25.

relationship between men and women that it puts forward. In striving to create an exemplar of the nataka (which demands, among other things, the happy ending), Bhavabhuti allows a woman who has been maligned to return to her husband who has loved her and missed her in her absence. Moreover, this maligned woman who is restored to love and to dignity is not only a queen but the goddess consort to the man-god that Rama has become by the time that Bhavabhuti was writing his play. It is certainly true that the idea of Rama-as-Vishnu is hardly overt in the play's action. Nor is it the driving principle of the *Uttararamacharita*, where, for the most part, Rama acts as and is acted upon as a king, rather than as a god. But that should not diminish the powerful counterpoint that the play provides to its own likely cultural and religious context. Either Bhavabhuti was writing against the dominant ideas of his time or his times were catholic enough to allow multiple narratives of a well-loved story and of an important theology. The *Uttararamacharita* shows us that there can be many and different answers, uttaras, to the questions that Valmiki's Ramayana raises, of which the Uttara Kanda of Valmiki's text provides but one possible set.

Bhavabhuti's knowing and deliberately evocative title suggests two ways in which we might understand his response to these questions from the Ramayana. One, that the *Uttararamacharita* is an account of Rama's later (uttara) life and deeds. The second – which I prefer – is that Rama's last act was to surrender to the love he had for Sita and to welcome her back into his heart and his public life.

# GLOSSARY OF SANSKRIT TERMS

| | |
|---|---|
| aditya | minor solar deity |
| agnihotra | sacrifice to the god of fire |
| agnishtoma | sacrifice in the name of soma, the celestial elixir |
| akshauhini | army consisting of elephants, horses, chariots and foot soldiers |
| ashvamedha | horse sacrifice |
| apsara | celestial dancer |
| arghya | consecrated water used in a ritual to welcome guests |
| ashvins | celestial twins who are horsemen |
| asura | one of a class of beings opposed to the gods |
| avatara | form of Vishnu when he appears in the world of humans |
| bahusuvarnaka | sacrifice at which much gold is spent |
| brahmin | priestly caste at the top of the fourfold division of Hindu society |

| | |
|---|---|
| charana | celestial singer |
| chhaya | shadow |
| daitya | demonic son of Diti; enemy of the gods |
| danava | demonic son of Danu; enemy of the gods |
| deva | god |
| dharma | basis for ethical action in Hinduism which includes ideas of duty, obligation and responsibility, and encompasses the concepts of good, true, right and just |
| gandharva | celestial musician |
| gomedha | cow sacrifice |
| gopi | cow herding woman in love with Krishna |
| guhyaka | chthonic being |
| kanda | book or section of a large text |
| karma | theory of retributive action in Hinduism and Buddhism |
| kavya | poem |
| kinnara/i | 'some sort of man', a mythical creature that lives on earth |
| kshatriya | warrior and ruling caste; second only to the brahmins in the fourfold division of Hindu society |
| kusha | grass used in religious ceremonies and rituals |
| Mahapurana | collection of Hindu myths from the classical period |
| maheshvara | sacrifice to Shiva |
| marut | storm god |
| maryadapurushottama | the ideal man, always with reference to Rama |

| | |
|---|---|
| naga | serpent of the underworld, often personified |
| panchama | undefined celestial being |
| pannaga | serpent |
| rajasuya | sacrifice performed by kings as part of the rituals of consecration |
| ramarajya | 'rule of Rama', a golden age |
| rakshasa | a race of beings opposed to the gods and oppressors of human beings |
| rishi | seer |
| rudra | howling creature associated with Shiva |
| sadhyas | deities who guard rituals and prayers, sometimes the sons of Daksha |
| sharabha | monstrous creature made up of different animals |
| shudra | serving caste at the bottom of the fourfold division of Hindu society |
| siddha | semi-divine being who is a 'perfected' individual; pure and virtuous person who lives in the sky because of the merit earned in his earthly life |
| tamasi | magical power to create darkness |
| uraga | serpent, sometimes identified with naga |
| vanara/i | monkey |
| vaishnava | sacrifice performed for Vishnu |
| vaishya | merchant and cultivator class; third in the fourfold division of Hindu society |
| vamsha | royal lineage, dynasty |

| | |
|---|---|
| vasu | elemental god associated with Indra, the king of heaven |
| Vedas | collections of hymns and rituals that are seen as the foundational sacred texts of Hinduism |
| vidyadhara | supernatural being with magical powers |
| vishvadevas | a group of gods |
| yaksha/i | chthonic creature associated with fertility |
| yojana | a length of nine miles |
| yuga | an aeon of which there are four (Krita, Treta, Dwapara and Kali) in every cycle of the universe's existence |

# CROSS-EDITION REFERENCE

## For Arshia Sattar's Translation of the Valmiki Ramayana

| HarperCollins India (2019) and Rowman & Littlefield (2018) Editions | Penguin Classics (2000) Edition |
|---|---|
| ***Childhood*** | ***Childhood*** |
| Chapter 1 | Chapter 1 |
| Chapter 2 | Chapter 2 |
| Chapter 3 | Chapter 3 |
| Chapter 4 | Chapter 4 |
| Chapter 5 | Chapter 5 |
| Chapter 6 | Chapter 6 |
| Chapter 7 | Chapter 7 |
| Chapter 8 | Chapter 8 |
| Chapter 9 | Chapter 9 |
| Chapter 10 | Chapter 10 |
| Chapter 11 | Chapter 11 |
| Chapter 12 | Chapter 12 |
| ***Ayodhya*** | ***Ayodhyā*** |
| Chapter 13 | Chapter 1 |
| Chapter 14 | Chapter 2 |
| Chapter 15 | Chapter 3 |
| Chapter 16 | Chapter 4 |

| HarperCollins India and Rowman & Littlefield Editions | Penguin Classics Edition |
|---|---|
| Chapter 17 | Chapter 5 |
| Chapter 18 | Chapter 6 |
| Chapter 19 | Chapter 7 |
| Chapter 20 | Chapter 8 |
| Chapter 21 | Chapter 9 |
| Chapter 22 | Chapter 10 |
| Chapter 23 | Chapter 11 |
| Chapter 24 | Chapter 12 |
| Chapter 25 | Chapter 13 |
| Chapter 26 | Chapter 14 |
| Chapter 27 | Chapter 15 |
| ***Wilderness*** | ***Wilderness*** |
| Chapter 28 | Chapter 1 |
| Chapter 29 | Chapter 2 |
| Chapter 30 | Chapter 3 |
| Chapter 31 | Chapter 4 |
| Chapter 32 | Chapter 5 |
| Chapter 33 | Chapter 6 |
| Chapter 34 | Chapter 7 |
| ***Kishkindha*** | ***Kiṣkindha*** |
| Chapter 35 | Chapter 1 |
| Chapter 36 | Chapter 2 |
| Chapter 37 | Chapter 3 |
| Chapter 38 | Chapter 4 |
| Chapter 39 | Chapter 5 |
| Chapter 40 | Chapter 6 |
| Chapter 41 | Chapter 7 |
| Chapter 42 | Chapter 7 (ch. no. repeated) |
| Chapter 43 | Chapter 8 |
| Chapter 44 | Chapter 9 |

| HarperCollins India and Rowman & Littlefield Editions | Penguin Classics Edition |
|---|---|
| ***Beauty*** | ***Beauty*** |
| Chapter 45 | Chapter 1 |
| Chapter 46 | Chapter 2 |
| Chapter 47 | Chapter 3 |
| Chapter 48 | Chapter 4 |
| Chapter 49 | Chapter 5 |
| Chapter 50 | Chapter 6 |
| Chapter 51 | Chapter 7 |
| Chapter 52 | Chapter 8 |
| Chapter 53 | Chapter 9 |
| Chapter 54 | Chapter 10 |
| ***War*** | ***War*** |
| Chapter 55 | Chapter 1 |
| Chapter 56 | Chapter 2 |
| Chapter 57 | Chapter 3 |
| Chapter 58 | Chapter 4 |
| Chapter 59 | Chapter 5 |
| Chapter 60 | Chapter 6 |
| Chapter 61 | Chapter 7 |
| Chapter 62 | Chapter 8 |
| Chapter 63 | Chapter 9 |
| Chapter 64 | Chapter 10 |
| Chapter 65 | Chapter 11 |
| Chapter 66 | Chapter 12 |
| Chapter 67 | Chapter 13 |
| Chapter 68 | Chapter 14 |
| ***Epilogue*** | ***Epilogue*** |
| Chapter 69 | Chapter 1 |
| Chapter 70 | Chapter 2 |
| Chapter 71 | Chapter 3 |

# INDEX

# ABOUT THE TRANSLATOR

**Arshia Sattar** holds a PhD in South Asian Languages and Civilizations from the University of Chicago. She teaches classical Indian literature at several institutions in India, and writes for a number of journals and magazines.